"Kramer has written a mischievous love song to a Vermont village."

—Stephen Long, author of *Thirty-Eight: The Hurricane that Transformed New England*

"*The Rise and Fall of the Republic of West Delphi* is as close to a sui generis narrative as I've ever read—that is to say its sheer levels of originality are stunning. Let me not fail to mention that we have a narrator who is a honeybee, which elevates the very notion of sentience, let alone how we humans should best be educated, to new spiritual heights. Kramer is a maestro of literary imagination as she deftly orchestrates community history, detective fiction, and existential treatise; her Vermont is fearlessly imagined. The story is largely set in the 1970s, but it's a timeless cautionary tale. 'The Great Chanterelle Murder Mysteries' sequence should be made into a PBS documentary. What a splendid writer Kathryn Kramer is."

—Howard Norman, author of *The Wound Is The Place The Light Enters*

"A romp through the author's experience of being 'summer people' in 1970's rural Vermont when the artists and academics who appeared from the city were regarded with both curiosity and contempt. Kramer fabricates a whole kingdom for her highly entertaining characters."

—Mary Hays, author of *Learning to Drive*

"The prose evokes such a peaceful and powerful sense of place, it's almost like being there."

—Laura Fillmore, president of Open Book Systems, Inc.

"In this beautiful and moving paean to place, Kathryn Kramer has crafted a memoir so distinct, insightful, lively, and surprisingly multivocal, it extends our very notion of the form itself. It is utterly absorbing, both in its preoccupations and the inventive and deeply felt ways it brings its vivid story to life."

—Laurie Sheck, author of *Cyborg Fever* and *A Monster's Notes*

"We live in times of great political upheaval caused by dictators and their sycophants. But what if another course of history ran parallel to this one, a history formed by autonomous microcultures buried deep within the woods of civilization? Kathryn Kramer's latest work has rescued the history of one such wood."

—Eric Levi Jacobson, director of the Vermont Center for Social Research

"Funny, warm, and wise to the tears of things, Kathryn Kramer's history of an imaginary republic in northern Vermont touches the heart and challenges the imagination. No one writing in English today can match the poise and sophistication of her prose. *The Rise and Fall of the Republic of West Delphi* bids fair to be one of the best books of 2026."

—Timothy Evans, freelance writer

"A hymn to rural Vermont, its buzzing, muddy, freezing, melting delights and challenges. A 'collective love affair,' Kramer writes, 'between people and place—there can be little that is more intoxicating than this.' Especially if the place is Vermont in the 1970s. Especially if the people are such charming dwellers in the realm of imagination, odd-ball utopians resisting the normal world's humorless work-a-day dreariness, visionaries attempting to 'make a grand occasion out of everyday life.' Even if, like most passionate love affairs, this collective one ends in some measure of disillusionment, the bitter-sweetness lingers on. A delight—sure to become a classic."

—Genese Grill, Robert Musil scholar and author of
Portals: Reflections on the Spirit in Matter

"Kramer has created a loving portrait of a small village in Vermont. That description in itself invokes the kind of ticklish presumption anyone with a smattering of Vermont experience is long-familiar with. Sacred cows are humorously deconstructed like slow dissolving lollipops. The many illustrious chapters...bring to mind the best of several Wes Anderson films (*Rushmore, The Royal Tenenbaums, The Grand Budapest Hotel*). The writing is subtle, farcical and contains enough smarts to house a small town. Many too-real-to-be-real episodes are pierced and punctuated with a disturbed concoction of flawed logic and whimsy, both striking with ruthless abandon. But Vermont history is not the full story as Freya's Reign—think the birds and the bees minus the birds—add Hercule Poirot, Sherlock Holmes, Phillip Marlowe and you've got a full-blown literary fantasia! There is endless joy in digesting the mountains of cleverness Kramer has climbed."

—Alonzo LaMont, playwright and author of,
most recently, "The Dynamics of Do-Gooders"

"Kramer's loving examinations of a few hundred acres of central Vermont and the people who have come to it, left it, and returned seem to me unique. As literature—and it is that—*The Rise and Fall of the Republic of West Delphi* is a tour de force of creatively deployed genre switchings: straightforward recollection, elevated mock-heroic and mock-formal reportage, a literal worker bee's first-person account, and detective metafiction: Doyle's Holmes and Watson, Christie's Poirot, and Chandler's Marlow all appear in these pages, together no less. And it is obvious that Kramer loves sentences. She is a master stylist of a breed now seldom found and even less often read: her supremely polished prose is meticulously and closely punctuated, with long, looping legatos of perfectly poised Jamesian, even Proustian, sentences alternating with Hemingwayesque staccato in a rhythm exquisitely pleasing. I adore her very syntax. Crucially, this book is also very funny."

—Richard Lehnert, author of
A Short History of the Usual and *The Only Empty Place*

"An original, gathered-together narrative, distinctly memoir yet with sometimes a curiously premised and searching fiction folded in—a rapturous pastoral elegy full of humor, intelligence, and history, beginning and almost ending in the land of Vermont yet always afoot the deep plans that might still survive in a rational and wise America. Kathryn Kramer's *Delphi*, with all its stories, threshold legends, treasured information, shows us once again how American writing might also be a state of mind, a way to be here, an oracle."

—Joseph McElroy, author of *Women and Men*, *Lookout Cartridge*, and *Plus*

"What happens when a colorful bunch of eccentric newcomers settles in a small Vermont village and establishes their own republic? A grown-up child of divorce has high hopes for this little Utopia and its promise of communal faithfulness. Kramer's affectionate memoir often taking the form of a post-modernist novel is composed of wittily fanciful tall tales and thoughtful disquisitions on the nature of communities as tiny as a beehive and as vast as our own troubled republic."

—Jonathan Strong, author of *Four Last Songs* and *Endpapers*

"Kathryn Kramer's love of her hometown is diffused throughout this fine tribute; an imaginative mixture of fact, fable, and fun."

—Chris Doyle, coauthor of
2025-2026 The Cruising Guide to the Northern Leeward Islands

"Kathryn Kramer has written a love story about a place and, as with any great love story, the condition eludes easy description. In this remarkable book she pulls off the sleight-of-hand, her trajectory consistently surprising—a honeybee narrator! a murder mystery involving mushrooms!—while at the same time managing to be both cautionary and celebratory, wickedly funny and profoundly sad, always holding 'two views, the long view and the short view, in companionable balance.'"

—Kathryn Davis, author *The Silk Road* and *Aurelia, Aurélia*

"Employing the bravado and wit of a mock-heroic tale, Kramer has crafted a memorial to a particular small place in the larger-than-life era of the 1970s and early 1980s. *The Rise and Fall of the Republic of West Delphi* chronicles the heady sense of being in the best possible place with the best possible people at exactly the right time. As the celebratory gradually gives way to the reflective, Kramer's generous-hearted memoir is suffused with a kind of wistful devotion that lingers beyond the final page."

—Catherine Tudish, author of *A Thousand Souls: A Novel in Stories*

"What a delightful and often tongue-in-cheek romp through the landscape of West Delphi, a village that breeds characters AND attracts character escapees from the "real" world that is always lurking on the margins of the stories. This book is very much a literary memoir, presented by an offbeat voice rich with description, observation and humor, confidently bound together by an abiding love and attachment to the special little enclave Kramer calls home."

—Tania Aebi, author of *Maiden Voyage*

THE RISE AND FALL OF THE REPUBLIC OF WEST DELPHI

Kathryn Kramer

Montpelier, VT

Release Date: July 28, 2026

Printed in the USA.

Paperback ISBN: 978-1-57869-307-8

Library of Congress Control Number: 2026910091

Published by Rootstock Publishing
an imprint of Ziggy Media, LLC
Montpelier, VT 05602

info@rootstockpublishing.com
www.rootstockpublishing.com

Book design by Eddie Vincent, ENC Graphic Services.

Cover art: Original painting by Friedrich Gross (www.friedrichgross.com), used by permission.

Postcard: "Our Lady Of The Large Zucchini At The Blessing Of The Zukes" ©1984 by Ken Brown, reprinted with permission.

This is a work of creative nonfiction. While many stories in this book are true, some have fictionalized themes interwoven. Some names and identifying details have been changed to protect the privacy of the people involved. In other cases, permission has been granted to use real names.

Dedication

To, of course, all the inhabitants of West Delphi who transformed it into the Republic. And with deep gratitude to my father, who first recognized "the farm" as a doorway to another way of life; to my brother and sister, who shared and remember the early times; and last but not least to my wonderful son, who grew up here and is now the Institute's custodian.

We owe no allegiance, we bow to no throne,
Our ruler is law and the law is our own.

—John Greenleaf Whittier, "The Song of the Vermonters"

I do not find that Plato pointed specifically to Vermont as the perfect state, but that was probably only because in Plato's day Vermont was not here to point to.

—Charles Edward Crane, *Let Me Show You Vermont*

I am as resolutely determined to defend the independence of Vermont as Congress that of the United States and rather than fail will retire with the hardy Green Mountain Boys into the desolate caverns of the mountains and wage war with human nature at large.

—Ethan Allen

You know, if anybody should die in a house where they keep bees, the master has to go to the door of the hive, and knock, and tell them about the death, or the bees will fly away.

—Beverley Nichols, *A Thatched Roof*

The Lord whose oracle is in Delphi neither speaks out nor conceals, but gives a sign.

—Heraclitus

CONTENTS

PART TWO

PART THREE

PART FOUR

Preface

One summer I left the village of West Delphi, Vermont, where I'd been living, to spend several months in New York City, and I looked for work as a typist. During my interview at the temp agency, the "personnel manager" explained to me how the agency expected its employees to dress. "Remember that you will represent the company to the public," she said. I observed her high heels, stockings, tailored blazer, and salon-cut hair and felt queasy. I could guess what she was thinking of me—respectable enough in skirt and blouse but no stockings, no heels, no coiffure, no makeup: *not professional.* I knew from experience that, even were I to copy her, I could never achieve the spit and polish of "executive" employees. Something would inevitably be awry. Hair straggling loose from its barrette, a smudge from a shoe on my bare leg, skirt too long or too short, blouse too tight or too loose. Not *put together.* Nonetheless I could type a hundred words a minute and had done this kind of work before. Rarely had I gone to fill a temporary vacancy at a company and not been offered a permanent job. Not only could I type, I could spell, a skill that, alone, appeared to provoke the desire to appropriate me. This time, as before, I anticipated being remanded to a bank or insurance agency, in one of which I'd usually worked, typing ad infinitum a particular form or two, deathly tedium only momentarily relieved by the whispered warnings of full-time employees at the water cooler or the copy machine. *Don't take the job if they offer it to you. Let me tell you, it's no picnic working here...*

Veteran prisoners alerting the newly interned.

On this occasion, I was dispatched to a music publisher in Midtown, in the Fifties, off Fifth Avenue, where I rose fifteen or twenty stories to eventually find myself in a small, cramped office, desks for three secretaries shoved against one wall, the bosses in rooms not as large as some bathrooms. No "public" anywhere in sight. The secretaries were comfortably dressed; one, I noted, wore blue jeans. Was this why I had been sent there? Where my flimsy imitation of business attire would not bring down the prevailing tone?

I was introduced to the head of the firm, a bulk of a man resplendent in a camouflage outfit, who informed me matter-of-factly that he was to be addressed as "Generalissimo Snowflake." "Sergeant Avery will show you around the office," he said. "Sergeant" Avery, another secretary, saluted and we left.

I can't recall if she said anything along the lines of "He's strange but nice," or "You'll get used to it," but if she didn't, I wouldn't have asked, it being my policy never to appear not to understand what was going on.

The next morning I arrived ready to work, pulled up to my desk, put on the headphones, and turned on the Dictaphone. I lunged for the volume control as martial music blared in my ears. After a long moment of this, a voice declaimed, "Good MORning, Private Kramer! This is Generalissimo Snowflake. Please take a letter."

And so it went. There was a certain amount of marching and saluting around the office. Reminders of Snowflake's being only one of four to have attained his rank. (Franco, Stalin, and Mussolini were the others I'd heard of.) He was occasionally overbearing, as befit his station, but also kind, funny, interested, and interesting—a *person*. Not *personnel*. At that stage in my life, my early thirties, a catalog of *Bosses I Have Known* could already have filled a small volume—from restaurant managers to bank officers to patent attorneys—and all had been men, most had been ceremonially preceded by the avant-garde of a paunch, and most had shouted. I kept waiting for this latest to reveal himself as true to type, however gotten up in generalissimo's clothing.

After I'd been working in the office for a couple of days, the Generalissimo summoned me to his office and demanded to know what the temp agency was paying me. Was this breaching protocol? I had the feeling I wasn't supposed to say. Nevertheless, I told him.

They charged him twice that, he informed me. "How about I'll pay you that for the rest of the summer and we'll tell them you don't work for them anymore."

What was the worst that could happen? So I agreed, and thanked him, trying not to show my incredulity.

"No, come to think of it," he said, "it's expensive to live in New York. I'll pay you..." And he added a couple of dollars to my already doubled hourly wage. What serendipity, I marveled, had landed me on the shores of this island of eccentric humanity in a sea of "appropriate dress" and "meeting the public"? I couldn't wait to go home and call everyone I knew and tell them of my incredible good fortune.

One morning not long after he'd persuaded me to go AWOL from the temp agency, Generalissimo Snowflake called me into his office, stood up behind his desk, saluted me, and announced, "Private Kramer! In view of your skill and eagerness, I have decided the time has come to promote you to sergeant."

I thought quickly and decided that the time had also come to reveal myself.

"Well, that's very kind of you," I said (unfamiliar with the more appropriate military response), "but I'm afraid that I'm already a general in the West Delphi army, and I'm not sure if I can be a corporal or any rank whatsoever, in fact, in yours."

An impeccably trained military man, Generalissimo Snowflake betrayed merely the faintest surprise (only a fellow general could have caught it).

"Well, General Kramer," he said, standing up and saluting, "it's a pleasure working with someone of your rank. We'll have to see what we can do."

The next morning, an even more elaborate ceremonious fanfare than usual greeted me on the Dictaphone, followed by a lengthy speech about the necessity, given my days of devoted service, of conferring a new rank upon me. For the rest of the summer, I was to be greeted by Generalissimo Snowflake's booming "Good MORning, General-*Admiral* Kramer," when I put on the earphones. He had made sure, in the course of a briefing, that although West Delphi in fact had a navy, I possessed no rank in it. Someone else headed that branch of our military. (Heads of military being, at least as of yet, all we had.) But I would now be an Admiral in Snowflake's forces.

This will not, however, be the story of my summer in the services of Generalissimo Snowflake, with whom I subsequently lost touch and who by now must have gone where all good generalissimos go—though I would prefer to think that he is still there, inducting new recruits into his army, teaching them how properly to salute, leading them in goose step down Fifth Avenue to buy them a ceremonial cocktail when they are posted to other outfits, as he did me. On my key chain I still carry the dog tags he supplied me:

GENERAL KATIE KRAMER
IF WOUNDED, CALL
GENERALISSIMO
SNOWFLAKE

No room for the ADMIRAL, alas. I looked at those words for years before realizing that they read more plainly as an admonition to me than as instructions to Good Samaritans.

Though this isn't going to be the Generalissimo's story, it's nevertheless a story about another island of eccentricity and sanity, where like every citizen of the Republic I became a commanding officer without having had to rise through the ranks, and it's dedicated to him and to all those like him, wherever they may be, who, however quixotically, subvert the expectations of artificial and unimaginative social arrangements to invent community, persevere in oddity, and confer honorary status upon the citizens of all other such enclaves when they encounter them in the wider world.

PART ONE

I

Annals of the Republic: Book the First

It was a dark and rainy night and the last thing the philosopher expected to hear as he sat reading by the fire was a knock on the door. He was startled, but not afraid. There was nothing to be afraid of here, other than the Jehovah's Witnesses who occasionally made so bold as to venture up his long winding road, and whom, he boasted, he had once kept standing out in the garage while he "got ready" to debate. Or was that the IRS man, improbably making a house call to audit him? These legends are sometimes hard to keep straight.

The philosopher never locked the doors. Anyone who wanted to get in would get in anyway. Once in the middle of the night his younger daughter's Siamese cat, who had become his responsibility (the children were always leaving things in the house; the attic was groaning under the weight of their possessions), had leapt onto his chest, hissing, ears back, hair on end, and he'd sprung directly up out of a sound sleep—not a stitch on—grabbed a golf club from the bag in his closet (he didn't golf, had bought them at a yard sale somewhere or someone had given them to him; who the hell knew how things came into the house?), and, club in hand, ventured into the upstairs hallway, and what should he encounter but a fisher, fixing him with a gimlet eye from the top of the stairs. Interrupted, clearly, in the process of making a midnight snack out of the cat.

The philosopher raised his golf club and yelled. He liked to think, in retrospect, that he had shouted a time-honored imprecation, something along the lines of what Achilles roared when he finally stopped sulking and went forth to battle—but it was more likely an inadvertent sound, half astonishment, half outrage. The next thing he knew, instead of retracing its steps down the stairs and out the hole in the screen door through which it had doubtless pursued the cat, the fisher veered to the side into the attic room (so called because a thick, planked, never-painted door led to the attic—all children categorically refused to sleep in this room, so it was yet another that relentlessly collected junk) and dove straight through the glass of the shut window like a grade-B stuntman. Or so said the philosopher when he told the story later. (So said the philosopher's elder daughter, repeating the story after the philosopher was no longer around to tell it. "'Like a grade-B stuntman,' he said.")

It certainly made a good story, as did all his other stories of encounters with wild animals, and he was a good storyteller. He came off looking somewhat hapless, but this was not unintentional; he was victorious in his wit. Amused by his own temerity in attacking with a golf club the only animal ferocious enough in the Vermont woods (assuming the catamount wasn't back; there was lively disagreement about that) to attack a man. To foil the woodchuck who was ravaging his garden, he stuffed down its hole a porcupine he'd had to shoot because it had barricaded itself in the cellar (which, like every other godforsaken part of the house, was porous to the elements); the woodchuck merely shrugged and dug itself a new way out, evidently finding the fresh shoots only sweetened by the taste of adversity overcome. He (the philosopher) had once attempted to do away with a raccoon who kept getting into the shed and wreaking havoc with the garbage by an even more ingenious ruse. One evening he set a pie tin full of wine in the backyard and waited for the raccoon to come along and get drunk, which it duly did, thereupon proceeding to dance around the yard "in honor of Bacchus." The philosopher drew the bow taut and let fly, but it was a bow bought for the children, the arrows dull, and the raccoon swatted them away like distracting mosquitoes. Yet the philosopher, far from being discouraged, cultivated this picture of himself as feckless and outwitted; it fit his view of the universe, as a place in which the decks were stacked against the poor goddamned human race, and all one really had to defend oneself with was one's sense of humor.

But on this dark night upon which our story begins, he had not yet told these stories to very many people. There weren't many people around to tell the stories *to*. There were neighbors in the village with whom he was friendly—loggers and farmers and Violet Sleeper, in whose immaculate kitchen he sometimes lingered for a cup of coffee—but it wasn't that kind of conversation he lacked. "Conversation" was not what you engaged in when you chatted with a neighbor about gardens and weather and the goddam property taxes, though he enjoyed these exchanges and was on good terms with people in the village. The philosopher was not a snob, in any conventional sense; he simply thought most people incapable of real conversation, which, by definition, was not brief and which explored the fundamentals: fluidly, eruditely, wonderingly, profanely.

All that, however, was about to change. The knock fell a second time, and the philosopher hoisted himself out of his low stuffed rocker beside the woodstove and went to answer the door. Who the devil was accosting him at this hour? It was November.

There, on the granite threshold, stood a young couple. The woman, the philosopher noticed with amazement, was wearing high heels. The philosopher had never seen anyone, in all the years he'd been coming to West Delphi, nearly a quarter of a century now, wearing high heels. She was also wearing a trench coat. He didn't pay much attention to such things but he recognized that she was stylish. How someone stylish had gotten into Vermont, and into this particular obscure corner of it, was a wonder. Vermont decked itself out in work boots and checkered wool shirts. Green pants and caps. At the college in the southern end of the state where he taught, the girls were still garbed in the Vermont chic of long skirts and hiking boots. The hippie sixties had lingered on into this, the next decade. At the college they had a joke: they don't graduate, they just disappear into the woods. Enough had remained faithful to the long-haired, a-material, communal, back-to-the-land, off-the-grid, screw-the-system ideal to endow this facetiousness with a certain amount of truth. The philosopher half admired this, half deplored it. Reinventing the wheel—he could tell them that everything had already been tried, everything. Recently he had argued that the program in international training with which his college was loosely affiliated should require a course in the philosophers who'd thought about politics with profundity two thousand years ago, but the program hadn't heeded his advice.

Of course, if you were a philosopher, you were used to people not heeding your advice. (Or perhaps you became one because they didn't.)

The man accompanying the young woman (which was how the

philosopher viewed most young men—pitying his female students, who had to wait for their male counterparts to grow up) was not dressed up, but his clothes were unnaturally tight-fitting. His sweater looked as if it had been through the wash by mistake and an inch or two of midriff advertised itself between the sweater's hem and the waist of his skintight jeans. What sort of statement did he intend to make, precisely?

When the pair had introduced themselves as Swift and Chantal (they had just bought the old church in the village, they said—what the hell were they talking about?) he realized that the woman was French. The philosopher would have been the first to admit that he was not overfond of the French. Happy to be bailed out by the Americans in '44, but how quickly they forgot the debt. Nevertheless he wouldn't take out his indignation on this attractive Chantal, who had so mysteriously arrived at his door.

"Come in, come in," he said. "Come in out of the rain."

He brought them through the front room—what the family had always called it—a repository for everything that had no place elsewhere: badminton rackets, croquet mallets, the chain saw (oozing dark oil onto newspaper), beer bottles (which the philosopher collected for his home brew), and who the devil knew what else—and into the toasty living room. Swift (who was not French) and Chantal stood by the woodstove, warming their hands. The philosopher offered them wine and soon they all sat, he in his customary seat beside the stove, Swift in the armchair directly across, and Chantal perched on the edge of the couch just beside the chair Swift occupied. Chantal admired the color of the walls—a rich deep green that was exactly, she said, the color of old France. Not of *rooms* in old France, but of la vielle France itself, as if the Second Empire—Napoleon resurgent—were suddenly laying claim to this salon in rural Vermont.

Swift and Chantal had come to see if they could rent the philosopher's house for the winter. They had bought "the Church" (it became clear that they meant the Averys' old barn; it hadn't been used as a church since the 1920s, when the steeple had been removed so that the milking of cows would not be sacrilegious, yet for reasons known only to themselves they persisted in calling it that), but because there were title issues that needed to be cleared up they wouldn't be able to move in until sometime in the spring. It also became clear (their conversation was very roundabout) that Swift was attending the new law school forty minutes southwest of Delphi; he and Chantal were moving up from New York. People were. The Vermont that had changed little since the philosopher had first known it in 1950, when he'd spent a year getting one of the few master's degrees that had ever been conferred by the college where he now taught, was about to undergo a population explosion of educated middle-class immigrants. He had thought that the village of West Delphi would escape but apparently not.

During the two decades that he'd been coming up here—spending summers with his family; then, after the divorce, except for the occasional descent of his children, alone—the village had changed little. The neighbors he'd known best, the Magoons, had moved to East Delphi, which might as well have been the other side of the country for all he now saw of them. Merle Magoon had helped the philosopher plant his grassy hillside with thousands of red pines, the crop that, at the time, county foresters promoted—worth next to nothing now they were grown (all over the state one saw these orphaned stands of pine)—but otherwise not much had changed.

Walt Avery had retired and sold his farm and built a modern ranch house on the main road—the first house visible from the philosopher's (was this a harbinger of what he had to look forward to?); but Violet Sleeper was still where she'd always been, in her low white house with the wraparound porch across from the cemetery (her house had been the store and post office when West Delphi had been the most populous village in the township of Delphi; incredible to think of now); Violet was retired from teaching (she'd taught in the little local school when it was still a school and not a summer house), and Elton from driving a truck. Elton's brother Alton, retired from logging, lived with them. (What idea had their parents entertained, exactly, or was it too much effort to change more than a single vowel?)

The Jewells were still there, farming (the only dairy farm in the village now. In 1957, when the philosopher first came, there had been four). So were the Hodges, up the hill from the Sleepers, in their tilted house (Lenny Hodge had done some logging for him recently). And of course the Lefevres down at the end of his road—Bucky Lefevre now living across the road in a trailer while Grace stayed in the house. "Better off apart," Bucky said, though he ran a power cord from the house to the trailer and Grace sometimes carried food across to him. A welfare scam, some said. Though this was not the kind of controversy it interested the philosopher to adjudicate.

One evening when the philosopher had gone out for a walk he'd found Bucky stretched out on the grassy median of the road, waiting for his nitroglycerin to take effect. "The ticker," Bucky said, apologetically. They had a pleasant conversation—the philosopher standing, Bucky lying down. Bucky apologized for taking up the road for the time being. The philosopher told him he was welcome to it. The philosopher liked Bucky. Bucky had a habit of coming out of his trailer and accosting unfamiliar cars that started down the road—on one occasion he'd stopped the philosopher's grown son, not recognizing him. The philosopher looked the other way when Bucky or his sons came up with a rifle and asked if he minded if they went out back of the house to hunt some "woodchuck." Once the philosopher had found a package wrapped in white butcher paper in his mailbox, bleeding through; he was pretty damned sure it wasn't woodchuck.

He explained now to Swift and Chantal that he couldn't rent the house to them because it wasn't winterized. He'd just come up for the weekend to close it down for the season. There was no central heating and the pipes would freeze. People used to live in it, true—it was a hundred and fifty years old—but they'd had several woodstoves and a fireplace, and must have spent all their time stoking the fires.

Though Swift and Chantal were disappointed, they enjoyed their new neighbor's company and he theirs. It was possible, the philosopher thought, as he listened to Swift elaborate upon his plans to soundproof a third-floor study, à la Proust, and write a book, and to Chantal upon their plans to redo "the Church," that they might be completely nuts, but they promised to liven up the neighborhood.

He cherished the quiet and isolation of the place (the "utter solitude" of the advertisement that had initially attracted him was exactly what he longed for after nine months of the classroom) and a philosopher, alone on a hill, can carry on quite a long time on his own, with the company of his library, but there are, after all, limits. He hazarded a guess that, despite their argumentative and high-flown manner of talking, Swift and Chantal might provide him with some interesting evenings.

When they mentioned that a friend of theirs, a fellow law student, had been the first to "discover" West Delphi (they spoke of him in the tone in which Ferdinand and Isabella might have boasted about Columbus) and decided to buy the Magoons' old place, separated by only one unoccupied house from "the Church," the philosopher foresaw a promising future for the village. Its name pronounced, he made sure to inform Swift and Chantal, with the accent on the second syllable, rhyming with "defy," not upon the first, as with the original. "Make of that what you will," he told them.

II

The State We're In

In the Republic of West Delphi, you'd never see an army advancing across a plain. If you have a level quarter acre to plant a garden in you count yourself lucky. Our neighbors the Jewells used to hay slopes that made tractor-driving look like an extreme sport.

Except for the river valleys on both sides of the state, there are few long stretches of flat land. One grasps the derivation of the term of scorn for outsiders: *Flatlanders.* They don't know what hard work *is.* Up here, folks farm on *ledge.*

Inland, between the river coasts, it's all hills, leading up to and away from the Green Mountains' central ridges, like ladies-in-waiting clustering around their duchesses. Settlements in hill valleys have an entrenched feel, as if the villagers have come inside the castle walls for protection. You don't necessarily know what's happening in the next valley over; as long as they keep their nose out of your business, you don't necessarily care. The old hill farms have the aspect of lookouts (unlike the nouveau ridgetop mansions that merely proclaim the profitable investment strategy and landscape tone-deafness of the newcomers) and people knew whom to leave alone. As Ethan Allen liked to say, "The gods of the valley are not the gods of the hills."

It's true. The latter are a lot fussier. Or maybe just bored. Like Zeus on an off day, they enjoy stirring up trouble.

Jealous, that's the word. They don't brook contradiction. And like the Olympians, they each have their own territory. Woe betide the hapless mortals who don't recognize whose is whose.

Snug in your citadel, you feel secure. Safe from invaders. But then at some point you realize that invaders have the advantage of being able to approach without your noticing. At any moment they could be creeping up with malice aforethought or—at the very least—*spying* on you. Calculating their next move. The disadvantage of this topography that persuades you you're the center of the universe is the underlying worry that someone will wrest your centrality from you. A quick reconnoitering trip into the next valley will, in fact, confirm your suspicion that this town, too, believes itself to be the hub around which all other encampments, whether they know it or not, revolve.

All over Vermont there are republics like West Delphi's, if more virtual and less articulated. They may not have had armies and navies and chroniclers as assiduous as ours, but, like us, they think their settlement the most unusual, most interesting, most envied of all the state. Or anywhere. The state, it may be said, thinks this about itself. From its inception Vermonters have been trying to persuade their neighbors of their singular identity, hypothetical though that may have been. Even the Encyclopædia Britannica says that "in many ways Vermont is a vigorous survivor of an earlier, simpler time in the United States."

I've read somewhere that Vermont has more numerous mountains and a more extensive mountain area than the White Mountains, the Adirondacks, and the Catskills combined. One of the world's finest horses was bred here—the Morgan. When President Monroe visited in 1817, he said the animal was a "noble one, fit to match Vermont's heroes." We boast the world's first expert on the snowflake. (Who knew there was competition?) And guess what? We sell more maple syrup than any other state in the country. We possess the largest granite quarry in the world and the largest underground marble quarry. Marble quarried in Vermont supports the US Supreme Court Building.[1] Ours is the country's smallest capital city. Moreover, the only one without a McDonald's. And all manner of world-famous folks have found their way to us—generals, presidents, presidents' wives, popes, famous dissidents, and refugees—but through personal connections, not official visits. They know we'll keep their whereabouts to ourselves. Vermonters don't brag about such folks to outsiders. We don't need to. We already know we have our finger on the world's pulse.

Even our landmass is different from our two neighbors'. The soil. The

1 A richly suggestive statement whose implications will not be explored here.

bedrock. We were once a seacoast and our climate was subtropical: fossils of tropical fruit and foliage have been found near Lake Champlain. Then something came along and pushed us up off the seabed. Says one account, "The squeeze came from the southwest, possibly from Washington." (How strange.) I once heard that New Hampshire and New York were originally part of what is now Scotland, whereas Vermont was part of South America. This, of course, explains not only the difference between our friendlier, more republic-hospitable terrain and that begrudged by the more forbidding mountain ranges to either side of us, but our peculiar New England–Latin American temperament. (I swear I heard this on Vermont Public Radio,[2] even though I cannot track down its source, and two geologists I've consulted consign this to the realm of fantasy. Perhaps the broadcast occurred on the first of April. Does it matter, in the end?)

The fact that the strict veracity of many of these assertions is in doubt should remind us that *strictness*—in storytelling as in life—is an element that the Republic of West Delphi, and the state of which it is synecdoche, have rebelled against. Veracity is not the point. A definition of "country" might just as well be not solely a group of people who hold the same truths to be self-evident but who like to brag about the same things. All countries are a state of mind, no matter how severely they attempt to police their borders, and Vermont's exceptionalism is real—but also myth, like the rest of the country's. Countries *are* myths; borders, except possibly oceans, are asserted: fictions maintained by force.

Before Vermont was a state it was a state of mind, fought over by its neighbors, who mistakenly believed that they could annex it. Even if the early settlers in fact emigrated from these adjacent territories, once they crossed the boundary rivers they knew they were Somewhere Else. Love of liberty and the desire for self-determination ran at flood stage through their veins. No one was going to run the likes of *us*! (Hence, among other things, our yearly town meeting—the only truly democratic organization left in the world, it's been asserted.)

Our official identity was in flux for quite a while, however. First we were part of New Hampshire, then New York said we were part

---

2 In the days before it annoyingly dropped the word "Radio" and retitled itself "Vermont Public."

of it. King George told the governor of New Hampshire, Benning Wentworth (think: Bennington), that he could hand out parcels of land in what became known as the New Hampshire Grants. (The ignominy of it!) New York, however, considering this to be *their* territory, wanted to "grant" land themselves. (Neither adjacent entity, it should be noted, was interested in helping out settlers; they wanted to use the parcels for speculation, if you can believe it.) New York petitioned the king who (eventually, once he finished fighting France) said that that state could have all the land to the western bank of the Connecticut River and so *they* began to give out titles. As may be imagined, we weren't pleased with this early flatlander interference. They rejected our claims to our own land and when they did recognize these they wanted to tax us, by gawd.

Something had to be done. So Ethan Allen and his brothers rode down from the hills and took care of those crooks. Once the Revolutionary War started, New Hampshire and New York had other things to worry about. Busy defending the newly concocted country of which they were each one-thirteenth, they weren't so preoccupied with that wedge of land pushed up between their two joiner selves. We took this opportunity to solidify our separate identity.

In the meantime the Green Mountain Boys got bored and decided to define their enemy more broadly: not just the small potatoes of New York, but all of England. Singlehandedly they conquered Fort Ticonderoga, that most impregnable of British bastions in the incipient United States. The size of an enemy's forces has always been of secondary concern to residents of the Green Mountain State. As the British general John Burgoyne is said to have remarked, "Vermont abounds with the most rebellious race on the continent."

This was in 1775.

For the next fifteen years, the boundaries of Vermont remained a bit fluid. In 1777 Vermont declared its own independence and became a republic. Until 1791, the state attempted to go it alone. The Republic of Vermont had its own money, postal system, laws, and citizenship. The motto on its state seal was (and is) "Freedom and Unity"—a fitting emblem for a collection of separate settlements all considering themselves the polestar of a new world. Some New Hampshire towns joined this newly invented country and Vermont claimed all the land in New York east of the Hudson. Congress didn't like this, if you can believe it. If we would give these fringes up, this venerable body promised, Vermont could join the Union—the "more perfect" one—but then rescinded the offer. (Incredible.) Instead, Vermont decided they'd negotiate with England. If England would recognize their Republic, maybe they'd remain an independent entity, or maybe they'd go back to being a part of the British empire. Even at this early date, a certain fancifulness about national identity may be noted.

This should not, however, be mistaken for indifference. There's a subtle but critical distinction to be made here. Early Vermonters seem to have recognized that there was always going to be some outside entity eager to put a label on us, so in a way it didn't matter all that much who it was. We'd have to get used to living in a state of public compliance and private contradiction. Remind ourselves that we're part of a larger entity—but only provisionally. Since 1791, when Vermont became the first state to join the original thirteen, we have never overcome a certain reluctance about this move. Allegiance to independent life remains staunch and suspicion of the Continental Congress and its motives endures.

Two centuries had gone by at the time of the founding of the Republic of West Delphi, but in some ways things had not changed all that much. Though in our innocence we new citizens thought we were unique, we were reenacting a time-honored practice in these here hills. From the Green Mountain Boys to the hippies who'd gone "back to the land" a decade earlier, everyone was fleeing the march of metropolitan values, advancing up the river valleys just as they had in the 1700s. As said Sinclair Lewis, he who gave small-town America a bad name in *Main Street*, Vermont was the first place he'd seen where he really wanted to spend the rest of his life, because we had a "population that is solid and not driven mad by the American mania . . . the desire for terrific speed and the desire to make things grow." (In the economic, not the agricultural sense, one presumes he meant.)

In recent years a movement to declare a Second Vermont Republic has arisen, and at its highest point some 13 percent of Vermonters have reportedly supported secession.[3] Just as when in the course of human

3 There is some disagreement about how we would constitute ourselves if we withdrew

events it became necessary for the colonies to declare their independence from the tyranny of Great Britain, the tyranny of a government too remote and out of touch with local concerns is now driving a portion of our populace to urge this step. Vermont must now declare its independence from the "tyranny of Corporate America and the US government."[4] As Calvin Coolidge famously claimed almost a hundred years ago, "If the spirit of liberty should vanish in other parts of the Union and support of our institutions should languish, it could all be replenished from the generous store held by the people of this brave little state of Vermont." Theoretically "even without recognition, Vermont basically meets the internationally accepted criteria for being an independent country." In keeping with this assertion, various politicians have declared, when pressing for new legislation, that Vermont will "show the rest of the country the way."

In our state legends, ever since the Green Mountain Boys set the example, we've been out in the vanguard demanding liberty. Purportedly we shed the first blood in the Revolution a month before the Battle of Lexington when a "young radical from Brattleboro" tried to prevent the king's court from convening in Westminster. Ours was the first state constitution to abolish slavery. We were the first state outside of the South to send men to fight in the Civil War. Our legislature voted funds for the First World War before the US had declared it and our impatience was so great by the Second that we declared war against Germany before the slow-moving United States did. We were the first legislature to recognize Civil Unions and the first state to legalize same-sex marriage without a court order. One town swore out a warrant for the arrest of George Bush II for war crimes. We had the first openly socialist mayor and then member of Congress and, lately, candidate for president.

How did this happen? Does the place attract particularly rebellious

---

from the larger republic. Some favor going it alone but others have proposed forming a new country along with Maine and the Maritime provinces of Canada. (It's not clear if their opinion has been asked.) (Or—for that matter—what would happen to New Hampshire? Perhaps the "Labrador Plow," a name given to the glacier whose retreat some years ago allowed Vermont to become Vermont, might be invoked to reassert itself and shove that irritating bit of intransigence out of the way.)

4 The language is the founder's, Thomas Naylor's.

individuals or do we get converted after we get here? Something in the water, perhaps?

Yet, though the spirit of liberty may spring up in our tree-guarded strongholds as eagerly as mushrooms after rain, and we be as grateful to recognize it and guard it as closely as we do the location of certain choice fungi, it, like some of these, may have unforeseen consequences when ingested. Liberty—we all hold it dear: West Delphians, Vermonters, Americans, human beings. It sounds good, it feels better, our hearts swell, anthems ring in our ears, we're ready to start marching. But—against whom?

What a dumb question! Why, whoever means to constrain us, that's who! We're on the lookout for *them*. There's always *someone* to resist. After all, what would we *be* without lurking invaders? How can you be the most rebellious, most liberty-loving—the *greatest*—if you don't have an enemy?

The spirit of rebellion, so always just born, so invigorating . . . so swiftly decaying into the spirit of nationalism, JOIN US! replaced by KEEP OUT! This chronicle of West Delphi's rise and fall is about that process. How we so innocently and ironically reenacted that time-honored journey. How our incapacity to conceive of an *us* without a *them* affects not only our social arrangements but the very earth and all that live on it.

III

Annals of the Republic: Book the Second

What forces could have been at work to summon the citizens to the Republic at this particular moment? From what and where could they have been in flight that sent them to this mountain fastness bearing (though they did not yet suspect this) the hopes of an increasingly endangered civilization? Just as Gibbon looked back upon Rome and with the hindsight of centuries identified the factors that led to its empire's rise and fall, so must we strive to distinguish those that did the same to the Republic of West Delphi.

If we commence our history one summer in the late seventies and early eighties of the last century, we will discover the cast assembling, the curtain about to rise. In a large blocklike building somewhere south of Boston, Massachusetts, the philosopher's daughter is typing memos. One of these reads as follows:

> I checked with the Chairman of the Ethics Committee on the notepad gift you received. Since the notepad is of no significant value and is personalized, so can be of no use to anyone else, it is proper for you to convert this to office use. It would be appropriate, however, for you to send a note to Tony DiNardo stating that you received this and that your understanding is that as long as it is something for office use of no significant value, that you may use it.

The philosopher's daughter thought that this was hilarious, when it didn't make her feel lonely and afraid. She particularly liked the phrase "as long as it is . . . of no significant value . . . you may use it," but there was no one with whom she could share her observations. *This place lacks a sense of humor,* she remarked to an invisible interlocutor—the appreciative listener she regularly conjured up to bolster her spirits as, over the past couple of years, she had eked out her living in a string of corporate offices.

"Nu Form Brand Flavored Yogurt," she typed, "has no sex because its delicious light taste is appropriate for: Husband and Wife, Father and Daughter, Mother and Son, Brother and Sister, Parish Priest and Nun . . ." Why did it not say "Monk and Nun"? The lack of ecclesiastical parallelism irritated her. Furthermore, who conceived of yogurt as having a sex? A belief apparently requiring rebuttal by the ad-men.

Not long ago, before she quit her regular job to be a Writer, she had worked in a publishing house, reading manuscripts, typing letters for a boss who certainly would have laughed at the self-important, rhetorically empty memos she was now copying. Everyone in that office would have laughed. In their four top-floor rooms of the old brick house facing Boston Common (the servants' quarters, they liked to say), they regularly rolled their desk chairs on their casters from doorway to doorway to read out particularly hilarious passages in manuscripts or cover letters that were continually arriving at their door.

> ___________ *is a novel set in Alaska, but it does not have dog races, Eskimo-wife-swapping, or any polar bears running through anybody's yard.*
>
> _____________ *is the story of my two years in Gestalt Therapy, where I used ordinary pillows to represent members of my family and others.*
>
> *I start the book in the third person, calling the protagonist "Little David," but when he is six years old I suddenly jump into the story in the first person and identify myself as him.*

It had been a cozy, congenial atmosphere, the kind of workplace where you might go out to lunch and find, upon returning, that someone had left a sheet of paper in the typewriter paten (we are in the days before the computer) on which had been typed in lowercase letters the single word "blitzkrieg." At the time everyone knew why this was funny. Once the heavy green front door with its large knocker shut behind you, it was a complete world, with its own urgent preoccupations, jokes, and myths. One might be acquainted with salient facts about people's families but they were like legends from a remote era. When they intruded—through illness, divorce, or death, or even a happy event, a wedding or engagement—it was disorienting, even shocking. People's private lives were not the point.

This early experience of the republic-founding impulse—a cloistered world protected by irony from the messy and humorless world surrounding it, a new country in which everything would be *different*—might have sounded a cautionary note to the philosopher's daughter, had she been in a state of mind to hear it, but in the corporate offices of Stop & Shop, she decides she's had enough. Enough of typing memos about yogurt, enough of temporary jobs, noisy apartments, no time to do her own work. She picks up the phone.

"Dad," she says, "I've been thinking I'd like to spend the summer at the farm."

Or maybe she didn't risk the conditional but simply said, "I am going to . . ." Squeamish memory draws a veil.

She needed a home, and West Delphi was the closest approximation. Surely, once she was there, she could find *some* way of making money. She wouldn't let her father's moods get to her. She was an independent person, after all. And she would be home, sleeping in her own room, waking to look out across the pasture through the window right beside her bed, falling asleep at night with the breeze blowing across her face.

There was a pause, of the kind termed "pregnant." Then the philosopher replied, "In fairness, you should know that someone else will be here as well."

"Oh," said his daughter.

It was clear that this "someone" wasn't going to be his long-lost uncle. That her father might have a companion was a possibility that hadn't occurred to her. She'd known that he'd had—well, liaisons—since he and her mother had divorced over ten years before, but no ongoing relationship, no one he'd ever mentioned. She'd become adept at guessing, from the tone in which he mentioned certain women, that they had been more than acquaintances, but she had grown used to her father's being alone and, except when her brother and sister were around, to being alone with him.

Sitting at her Selectric typewriter, staring at the page in the roller, the child rudely confronted by the fact that the parent has a life that does not include her, she wondered, Now what? But she had no other plans, didn't want to make any. And West Delphi was home. It was *her* home. It had never seemed more so than it did now, when its status was threatened. That she might not *have* a home was too unbearable to contemplate. She'd build a tree house and live in that, she decided. Return to the house only for bathing and cooking. Or she could bathe in the brook. She wasn't sure about typing. Could a person type in a tree house?

When a day or two later the phone rang and it was the managing editor of the publishing house where she'd previously worked wondering if she'd be interested in being the reader of their unsolicited manuscripts, she asked if she'd have to read them in the building. When he said no, she could pick them up once a month and read them wherever she wanted, she knew it had all been meant. She'd taken a leap of faith, and it had been rewarded. Fortuity, as would soon become apparent to all the founders of the Republic, had been hiding Predestination.

Meanwhile, Chantal Meunier and Swift Newman, as has already been noted, looking for an inexpensive place they could fix up (and, Sacrebleu, could they fix this up . . .) had put a down payment on the "Church" (soon to be liberated from quotation marks). Chantal and Swift's friend and Swift's law school classmate, Ben Metcalf, had bought the Magoons' little house from the people who'd bought it from the Magoons when they'd moved to East Delphi. The Osgood place, a mile up a hill, long abandoned to the elements, had been bought by someone reputedly with a trust fund who could afford to restore it. The old schoolhouse, for years owned by people out of state who rarely came up (visitors, it should be noted, nearly always came *up*, there being few places within the borders of the whole larger republic to come down from), had been sold to a woman from New York. "She's very vivacious—you'll like her," Violet Sleeper promised the philosopher's daughter, who xenophobically wasn't at all sure that she would. Who *were* all these people, and what did they want with West Delphi?

These were not summer people; they were *like* summer people, in that they were not natives, had spent more years in school than most long-term residents, and worked at professions, not just jobs, but there was a disturbing blurring of boundaries: summer people turning into year-round residents. They were trespassing upon a liminal space, before the Threshold Institute even taught us what one was. (Founded by the philosopher, the Institute will be described in due course.)

Summer people—it's a term with moral overtones. They are essentially visitors; they skip the character-building winter. They lack fortitude; are limestone, not granite. Where will *they* be when your car gets stuck in the mud or you have an ice dam on your roof and water is running down into your kitchen? Drinking lattes in Starbucks, that's where, or doing whatever the 1970s equivalent might have been.

Summer people, living in summer houses.

IV

Ancient History

This is also a story about love of place, another tributary that has always fed and justified the nation-building impulse. Well before the glimmer of the Republic's dawn, in all its convivial self-ironic glow, the philosopher had had a family with whom he spent summers in West Delphi. He was a father; a husband, however half-hearted; the driver of a pale-blue Ford station wagon named Rocinante after Don Quixote's long-suffering steed.

Up before dawn, last-minute items crammed into the already overfull car, the family set off north, escaping the sticky Annapolis summers where it was often too hot even to sleep, exchanging them for the cool evenings rich with the smell of newly mown grass and the gently operatic trill of the thrush. Tomato plants, a foot tall in their peat pots, started from seed and ready to be put in the ground, took up the top layer of the far back. "Can't see a goddam thing," the philosopher would announce, as if this state of affairs had been orchestrated by an unseen fate. To pass another car on the highway required a group effort—"Safe over here!" "Nothing on this side!"—which was inadequate, however, to preserve other drivers from his imprecations. "Bloody nincompoop!" "Goddam son of a bitch!"

We philosopher's daughters (though not yet aware that we were a philosopher's daughters, who might have been expected to behave philosophically), unseatbelted in our allotted half of the back seat (the other taken up by boxes), were so furious at each other by the time we'd gone fifty miles that we divided the already reduced section of seat even further with a Kleenex box. "Your elbow's over the line!"

"It is not!" "Girls, please!" This from our mother, feebly attempting to make peace from the front. Our father simply ceased to take things philosophically and swore. All of us, in our only recently fresh travel clothes, stuck to everything, the hot breath of Delaware and New Jersey assaulting us through the open windows. There's no air-conditioning in cars in the late fifties.

We've learned the landmarks by heart: the Baltimore tunnel and, after it's built, the Chesapeake Bay Bridge; the high, scary Delaware Memorial Bridge; and then—the point of no return—the vast green sign: NEW JERSEY TURNPIKE, ALL CARS RIGHT. So thrilling, so commanding, the threat plain: if you don't get into the correct lane, you're doomed. Inexorable and frightening—exalting—as we glide beneath that pronouncement and give our fate over to NORTH. It's the sign that tells us we're starting to get somewhere—though we're not safe yet. Not until we get off onto the Garden State Parkway and head into upstate New York can we begin to relax. There are so many disasters that can befall us before that, wrong exits inadvertently taken, or, god forbid, a breakdown. As if in reward for having escaped these calamities, we're allowed to stop for dinner at the silver Rutland diner, which offered what I then believed to be their own miraculous invention of a hot roast beef sandwich.

Then on, on into the gathering dusk, up into the Green Mountains, over the increasingly narrow roads, which finally turn to dirt. Then, no matter how tired and sleepy we are, Mary and I (and, in early years, our older brother, George) wake up. We sit up straight, leaning toward the open windows to breathe in the cool night air. There are few cars now and only the occasional house, its lights shimmering. Strangers, but not quite. They *live* up here. People do. It's not solely the dreamworld we pine for during our long winter exile.

And then at long last the unbelievable occurs: we're heading up the final slope into the village, having seen no car for miles; turning onto the as-yet-unnamed road that the Magoons live on; crossing the old iron bridge over the brook; gliding to the right, onto our road. Our driveway, but also a town road, half a mile still to our house.

First down, then up, around the sharp curve, as in the back we now sit forward, pressed against the front seat: HONK YOUR HORN! the wooden sign there warns. "Honk the horn!" we plead, and our father usually obliges. Placating the hoi polloi, that's the general implication. Then comes the gentle acceleration beneath the dark maples overarching the road, along the field we've always called "the pasture"; next the slight hesitation as the car pauses, as if deliberating, before the turn down into the yard, the dip, and then: stop. The engine dies. Doors lurch open. We inhale. Stretch. At last.

Back safe in this other world, our trial-by-turnpike rewarded by this deep quiet. We unlock the door and go inside. And, oh, the smell of that house, as if quiet could have a smell: old wood, decomposed mice, dust—the very elixir of peace—in synesthesia with the way it looks: the long dark-green living room that Chantal Meunier will later pronounce the color of the true old France, the narrow four-paned windows with their antique rippled glass, the kitchen with its massive wood-burning cookstove, the dining room with its heavy squire-of-the-manor table. Everything is so convincing. We've lived through a whole year, we've grown and changed, but here it still is, just as we left it. Waiting. Waiting—waiting for us!

Our father goes into the basement with a flashlight and turns on the electricity. If it's late, he'll wait until the next morning to turn on the water, a ceremony of banging and invoking the deities, as we, the acolytes, stationed at the faucets on the first floor and in the upstairs bathroom, await revelation. A shout from the cellar—"Anything yet?" "No!" "Now?" "No!" "What the hell!" But always, finally, it happens: first spluttering, then startling bursts of air; a trickle, more violent air spurts, a stronger flow, and then—water. Clear spring water—though occasionally it tastes strange—and then he slides the wooden cover off the spring and discovers the mouse or chipmunk (and once, woodchuck) that over the winter got in through the loose boards and drowned. After that the water tastes for weeks of the bleach he pours in to purify it.

How did a philosopher know how to do these things? Fix the byzantine plumbing, run the rototiller, the lawn mower, the chain saw? Not only run them, but often repair them? Make beer and root beer, and, later, wine, bread, cheese? He already made spaghetti sauce; the recipe, along with clams on the half shell, was taught to him by his college roommate's Italian mother. He engaged in rudimentary carpentry, we knew, but one day (this, much later) he still amazed us by deciding to take out the side door and replace it with the pantry window and vice versa, thus transforming the essentially useless space of the front room into the dining room, and the original dining room into a study. Until then his study had been in the attic bedroom through whose window the fisher cat[5] had legendarily leapt the night he went after it with a golf club.

The door was a little off the horizontal, but what of that? It worked. It hadn't cost anything. Not to spend money unnecessarily was, for a child of the Depression as he was, a hardwired impulse. He never forgot working in the celery fields in Michigan for seventy-five cents a day (which his children, on whom this fact was impressed, have never forgotten either), or the way his mother would go around the table and take a little food from everyone's plate to give to someone who'd come to the door asking. He would buy large containers of discounted spices in order to save money, ignoring the fact that they were discounted because they were stale. (My son, staying in the house a few years ago, threw away the last of these, more than two decades after his grandfather died.) Said grandfather exulted when he'd saved enough Green Stamps to acquire new plates and glasses for the house. He came home pleased with the world because he'd found a pair of sneakers for five dollars. ("Don't tell Dad I need clothes if he asks what I want for my birthday!" my sister exhorted me once.)

But what did we do throughout these pre-Republic summers? The time passed, not always fast. There were rainy days without playmates, when Mary and I moaned with boredom. George was around some of the time, but he was already a teenager, and off on his own pursuits. Mainly I seem to be sitting on the wicker-backed sofa, with its scratchy brown velveteen embossed cushions, my legs out straight in front of me, reading. One summer *The Hobbit*, whose Misty Mountains coalesced in my mind with the New Hampshire Whites in our eastern view, just as Birchwood, the nineteenth-century hotel that burned right before we came up our second summer (in the village Violet Sleeper had thought it was our house, when she saw the smoke from up that way) became forever mixed with the enchanted East Dene of Walter de la Mare's "Theotherworlde" in his introduction to his collected poems, *Come Hither*. Long before it officially happened, I had already become a citizen of that country where it's possible to live in the world and the world of the imagination at the same time.

---

5 A fisher cat, it should be noted, neither fishes nor is a cat, and how it came by this name remains a mystery. Of course, what could be more suitable than that the most ferocious animal around preserves its origins surrounded in obscurity?

Then, as now, this place I love more than anywhere else in the world is up a back road, outside a village of fifteen-plus houses (depending on whether or not you count the maybe half dozen straggling out from the edges), with no stores, no post office, no school, a population of under sixty. This is less than 5 percent of the township's population of about 1,450, which is less than one-quarter of one percent of Vermont's population of almost 647,000, which is itself one-fifth of 1 percent of the 333 million-plus of the country as a whole.

Three roads lead from elsewhere into the village, all of them dirt; the closest pavement is two miles away. GPS and Google Maps and the like can't get you here from there, which pleases us, to be unfindable by such newfangled devices. First-time visitors often don't believe this, and regularly end up being directed by their GPSs around by Birchwood or up to the abandoned copper mines, which haven't been worked since the 1920s. It astonishes and entertains us that people from away can trust this electronic information over the evidence of their senses. These smug search engines can't distinguish between an unmaintained track and a state highway. This, rumor has it, is not solely because these entities aren't as bright as they think they are, but because the state doesn't bother to mention to the Feds that these stretches of road are not kept up lest whatever regulatory body regulates such things reduce our funding accordingly. What body this is precisely and what funding they provide we don't know, but this does not undermine our conviction in the existence of such entities. Forces are always mustering on our borders, plotting to impose their nefarious designs and deprive us of our independence.

A few years ago a woman appeared at the edge of my yard, calling "Hello?" in a quavery voice. I was in my kitchen and went to the door.

"Are you lost?" I called cheerfully.

I walked up to the road and she said, "I'm so scared." She was shaking from fear. Until that moment I'd always assumed that that was simply an expression.

At the time, late spring, the back way from the Birchwood Road to my house is often washed out. There's a three-foot-deep mud bog on the slope down from the top of the hill that even four-wheel-drive pickups can't always get through, and she had a smallish SUV. She'd plowed through coming down, but, as she'd realized, she'd never in a million years get back up.

I put an arm around her and asked her if she wanted to come in and have a glass of water—or whiskey. "No, just water," she said, but she laughed and began to relax.

It turned out that she'd driven over from Maine to attend a weekend retreat offered by marriage counselors who at the time lived in the village and her GPS's ladylike voice couldn't tell her, as I now did, that from here on down to the village the road was in good shape, that the couple who offer these couples' retreats live just a quarter mile on from the end of our road. This was her last hope of saving her thirty-year marriage, she told me.

At my kitchen table we chatted for ten minutes or so—about her marriage, our children (away from home now); we didn't mess around with small talk—and when she left I was in a much better mood than I'd been when she showed up. Serendipity had provided me with a stranger—that magical beginning of so many stories: a lost person—and all unexpectedly a real and meaningful exchange had occurred.

But—wait a moment . . . serendipity? And already I am telling other Delphians the story of this stranded woman and how she came to West Delphi to save her marriage; this story naturally prompts us to revisit other stories about the marriage counselors, such as the time, driving down our road with my sister and encountering a zombie-like couple walking along (they were enjoined, I'd been told, to walk during their breaks from counseling but forbidden to speak), Mary spontaneously took one look as we passed and exclaimed, "Dump him!" The car window, luckily, was up. (Or possibly not.) Or the time Bess, who lived next door to the marriage counselors (when they first arrived and were renting the church), weary of hearing the couples shouting "I hate you!" at each other (another exercise, apparently), stood in the middle of the road and shouted at the top of her lungs, "I hate you too!"

The stranger's arriving at my door has already joined the larger narrative of all the people who have accidentally[6] found their way to this village, like the time the hot-air balloon landed in Fred Darby's field and, having lost its pursuing car, had no way of knowing where it was.

---

6 Really?

Citizens of the Republic, upon espying a balloon in one of the Republic's fields, naturally went out to greet it. This welcoming committee was comprised of Otto, who is Swiss; Chantal, who is French; a visitor who was Dutch; and one other person, who may or may not have had an accent. "Welcome to West Delphi," said Otto, in his cordial way. Others also greeted the balloonist, who looked about himself in astonishment.

"Where *am* I?" he said.

When Otto tells this story, details differ: the balloon did not come down in Fred's but in Hiram Jewell's field; Mike Caponegro was there, and he's from the next town over and as non-accented as a North American can be. Perhaps the balloonist said, "Could you give me a hand with these ropes?" But we are storytellers; the Republic could not have come into being otherwise, and yet, even controlling for exaggeration, it is an article of faith with us that some vortex pulls certain people into our sphere. There is *something* about this place, something that distinguishes it from all others and—thus—us.

When evidence to the contrary presents itself—as, for instance, when a neighbor's hyper-allergic daughter-in-law was stung by a wasp and the 911 responder described in detail the cars in the driveway, perfectly visible to her by satellite—we don't dwell on the fact that we are not as immune to discovery by technology, as remote from and inaccessible to the prosaic world as we prefer to believe. Instead we simply revert to an apparently opposed but in fact complementary way of thinking: we are the center of the universe, and everyone, if they but knew it, would give anything to live here. But it is not every man's lot to gain Delphi, as my father, altering the quotation slightly, liked to say. Long before the Republic had reached its zenith, he maintained that the jets that flew overhead around noon each day were the Strategic Air Command, their route over our house merely confirming the fact that our importance was recognized, even if never spoken about, at the highest levels.

Solitude does this, it can be argued; if no one is around to contradict you, you can think whatever you like about yourself. But if other people think it *with* you . . . what is this, then? A group megalomania, the madness of the crowd, a *folie à* . . . whatever number of storytellers it takes to found a Republic? Your army may be invisible, your rank purely nominal, your constitution unwritten, but what difference does this make as long as your fellow citizens subscribe to the same beliefs? Combine this patriotic fervor with an allegiance to the place itself and—how could you want to live anywhere else?

V

Annals of the Republic: Book the Third

If the American obsession with getting *On the Road* contains, in addition to the exhortation *Go West*, the diluted essence of the European Grand Tour of earlier eras, so does the summer house hold in germ the cultural memory of the English country house life, once the essential component of an upper-class existence. There was the house in town, for when court was in session, and for the season, when daughters were brought "out" and husbands sought; and then there was the county seat, which gave the head of the household his mandate. Landed gentry—those who had estates conferred upon them by the crown as a reward for loyal service. If you owned land, the implication was, you'd done something to deserve it. Being a landowner anchored your position in society—it *gave* you your position. You held the *same name* as your land. You were referred to as "Cornwall" or "Devonshire"; you weren't separate from it. In other words, you can't expect to just show up and *claim* a relationship with a place. Like a newly minted tycoon's construction of a family seat, there's always been something flimsy about summer residents' provenance, however much their attachment to the place may have convinced them that it was somehow entailed.

Besides recalling this aristocratic archetype, New England summer houses are also memorials to a pre-automobile world, when families who could afford it would come by train to spend the entire summer at the seaside or in the mountains, often in grand resort hotels that nearly all perished in the Great Depression, like Birchwood, up the road from West Delphi. At least the mother and children would, while the father continued to strive in ungenteel commerce in the metropolis.

Summer houses thus mix the aura of both heritages: the dynastic family seat that's always there, conferred and incontrovertible; and the resort, at which you're a visitor and thus not ultimately responsible. Summer houses are home—yet escape. It's how we think life ought to feel—endless days full of possibility—yet mostly doesn't.

Add to this that by the 1950s it was often artists and academics who had work schedules that allowed them to take a whole summer away from a workplace—from the grubby obviousness of striving for a living—to believe, still, in these private kingdoms. And there arises the implication (though the clever children of philosophers could pick this up) that it's people who *make things up* and *think* who live this way, and summer in the country is where you go to think clearly. *What did it matter if these two categories became confounded?* the philosopher's daughter thought blithely, as she threw caution to the winds (such winds as could blow in that building without windows, filled with cubicles) because—well, she wanted to. Perhaps thinking and invention were, in fact, simply two aspects of the same process, and when you got tired of beating your head against the wall as you tried to figure out what to do with yourself you just took a leap and—made something up.

But what was the big idea of these new immigrants to West Delphi, fudging the existing categories? Before their arrival there had been the people who lived there year-round—the Magoons, the Averys, the Jewells, the Sleepers, the Hodges, the Lefevres, the Darbys—and, in the summer, her family. Now, besides the philosopher and his daughter, there was his former student, now girlfriend, Sasha, all ensconced up on the hill. The vivacious woman's boyfriend, Otto, a Swiss painter with a charming accent, was going to live in the Schoolhouse for the summer. The vivacious woman herself, Gilda, would come up on weekends. Ben Metcalf, the law student friend of Swift and Chantal's who'd "discovered" West Delphi, and who'd already come up the hill and introduced himself, as if the philosopher and his family were the landed gentry on whom it was incumbent upon newcomers to leave cards, soon brought Otto up to the farm and introduced *him*.

"We ate some asparagus from your garden," Ben announced, in his frank, engaging way that invited confidences in turn (a manner that would serve him well when he became a reporter), confessing that they'd harvested it before the philosopher came up for the summer.

"They were delicious," Otto divulged, generously conferring individual identities upon the stalks.

An obliging, affable, magnetic person, impossible not to like, Otto befriended everyone. He was soon visiting Violet Sleeper, his next-door neighbor, almost daily, sitting at her oilcloth-covered table and eating doughnuts or a slice of pie. Violet was widowed now, both Elton's and Alton's existences attested to by shiny granite headstones in the cemetery directly across the road from her kitchen. She could sit at her kitchen table and keep an eye on them, much as she'd seemed to do when both of them, retired, had sat at the table while she moved from stove to table to sink and back again. She was glad to have Otto's company. Miss her husband she did—her eyes filled with tears when she spoke of him—but Violet was not one to shroud herself in solitary mourning. Hers was the house at which you felt welcome to drop by anytime; the wraparound front porch, its whole length introduced by a single riser up from the road, practically insisted that you go up and knock on her screen door.

Violet was rarely too busy to pause in her baking or cleaning or sewing and sit down with visitors to chat, offering coffee and doughnuts, or pie, or zucchini cake, sometimes enjoining a game of Yahtzee or Scrabble. In a notebook kept under the telephone directory she logged her visitors (and, according to Ben, the number of cups of coffee each drank) and would incontestably have been the most visited person in West Delphi. At least until Otto came along.

"I don't know how he gets any work done," the philosopher said wonderingly. "He's so damn gregarious."

There were always cars outside the Schoolhouse in the evening, or else Otto's was gone. (If he were a millionaire, Otto once avowed, he would buy everyone in Delphi the same model and color car, so that no one would be able to tell who was visiting whom.) Otto met people everywhere, and invited them over the borders. Yet somehow he managed to keep producing the whimsical folk art furniture, and later pictures, that he painted. Mythological-feeling scenes of country landscapes and animals, one of these portrayed a story called "Stanley's Dream" on a cabinet, commemorating his neighbor Stanley Jewell's longings: for a house of his own up on the hill, with a tower, a comely wife, and a herd of fat cows.

Nearly every evening Otto walked across the road to help Hiram and Stanley with the milking. Coming from a highly orderly society in which, as Otto avowed, even the cats were required to take out hunting licenses before catching mice, he couldn't comprehend what seemed to him the slovenliness of the Jewells' barn. How could they function like that? What prevented them from simply cleaning it up? Or making their farming methods more efficient? When someone recently had painted graffiti in the Zurich subway system, it was such an extraordinary act that the perpetrator, instead of being punished, had been pitied, deemed in need of psychiatric help, and eventually rewarded by having a book published about his exploits. Coming from this welter of propriety, Otto, held up at knifepoint when he first moved to New York, had begun to remonstrate with the mugger in Swiss German—sympathetically, for he believed him to be deranged—until the mugger gave him up as a hopeless victim and rushed off in disgust. That other barns in the area might have looked the same and for the same reasons—not enough money and help to get more than the basics done every day—didn't occur to us as an explanation, reclining as we then were in a worldview as yet unvisited by questions of economic disparity. It wasn't, after all, as if we were sitting around doing nothing.

Otto was painting (and painting the Schoolhouse); painting Violet Sleeper's oversize mailbox with a scene starring her large black-and-white cat, Wilbur; building a barn, where he would keep the first of the many horses he would acquire. Chantal and Swift and Ben were fixing up their houses, undertaking even such massive jobs as replacing the rotting sills of the Church. Swift could frequently be seen hauling a giant beam across the yard, looking like a penitent on the way to Calvary. They did everything themselves, learning as they went. Often they joined forces and helped each other. It hardly seemed like work, at least to those of us watching from up the hill, so cheerfully companioned were their labors. There did not seem, anymore, to be jobs that only other people could do. You didn't *hire* people to work on your house for you. Driven by financial expediency, this belief yet acquired a moral overtone. It was perhaps these new residents' enterprise that inspired the philosopher (given to expounding upon all the things that *ought* to be done) to, one day, get the idea of exchanging the pantry window for the entry door, which instantly added an entire new usable room to the house.

One evening, driving through the village, the philosopher's daughter happened upon two figures swathed in white, robed and turbaned like Sikhs, proceeding in single file down the short slope between the Church and Ben's house. The foremost and smaller of the two figures, whom she recognized as Gilda, bore what looked like a blender, held out before her as an acolyte would a taper. But—a blender? In that getup? The philosopher's daughter didn't recognize the larger figure. She considered stopping—but the gathering looked clandestine and she was already feeling a little excluded by this new society developing in the village. Some strange cult, it appeared, she told Gilda later, with which she was reluctant to interfere. "You might have been being abducted, for all I knew. But I just drove on by!" The taller figure was Chantal, it turned out; they had been insulating the eaves of the Church and had swathed themselves to guard against the fiberglass fibers. The blender Ben required for yet another batch of his inventive pesto. (Cheddar and peanut was one particularly notable combination.) Culinary experiments were being embarked upon and reproduced in the kitchens of the Republic with the alacrity with which less savory regimes compete in an arms race.

Up on the hill, a half mile from the village, the philosopher and his household observed all this activity with intense interest. Chantal, who'd grown up in a French village and accordingly claimed to feel right at home in West Delphi, had, like Otto, formed an alliance with Violet Sleeper and, during the academic year, when she taught French at a local high school, stopped by every afternoon for coffee. Ben, on his way home from law school and then, later on, from the newspaper where he worked, visited nearly as often. They bought pies and zucchini bread from her, and helped her with chores around the house.

"The village . . ." we'd always said—we, up on our hill, by implication not quite being part of it. We had known everyone in West Delphi for years; when young, Mary and I had played in the Jewells' hayloft, had helped the Magoon boys drive their cows home in the evening for milking. I'd sat on Hiram Jewell's lap while he drove the tractor back and forth across the pasture, cutting hay. Ernie and Billy Magoon and Stanley Jewell had played up at our house. George had been friends with

Violet and Elton's son, Leroy, and joined a local Bible church because he was sweet on a girl who attended it. But then, when I was twelve, we'd moved from Maryland to New Mexico and had stopped coming back in the summers. What might have been a natural development, one way or another, had become a hiatus. Our relationships with the "villagers" had remained warm, but intermittent.

Now here were Otto and Chantal, seeming to make no social distinctions between farmers and college professors. Chantal confided in Violet Sleeper as freely as she did in her friends, and Otto was as at ease assisting Hiram and Stanley in persuading their small and exceedingly unenthusiastic bull to mount a very large cow as he was discussing the art world at the philosopher's dining room table. It was an odd feeling. We had been there for twenty years and other than the villagers had seen few people—visiting relatives or out-of-town friends: people who either came to stay with us or other academics, colleagues of my father's, who with their families rented houses in nearby towns for a summer or two. Now it was as if someone had come into the living room and drawn aside draperies to reveal a window we hadn't known was there. Were the newcomers' friendships with the Jewells and Violet Sleeper livelier simply because they were in town year-round, living next door? Or had we, without acknowledging it, conformed to social gradations that foreigners were too culturally tone-deaf to pick up on? Was this an *American* problem? And yet Ben Metcalf, also American, made no distinctions. Were we, up on our hill, simply snobs?

Feeling left out was a new feeling, in West Delphi. There'd always been isolation, especially after the Magoons moved to East Delphi, but there had been no one in particular to feel isolated from. No group. I'd visited Violet and the Jewells, but it had never occurred to me to wish that our house were closer in, to envy Violet Sleeper her proximity to the Jewells, for example. Now it seemed that everyone besides us was right in the heart of things, within sight and shouting distance of each other. They could see each other when they went out to work in their gardens, and at night look out their windows and see each other's lights. Otto and Gilda, Chantal and Swift, and Ben, and their perpetual streams of visitors, were continually in and out of each other's houses. For our household, dropping by was less casual. To descend from the mountaintop required an intention, or an invitation. The philosopher, seemingly untroubled by the side effects of remoteness, merely remarked, "There may be hope for this village yet."

Gradually, however, almost despite ourselves, we began to be drawn in, to be invited down and in turn to invite up. We lost our timidity, and felt comfortable dropping by. Ben, Chantal, and Otto were so welcoming, like Violet interrupting whatever they were busy with to offer coffee. (Another catalyzing revolution: these newcomers all made coffee in Italian espresso makers. The philosopher got rid of his automatic drip pot and bought a Moka.) "This village is looking up," he repeated. "What we need now is a pub."

In fact, there was one: a rotating one, with dinner. Dinners at the church, dinners at Delphi Industries, as Ben had incorporated himself in order to enable him to buy things wholesale. ("What *is* this Delphi Industries?" a supplier questioned him. "What do you *do* there?") Dinners at the Schoolhouse. Dinners at the Threshold Institute, as the philosopher's household was now referred to.[7] Chantal, an accomplished cook in the French style (in the summers she worked as a chef at a local lake resort), baked baguettes and made cassoulet. One fall, she and Swift and Ben went in on a side of beef; wrapped in butcher's aprons, with Chantal's *Larousse Gastronomique* propped on the counter before them, they attempted to divide the carcass into the classic pieces. Otto made *hasenpfeffer*—rabbit stew—from his own rabbits. The philosopher's daughter, for reasons now obscure, learned to make Sacher torte. The philosopher made his trademark spaghetti, or chicken livers in wine sauce, and expanded his

7 An abbreviation of the Institute for the Study of Threshold Phenomena, a quasi-dimensional think tank founded by the philosopher and ratified by compatriots. The Institute had come into being in the way entities tended to in the Republic—as a joke, a fancy, but thereafter referred to with enough frequency that it came to be taken for granted. When the philosopher had been dean of the college where he also taught, he had hired three psychologists ("Three for the price of one," he liked to say) and they had introduced him to the concept of "threshold phenomena": thoughts hovering on the border of consciousness. The Institute also signified to the philosopher a merging of disciplines, the location, for instance, where literature and philosophy crossed over into each other, or literature and politics, or politics and religion—the ill-defined, or undefined, areas where intellectually he liked to roam. (The fact that, as with Ben's Delphi Industries, having an organization through which he could order beer- and wine-making supplies more cheaply than as an individual was, if not strictly the motivation, a handily furnished justification.)

repertoire to include coq au vin (which, on principle, he refused to call by its French name).

Besides splendid meals, the citizens of the Republic made bread, cheese, cakes, and pie; put up dilly beans and pickles, jams and jellies. Violet was the guru of baking: her recipe for zucchini cake made it, via a visiting reporter friend of the philosopher's daughter, into a national newspaper. The philosopher kept bees and persuaded Ben to. He and Ben, as has been mentioned, made beer and wine. The philosopher's daughters stained their fingers yellow picking dandelions for wine: it was a beautiful pale gold that tasted like its color—not sweet, but like the essence of flowers. The philosopher also made wine from rose hips, blackberries, and raspberries and bought cabernet sauvignon concentrate when he ran out of fruit. The wine, fermenting in carboys—large heavy glass containers, a yard tall, the tops corked with a Rube Goldberg–looking contraption that released carbon dioxide—sat on straight chairs around the living room like stiff, taciturn guests, burbling disapprovingly at regular intervals. Everyone tended vast gardens and kept chickens, and then Chantal and Swift acquired a pig—Cochon, greatly beloved by Swift, though one fall day, Cochon took off "for Istanbul," whence he reportedly sent regular postcards detailing his adventures. Otto had acquired one horse, then another; in the beginning he rode them, then bought a buggy in which he gave everyone occasionally hair-raising rides along the narrow back roads.

In my plan to build a tree house, I had persisted so far as to carry several boards out into my favorite field, three stone walls away from the house, before I gave up. The remnants of a small platform stood for many years as a monument to my early, abortive attempt to erect a separate shelter on the land. I stayed in the house, and our household of three got along, thanks in large part to the friendly and open personality of the "someone else." Sasha, a few years younger than I, was lively, a sympathetic listener, generous with her laughter, not one of our moody breed. I understood why my father liked her. I liked her too. Everything was fine—especially when I didn't think about the situation: living alone on top of a hill with my father and his young lover. When I did, I was so preoccupied by my own discomfort that I didn't devote much thought to theirs. Or, more accurately, I couldn't bear to think about it, to perceive myself in the role of spoiler to their summer idyll. Generously they didn't make me feel unwelcome; Sasha's presence made my father cheerful. I had never seen him in such a buoyant mood, in fact, and I worked hard to be entertaining.

During the day we went our separate ways; at dinner, which we took turns preparing, we sat around the heavy dark table, which gave to any meal a feeling of a meeting convened, and watched the *ABC Evening News* as we ate. Pre–satellite dish, ABC was the only channel that came in. How Peter Jennings eased conversational awkwardness over the years at our dinner table! Was he balding? we speculated. Was he wearing a toupee? Peter wouldn't do that, we concluded—he had too much integrity.

When we weren't discussing Peter's hairline or reacting to the news with convivial rancor—"Those goddam idiots in Washington," the reigning pundit pronounced—Sasha and I listened as he held forth about Joyce or Conrad or Derrida. Or—and this formed the liveliest intervals of our conversation—we recounted with joyful incredulity the latest news from the village. To bring a fresh object of local wonderment brought more inebriation to the dinner table than the philosopher's home brew.

"Did you know that you can drive Swift crazy by asking for a match? He counts the matches in a box and orchestrates their dispensation to coincide with the number of cigarettes in his packs, and he'll go for another box, rather than have his arrangement disrupted. Otto asks him for one just to see what he'll do." (No one had heard of OCD in those days, and this was considered a lovable eccentricity, as, at this halcyon moment, were all personal foibles.)

"You know Ben's satellite dish? When he first got it, Swift and Chantal told him that 'Meshdish' was the name of a town in Iran"—where Ben had once taught English—"and he spent all afternoon looking in his atlas trying to find it."

"Swift is now claiming that Cochon has bought a villa in Istanbul."

"You know what? Some of the other reporters at the *Darby Gazette* told Ben that this area is called Oz. 'Oh, you live in Oz!' they said to him. As in *Wizard of*. . ."

Which, of course, merely confirmed what by now we'd already understood: we were a place apart, an unknown country upon which adventurers could stumble. The Republic was nascent. We ourselves were such adventurers, who'd stumbled upon a kingdom of kindred spirits, our intoxication with our good fortune continually renewed by the taking of a kind of citizens' communion in our repeating of these stories, our founding myths, our constitution.

VI

The End of Freya's Reign: Part the First

An apparent detour in fact leading the traveler back to the high road.

It is said that the legendary Queen Radegund was softer than rose petals, that her courtiers fought to press against her, and that in wintertime many were crushed to death, so fierce was the competition. Once you had smelled her you could think of nothing else, so that the drones complained of workers leaving their jobs undone: dead bees in the hive, larvae unfed, pollen left to pile up in the entrance, inviting robber bees to invade. It is said that Queen Radegund acquired her magical scent because in the summer of her birth the plum tree in the garden of the big yellow hive bloomed for the first time, and that year there were more flowers than ever before: poppies and marigolds and hollyhocks and bachelor's button that the beekeeper planted in front of his hive, as well as the lilac and mock orange and tiger lily that bloomed each year on their own. In all its history, our hive had never known such abundance. Sometimes we had had to travel far afield in search of wild apple blossom, clover, Queen Anne's lace, purple loosestrife.

Queen Radegund reigned longer than any queen in the history of our hive, and even in her last battle she put up such a fight that her successor nearly succumbed. The new queen, our beloved Freya, had to be coddled and nurtured for weeks after her victory before she could take her first flight. Morale was so low, anyway, after Queen Radegund's death, that the population died off like flies. (Repulsive scavengers.) If the new, young queen had not finally rallied it could have meant the end of our colony, yet although we endured, the end of Radegund's reign marked the beginning of a decadent period in our hive, which, some say, continues to this day.

During Radegund's reign, the workers grew careless and did not raise as many queen cells as they had before, and this left the hive unprepared in the event of an emergency, such as the invasion by an alien swarm. Certain factions claimed that this was because Queen Radegund bribed the workers with promises of eternal proximity to her scent if they would not breed competitors, but I have never believed those stories. Queen Radegund's first concern was the welfare of the hive—as it is all of ours. I think that the workers had grown lax because they had come to believe that the old queen was immortal. No one alive could remember a time when she had not been queen. Secondly, it was during the last year of Radegund's reign that the beekeeper's garden was not replanted: where there had bloomed sweet pea and cosmos was now tangled with grass and burdock and maple saplings, and the workers, unused to having to travel far in search of pollen, were not prepared and barely managed to store enough honey to last the winter. If it had not been a winter of much snow, blanketing the hive and keeping the workers drowsy, we would assuredly have perished.

Queen Radegund will always be remembered for the bravery she showed in her last battle. The workers who were standing about the old queen when her successor, still glistening after her emergence, gave her shrill invitation to combat, said that Radegund trembled, even though it was such a warm July day that workers were taking turns lining up and batting their wings to keep down the temperature in the hive. Radegund must have heard something in Freya's voice that told her she would not be able to win this contest. Alas for poor Queen Radegund, softer than rose petals . . . But it is not like me to be sentimental. "The queen is dead, long live the queen" is a slogan that beekeepers have borrowed from us.

The second year that Freya ruled, it seemed as if the queendom might regain the splendor it had known at the height of Radegund's reign. It was a balmy year, raining just the necessary amount, and the workers foraged far and wide for pollen. The stores of honey grew. But, alas, the hive grew crowded and the workers grumbled. Where was the honey to go? Sacks of pollen were piling up inside the hive. That was when, in secret (instead of killing her, as in loyalty they ought to have done), the workers nurtured a new young queen, fed her upon the choicest honey, and then incited her to rebellion. The vengeful Lilina . . . One day, soon after her birth, the courtiers who had raised her led her forth, and, without even bothering to challenge Freya, Lilina gathered a swarm about her and departed the hive forever. She and her subjects settled in a hollow tree two miles away and are there to this day, though the workers there have forgotten their origins. They are an untutored race who keep no memory of their history, have never heard of Radegund, and know nothing of beekeepers. Were one of Queen Freya's subjects to dare to cross the threshold of their uncivilized hive, she would meet with an instantaneous and brutal death, for Lilina's workers regard us as their enemies. Thus, too, must we regard them.

After Lilina and her followers swarmed, Queen Freya did her best to rally her workers' spirits, but they were resentful of the additional work they were now burdened with in order to prepare the hive for winter. In the beekeeper's heyday, Freya told us, this could not have happened. He would have seen how crowded the hive had become and would have built an extra story on top. Sometimes he would take the honey away to make room for more. He never took so much that he did not leave us enough to last through the winter, and if it was a hard winter he would reappear from wherever he migrated to, to feed us with jars of sweet syrup until spring came and we could again begin to make honey.

Queen Freya liked to tell the story of how, every summer morning except when it poured rain, the beekeeper would visit the hive, sit motionless on a large rock nearby, and watch the workers come and go. For a while workers were assigned to watch him at all times, and to sound the alarm should he show menacing intentions, but it grew clear to them that he meant no harm. He wouldn't kill a fly! they said in disgust, even when the fly continually provoked him, conducting forays against his face, landing in his hair, and buzzing like a drunken bumblebee as it tried to disentangle itself. The beekeeper merely rescued the revolting creature from its hapless predicament and tossed it into the air. After a time the workers lost all fear of him, and some even alit on him, and he never moved, never tried to frighten them away. Only once was the beekeeper stung and that was when a young bee, skittish, became alarmed when the beekeeper lifted the roof off the hive as he sometimes did, according to our history, to make sure that all was well within, and, in mistaken heroism, gave her life in defense of the hive.

Queen Freya is very wise and knows many things and no one has ever doubted her sincerity, yet there are nevertheless many among the workers who scoff at her stories, and say that the beekeeper is a myth, that he has never come down to our hive from his enormous one and watched over our existence. Even if he did, they say, it was in days so long ago that it makes no difference now. He is never coming back. It is sad to think that this might be true. I, Honeysuckle the Ninth, born in a cell on the fourth tier of the north side of the hive, have always longed to see our beekeeper. Even as a very young worker, when my companions were flitting back and forth in the sunlight, staging mock battles with imaginary wasps, pretending to take orientation flights even before they were old enough, I preferred to remain at the entrance with the guards, listening to the stories the scout bees told when they came home from their expeditions. Perhaps it would have been better had I been born a drone, as my companions have often taunted me, so given am I to dreamy contemplation and, they say, fruitless imaginings. Yet I cannot help but think that it would serve us well to know more about the habits of beekeepers, if they can exercise such an influence upon our lives. And I cannot bring myself to believe that our beekeeper has died or abandoned us for another hive.

VII

Interlude One: Summer

Daylight wakes me and, because I don't have to, I get up. My room faces the pasture, which stretches from the barbed wire fence below the lawn to the stone wall that marks the southern boundary of our land.

The Jewells' heifers, kept here for the summer, regularly break through the fence and we drive them back and then call Stanley who comes up to mend the barbed wire again. For many years the pasture stayed green all summer when other fields turned tawny because the cows kept it cropped. I lie in bed and gaze out at this green sweep, as level as anywhere on our property gets, and wait for it to smooth out my thinking.

The room is small—there's a square space the size of two pickup truck beds where there's a dresser and a miniature armchair; a narrow fold-out desk where I used to keep a letter from J. R. R. Tolkien with his signature in Elvish, responding to the only fan letter I've ever written until either someone made off with it or I hid it somewhere I've never been able to recall; then an alcove that just fits the single brass bed. A virginal room; the bed's not big enough for two people regularly to sleep in, though I have shared the bed, and it's the room to which I brought my newborn son, pushing the bed against the wall so he wouldn't fall out, sleeping carefully on the outer edge so I wouldn't roll onto him.

It was always a refuge, this room—safe in the house and yet surveying the pasture, the world; a luxury of retreat in the afternoon when I drowsed in its sunny quiet and listened to the comforting murmur of other people busy with life downstairs, or at night, when the sky was vivid with stars and the velvety breeze blew in through the screen and bathed my face.

It was this room I'd think of when, in various noisy city apartments, I couldn't sleep. I'd pretend I was there, and once in a while this ruse would permit me to drift off.

I tiptoe down the stairs and make tea, careful not to let the kettle whistle. The outside doors have been left open so the cat can come and go, in defiance of whatever wild animals might like to venture, and sometimes do, through the hole in the screen. Once a raccoon and Henry, the cat who afforded the fisher his role as grade-B stuntman, burst simultaneously through the kitchen screen, raced toward the living room side by side—unclear who was chasing whom—whence in mutual horror they fled in opposite directions. My brother was there and our father said, "Get the gun." When the raccoon took refuge in the pantry near some recently bottled wine, he said, "Wait." It wasn't until the raccoon fled back to the living room and began to scratch the brand-new stereo speakers that he gave George the order to fire. I think of this story nearly every time I look at the hole in the screen.

Carrying my tea, I go through the living room with its regiments of books and onto the front lawn. The wet grass is cold against my bare feet. To the east, a sea of fog fills the valley. The mountains rise out of it like low-lying islands, and the sun is a pale disk, hovering above the horizon as if it might change its mind and sink back out of sight. Not triumphant and willful, as it looks on a clear morning. I am the only one awake.

I sit in one of the white wooden lawn chairs, cradling the warm mug. The pair of these chairs always faced south toward the pasture, even though the more spectacular view is to the east: the nearby gentler slopes lightening to blue as they cross the invisible Connecticut River and become mountains. Nothing to bruise the eye, as if we're living on in a time before factories and electric lines and radio towers have even been thought of.[8] We turn our heads to look at the view at junctures in the conversation, or when we want there to be junctures. As if to say, *Excuse me if I don't attend, but, you see, the mountains . . .*

Until decades later when I was startled to see that tenants had turned the chairs to face the view, I never wondered why we oriented them to look at the pasture. More conducive to conversation to contemplate that soft green expanse, perhaps. There's something so adamant about the blue

8 Cell phones had yet to impinge on anyone's consciousness.

shapes, like a crowd of whales rising from the deep. *So that's it.* Even if what they articulate can't be translated into human language.

When I came to build my own house, up the hill from my father's, I oriented it to face the mountains. No gentle sweep like the pasture's leads away from my house; it's anchored on a slope between woods rising behind and a field falling before. There'd be no level space at all had I not had sections terraced by a bulldozer. The house looks directly at the mountains over a steep valley, and more of the light-blue ones are visible than down at the other house. So that I could lie in bed and see the mountains, the carpenters I worked with in building the house held a plank and I lay on it; they lifted it up and down so that we could gauge at what height to put in the bedroom windows. It's a grand and splendid view—so extravagant sometimes, especially on fall mornings when the mist interleaves the nearer valleys, that I can scarcely believe it exists, let alone that I'm looking at it. But it's demanding. It isn't going to cut you any slack. It exalts you, but you have to live up to it, whereas the soft rolling green at the house down the hill, even the mountains there, being more closely framed, are reassuring, benevolently letting you go about your human business. To sit in the white lawn chairs—gone now, disintegrated, finally, after many years of wear—was to hold these two positions, the long and the short view, in companionable balance.

In the field down below the chairs' lookout point used to be the vast vegetable garden, where one morning after being woken at dawn by the sound of a deer snorting, I looked out to see Henry, in his Jersey-cow-colored Siameseness, planted firmly on his haunches staring up at the deer while she pawed the ground and repeated her loud, insistent exhale, demanding, it seemed, that this peculiar small creature account for himself. What manner of animal was he, and what were his intentions? *Speak up, now.*

Henry was legendary not only for ushering the fisher into the house in the wee hours, but for traveling, by himself, from Vermont to Maryland, disappearing one day when my father, who'd inherited him from my sister, took him to southern Vermont for the academic year. We thought he'd been stolen, hit by a car, attacked by something. Or just run off in high dudgeon, not pleased at being taken away from his happy hunting grounds in West Delphi.

Two months later, the household in Annapolis where he'd lived as a kitten called up. "You're not going to believe this," they said. They had a German shepherd and another cat, both antagonistic to strange animals. "Oh, hi, Henry," these two said, as Henry walked right into the house, past them, and directly to his food dish. My father drove down to Maryland to pick him up and maintained that Henry cursed all the way back up the New Jersey Turnpike. (That unwitting stretch of highway has never met with much favor from anyone in our family.)

How did he *get* there? we wondered. Specifically, how did he cross the Hudson? We heard there was an "animal trail" down through the Adirondacks—had he gone west from Marlboro and somehow crossed the Hudson by bridge in the wee hours? The vet in Annapolis was amazed at what good shape he was in, given his ordeal. Had someone abducted him and he'd escaped or been released farther south (the abductors weary of his profanity, perhaps)? Our favorite theory was that he'd gone due south until he'd hopped a fishing boat in Long Island Sound and ridden down to the Chesapeake in style.

Henry was in a bad mood for a long time after his odyssey, but stayed around for a few more years and through several more winter houses, until he disappeared with my cat, Kip, whom I'd left with my father at his winter residence while I was traveling. Though we'll never know what became of them, we speculate that the two may have headed north together for the farm.[9] We always thought that this was where Henry had set off for the first time but, finding it unoccupied, had then turned around and headed back south. There's something about the spot that everyone, but animals and small children especially, immediately recognizes. Human and beast, they emerge from arriving cars, look tentatively around, sniff, literally or figuratively, and then all at once the realization dawns: it's safe here. The serenity is real. No cars, no asphalt, no *noise.* Nothing but fields and woods and mountains—and you. You will not be interrupted, or waylaid, or gainsaid. To roam freely—simply to *roam*—the desire to do this was there all along, but buried, forgotten. And now there's all the time in the world to do this, and it's yours.

Animals have methods of finding their way that are closed to us, either by design or because we've lost the knack. Believers in geomancy, a

9 As we'd always called it, despite our never farming anything except stands of red pine.

method of divination that interprets markings on the ground, think, for example, that what have been called the "old straight tracks" in Britain—traveling routes linking monuments and hills—were not only early pre-map traveling aids but laid out in response to underground water currents or electromagnetic lines. UFOs, some people assert, use these tracks for navigation. Bees performing their aerial pantomimes, migrating birds and butterflies, spawning salmon, not to mention longing cats and dogs, going after families who have left them—all respond to signs in the landscape that people cannot, or can no longer, apprehend. The dowser's knack of locating underground channels of water, and sometimes other things, assuming you believe in this ability, are vestiges of this long-lost ability to read the earth. My brother once took hold of a dowsing wand Alton Sleeper was holding and he could feel the force with which it pulled their hands down toward the ground. Recently I've witnessed this myself—and there is no way that the hands holding the stick could simultaneously have tipped it toward the ground. They strove, in fact, to hold it back. Not everyone has this skill, or the understanding of the forces that ply it if they do. But there are things we can discern in a place even if we don't know what they are.

In Delphi there's an area called Bryce Hill where there were once copper mines. At the site of one old mine the ground is bare and russet-colored from the tailings. The hillside is punctuated by birch trees, which look innocently bucolic until you know that they're a tree that grows more readily than others in the copper-polluted ground. Then they seem like strikers crossing a picket line. Halfway up the poisoned slope is a narrow declivity that leads to a cave that leads to a mine shaft. A jagged sign warns: KEEP OUT, DANGER. Beer cans are strewn around the mouth of the cave: evidence of observance of the sign—or the opposite. Snow can hang on in this tiny gorge into June and there's always water on the floor of the cave, water oozing from the roof, and as you draw near you are struck by a chill breath from the deep. Before you reach the molten heart of things, it must be pretty damn cold down there.

Bryce Hill is a spooky place, sinister and sad. Hundreds of people lived up there once, and a new road had to be built between the mines and Center Delphi to carry the copper ore. In the late 1870s the Delphi mine was one of only a handful in operation in the entire country; but then the price of copper fell, the mine closed; reopened; copper went up during the First World War, but by 1920 the Bryce Hill Mines had closed for good. Now they're on the official list of Superfund sites, ecological disasters that the federal government is scheduled to clean up.[10]

But even before the hill was mined, settled, and fell into ruin, there may have been something in the disposition of the hills that gave Bryce Hill its uncanny quality. That may have suggested to earlier settlers: *There's more here than meets the eye.* Years before I first climbed up there, Bryce Hill was a place unimaginably beyond Birchwood, the old hotel that burned, which itself already stood in my mind as the outer reach of civilization. Civilization *past.*

There's nothing back of us for miles was something we said to people in describing how utterly quiet and isolated our house was. The "Last Homely House"—I'd read about it in *The Hobbit.* Birchwood was de la Mare's mythical East Dene; it was the magical château in Alain-Fournier's *Le Grand Meaulnes* to which the title character travels. "Utter solitude" indeed, as the real estate ad that originally drew my father had claimed, though the place feels nothing like the drastic sound of that. Visitors ask, "Don't you feel isolated up here?" and I shrug and say, "You can feel isolated anywhere," or "Ask me in mud season."

Of course one can, and I have, but how to explain the intoxication that's like a drug you want more and more of, of being alone and hearing the summer world start up with the first annunciatory bird, and then the corroboration of the others—the chorus of the sun on the grass, the breeze in the trees around the edges of the yard, the smell of the morning. All of this up to its own devices, all day long, without any initiating by humans whatsoever—this gift, how can one not but feel—on into the night, into the chirping of crickets and the particular way the warm air feels, cooling down, the fireflies blinking around the lawn like apprentice stars while, up above, the real thing, more than anyone could possibly ever name—it all makes me recognize over and over the inadequacy of my language to respond in my helpless love to what all of this knows.

Once, here, was the opposite of isolation; West Delphi was the most

10 As I write, the EPA is preparing to sequester the poisonous tailings in mounds, which will involve about five thousand trucks worth of material moved in and out. Needless to say, the people who live on the access road have a lot to complain about.

populous of all the villages in Delphi township. Cellar holes mark where several houses once stood along the now-uninhabited road between our house and Birchwood, and Birchwood itself stood on its rise, surveying the valley: a grand two-story house with an ell and a wraparound porch. There were summer guests, pursuing lazy pastimes: strolling, going for buggy rides, sipping sarsaparilla in rockers on the porch, bowling in the wooden bowling alley that stood for many years, even after the hotel itself burned, disintegrating gradually until the floor had so merged with the ground that morels grew up through it one spring. (I have almost forgiven Otto for being the one to discover them.)

I never saw the hotel standing; my brother did, that first year in Delphi, but my sister and I were too small to hike that far and in the early days the road was impassable by car. It remained a Shangri-la of a destination whose reality could never live up to its enchanted reputation, but it didn't have to: by the time I got there it was so overlaid by the stories I'd heard about it and the geography of my own imagination that an actual building would have been more of a hindrance than a satisfaction. It was almost inevitable that one day I'd set a novel there, adding yet another layer of invented life to a place that in many ways had, for me, never been other than invented.

All over Vermont, cellar holes bear witness to the fact that early builders knew how to site a house; they knew the value of a view, long before towns got the bright idea of taxing them. One of the uncanny things about Bryce Hill is the viewlessness of so many of the houses that are on hillsides and *ought* to have views. You look out to where you expect there to be an opening to the wider world and there isn't, or it's obscured by another hill or by trees. Fields, unhayed, have grown back to forest. A hill farm—these places on the slopes of hills, alongside a road: it's defiant and risky for a house to insist on staying level, sideways, on a slope. There's something plaintive and insufficient about them, as if they'd wanted to ascend to the crest but couldn't.

In the spring of 1958 our parents came back up to Delphi to decide whether to buy the house we'd rented the previous summer or another—the same price, with double the acreage and a pond—on Bryce Hill. In Annapolis, my brother and sister and I sat waiting for the phone to ring. Our hopes were all on the place we'd already come to love, attaching ourselves to it as quickly as if we'd recognized it. There was a certain glamour to a pond, and we supposed more acreage was a desirable thing, but we had campaigned for the place we'd already sworn allegiance to. When at long last the inert black object produced its jarring noise and George assumed the eldest's prerogative of answering it, Mary and I listened anxiously, attempting to glean the verdict from his cagey monosyllabic responses, though it couldn't have been very long before he hung up and divulged the news.

"It's the farm!"

We all cheered. We had already taken over from the previous owners—adopted a giant doll they'd left, whose stuffing was coming out to the extent that he now bore bandages over much of his limbs; I had appropriated a birthday book, crossing out the names its former owner had entered and inscribing my family's and friends'. What we'd known, if our parents hadn't, was that the place was already ours.

Bryce Hill is thus also, in addition to being beyond the furthest point of civilization, somewhere we might have lived. A memorial to a life that didn't happen. The vague fear that attaches for me to that part of town may in part be due to the recognition that I might easily not have had this deep and abiding relationship with our land, more incontrovertible, if not always more comforting, than any human one. Whenever I drive up to Bryce Hill I try to figure out which house it was that my parents almost bought; I toy with thinking how our lives might have been different. Whom would we have known? Whose barn would we have built hay forts in? Where would we have bought milk? If it hadn't been from the Jewells it would have been from someone else, but the Republic could never have been formed on Bryce Hill, nor the Threshold Institute founded. No dreamy reverie can encompass *that*.

It was predictable that one day a character would stride down from Bryce Hill and into the novel I'd set at the old hotel, and then a character went back up the hill and sat beside the chill mine entrance when in a despairing mood, and now when I go there I sometimes realize with a start that the events I'm recalling as having occurred in that spot are of my own devising.

You learn that it's impossible to see any place plain, free of human associations and expectations. The very notion of place is bound up with naming, distinguishing one patch of earth from another. It's expedient—hard to give directions without identifying places by name—but inevitably mixes up the name with the thing. It's easiest to see this with cities. Few Americans, for instance, can see Paris or Rome not overlaid by "Paris" and "Rome," places usually encountered first in literature and film. And what would that mean, in any case, pure apprehension of place? Rarely is there such a thing as a landscape plain, anyway, if by that we mean free of human interference. The disposition of fields, the patterns in which houses have been situated, the way forests have grown back, or not, are the result of someone's decision, of economic necessity, of the method used to lay out property in the old country, of complying with topography, soil, and water. You try for untrammeled perception, to listen to what the place is telling you—the message in the way the hills overlap or the stars have arranged themselves right over your house—but what you mostly hear are the stories of the people who have lived here before you. Only at a distance—far enough to turn green mountains blue—can you reliably see the land untouched by human meddling. Yet even supposing we were somehow transported to such a pristine landscape, about which no one had yet said anything, our minds would strain at the leash to start sorting and defining.

Even so, though, even so, something intrinsic to a place determines how people settle in it, which in turn affects those who come after them. Obvious factors, like climate and the lay of the land: fertile earth and level fields in the river valleys inviting farming, the poorer rocky soil of the hills and the shorter growing seasons making that land more suitable to grazing sheep so that when the sheep-farming fell off, undercut by lower pricing elsewhere, the forests took over. But there's something beyond these things, qualities in the land—in the arrangement of hills and, more ungraspably, in the ground itself—that bring an influence to bear, first incline a settler to say not there, *here*.

Sitting out in the early morning, I look to my right: spread across the damp lawn are croquet wickets, glistening with dew as if they've grown up naturally, springing up overnight like mushrooms. They have a profound air of waiting about them, even though, to be truthful, they also look indifferent. If your sole purpose is to await a ball rolling through you it is easy to see why you would express a certain ambivalence.

The wickets are set up not in regulation order on a grassy space the size of a tennis court, as they would have been at the old hotel, where men in boaters and ladies in expansive straw hats would have bent genteelly to tap their mallets, but are placed strategically around the whole yard in a combination of croquet and golf that, had my brother and sister and I been enterprising types, we might have attempted to advance onto the Olympic rosters, like curling. You have to hit long distances, go around the far side of the chicken coop, whereupon, if you're lucky, and aim perfectly, and strike with just the right amount of force, when the ball reaches the piece of bedrock just past the swing, instead of vaulting over it, it will pause and then, as if changing its mind, roll along the length of the rock and slip with a deeply satisfying casualness through the wicket at its base.

The swing, which for years hung from an outstretched branch of the large butternut, is gone now; the tree—like the other two butternuts that marked the corner of the lawn by the white chairs—victim to a disease that has killed off most of the butternuts in the area. My father planted a maple beside the chicken coop instead; by the time he died it was sixty feet tall, though recently, itself victim to some illness, had to be cut down by his grandson. The red pines that he planted with Merle Magoon, spaced evenly apart with the regularity of headstones in a national cemetery, are three times that height and completely cover the hillside that was open all the way to the top of the hill when we arrived. "If you don't plant it, it will be taken over by junk" was an axiom I grew up hearing and of whose coming true I live in dread: wild cherry and sumac and poplar infiltrating unmowed grass and before you know it, there goes your field.

Inside the house, the refrigerator coughs itself to life; the pump goes on; lightly lifted by a breeze, the screen door slams gently against the frame. Outside, early in the morning or late at night, there are no sounds except the ones the universe makes. No cars, even over on the main road, no voices. Only birds making their announcements: warblers and robins and maybe a woodpecker tapping; the ruffed grouse making the sound of a distant truck engine starting up and dying out: its mating call. The low rider-driver of birds. Until you learn what the sound is, you wonder what on earth is going on—what eager logger is revving up a chain saw in the woods this early?

At night there are barred owls, with their alarmist calls—hollow sounding, which is an odd characteristic to ascribe to a sound, but it gives the impression that there's empty space inside of it. Maybe there is—a deep-diaphragm projection that opera singers strive for; to someone lying in the dark listening to it, it communicates an urgency to *do* something instead of just lying there like a hapless idiot. For years I thought they were "bard" owls—a spelling that acknowledged their premonitory wisdom, if only we had the sense to interpret it. Our dog Archer, before he became too deaf to hear it, always barked disapprovingly in response to this arrogant, cryptic warning. My son, at eight, assaulted by this doomsaying tease who had taken up its post in the huge maple just outside his bedroom, urged me under no circumstances to let the dog out because there was a wolf out there. "Mom, there really *is*!" he admonished his dim-witted mother.

There aren't any wolves (though their reintroduction is darkly rumored—some damn fool in some branch of the damn fool gub'ment deciding to bring back what it took so long to get rid of; Merle Magoon used to wax eloquent on this subject), but there are coyotes in their covens, sometimes quite close to the house, and I hope not as devious as the ones in New Mexico, which my brother told me send a female in heat to seduce domestic male dogs to leave their homes and follow her, thereupon to walk into an ambush and be devoured. One fall when my son and I were staying in my father's house, I looked out the window and saw two coyotes at the crest of the driveway, where it turns from the road to come down into the yard. Later on, I saw our cat Catnip up there, as if challenging them to come back, convinced he could make mincemeat of them if they dared. Summers nowadays are an ongoing struggle to keep cats from getting eaten, since what they love best in the world is to be out on a summer night. Not only coyotes and fishers kill and eat cats. Raccoons, bobcats, sometimes owls kill them. I don't know how tasty they find them. November is the worst time—game is getting scarce. I lost one cat to some predator, having made the mistake of thinking he'd be safe out at night if he had a cat door to get back in through. A neighbor came home one day to find her house splattered with her cat's blood and her cat gone, a fisher having pursued him in through the cat door. Her husband had to watch helplessly while a fisher chased another of their cats onto the roof of the house and killed it in front of him. I'd used to wonder heretically if my father's tale about the fisher who chased Henry upstairs were strictly true, but after hearing these stories I no longer doubted. Originally introduced into the state in the late fifties to bring down the porcupine population (goddam "experts" fiddlin' with Mother Nature), fishers have flourished, since they have no natural enemies, and there is talk of allowing them to be hunted, or trapped. They are sleek, beautiful animals, in size between a mink and an otter, both of whom they resemble, though their closest relative is the wolverine, which lives farther north. Their faces, snarling, are wicked and intransigent-looking. They are not the creature you'd like to come across in a dark alley.

I'm not scared of fishers for myself, and of bears only if I see a cub and not the mother—though I've been told we live in the center of the highest concentration of them in Vermont. (Of course, I think, why wouldn't we?) I don't see them often, mostly evidence of their presence: their droppings, blackberry bushes flattened and broken off after they've rampaged through them, their tracks in spring snow, their scoring of tree trunks with their claws as they look for grubs. I'm not scared of moose, or of catamounts (yet)—which game wardens insist aren't around (people must be mistaking them for dogs or other escaped pets), though several reliable witnesses I know on both sides of the state have seen them up close. Nevertheless, I am aware that there are animals out there who would not be pleased to see me if I were in the wrong place at the wrong time. One night I opened the door to let Archer out and right up on the road, not fifty feet away, a coyote gave a confrontative and lascivious cackle. I've always loved to walk at night here but now do so uneasily, especially since Archer died. I *am* scared of rabid foxes and raccoons. Even woodchucks. Having been told of a rabid woodchuck that chased a man onto the top of his car, the only place he could get away from it quickly enough, I've never looked at a woodchuck the same way since. It held him hostage as it growled and leapt at him from the ground. He could still be up there.

An awareness of elemental danger is something I never experienced here when I was young. Most of these animals weren't around then: fisher, bear, moose, coyote. The land was still open and farmed. Moreover, it was always summer. I walked down the road at night in the velvety darkness with no thought except for the richness of the country dark.

But then as now you can never be unaware of animals for long. Even if you have no pets or livestock, and I know scarcely anyone who has neither, there are mice in the house, running in the walls; a phoebe nesting on the porch; a common yellowthroat pecking at the window to vanquish its own reflection; a bat (when there were still bats) scritch-scratching its way under the eaves to sleep off its night's labors on the shingles above my back porch; a garter snake slithering its way into the kitchen to cool itself on the tile floor; porcupines gnawing the molding of the front door. Hearing the telltale sound one evening not long after the first such event, I opened the kitchen door to see two young porcupines standing on their hind legs, chewing on a freshly painted piece of board around the dryer vent, looking at me as if they were at an espresso bar and I a newly arrived and not particularly welcome customer. I'd been advised by someone at a party (a male someone) that the best thing to do was to pee on them, but not being anatomically equipped for this method I instead threw a cup of vinegar at them and they spluttered and then toddled off, muttering. One morning I found all but one of my ten nearly ripe butternut squash half consumed by who knows what marauding squash eaters. Probably moose, since the previous year one had bitten heavily into the *three* that were all that grew; I knew because she loped out of the yard just as I drove up, then turned around and looked at me challengingly, as if to say, "Yeah, and so? What are you planning to do about it?"

That my house and the gardens I've planted around it are of interest to these other species only so far as they can make use of them reminds me on a regular basis that my species is not alone in the world, and that the world was not created for our benefit, or even with us in mind. I believe this and yet—when I am out in it, part of it, whether digging in the dirt, watching the trees move, or lying in bed at night, listening to the wind come up when it's about to rain, privy to language that I couldn't have learned any other way except by being here—I feel—not that it's speaking to me, exactly—but that I'm meant to listen.

The breeze comes up and the mist dissipates. The day begins. It's deep summer now: sunny and breezy, a few insomniac crickets chirping, birds signaling, bees ministering to the bee balm. A chipmunk appears on the stone wall and vanishes. A chain saw hums in the distance. Then the day is much like a day anywhere. There are things to be done. Inside: writing, reading manuscripts, doing dishes, house repairs, phone calls, insurance company forms to be decoded. Whatever it takes. Outside:

weeding, harvesting, transplanting, the eternal lawnmowing. It's not till late afternoon that there's time again for contemplation.

Then for the second time I go sit in one of the white lawn chairs and my father comes out and offers me some home brew. "Sure," I say, and he goes back in the house to pour it.

Come away, O human child! I hear him reciting.
Come away, O human child!
To the waters and the wild
With a faery, hand in hand,
For the world's more full of weeping than you can understand.

He's in a good mood. He likes it when I drink with him. "This'll cure your insomnia," he says, handing me a glass of the amber-colored liquid with its three-inch-thick foam. When he makes dire pronouncements—"Things aren't like they used to be," or, shaking his head, "The poor goddamned human race"—he's cheerful. Bad moods leave him inarticulate, grumbling to himself.

We sit and gaze at the fields. Talk desultorily about the weather, the garden, the lawn. The talk is like a chain saw or lawn mower starting up. You hope it will catch and you can embark upon an engaged conversation.

"It's starting to slow down a little," he says hopefully, looking at the grass.

He lives in religious fear (inculcated in me) of the grass's "getting away from us," growing too long to mow, if too much rain or a broken mower befall us.

Periodically we gaze over at the mountains, as if we might be absorbed into the view by pure looking.

People are coming for dinner. Fellow citizens. Inside is simmering his marinara sauce, whose rich smell fills the house, or chicken with wine and potatoes (not, he'll remind Chantal, *coq au vin*, in their good-natured rivalry about who invented cooking). Sasha or I may have made a pie. Raspberry, if they're in season, or apple. Later on blackberry, if it's a good year. My father, who may have changed into a clean short-sleeved shirt and khakis from his green work pants and T-shirt, brings out a bottle of wine, maybe his own. Guests have brought more bottles. We pull the upholstered chairs up to the heavy carved table. The upholstery is fraying, or else it's after I've made slipcovers—an old-fashioned fabric with large, splayed flowers that goes well with the Hapsburg-yellow walls and blue floor. The philosopher sits at the head of the table. His is the only chair with arms. After his death, it took a while before any of his children felt comfortable sitting in it, though we didn't like looking at it empty either.

The conversation is general—the citizens are good talkers. So much is happening! Stories begin in the village but range far and wide. Otto tells a story about something that happened to his friend Hans Furness's father. Hans, Swiss like Otto, also lives in New York City. Hans's father, visiting from Switzerland, is in a wheelchair. Hans left his father outside a store while he went inside on an errand. It was warm in the sun and his father fell asleep. When Hans came out of the store and woke him, his father discovered that people had left coins in his outstretched palm. We laugh and marvel about this. We talk about America. We talk about Switzerland. Before long Otto and the philosopher start in about the "Heidis"—their plan for converting the Institute into a country getaway populated by buxom young women in dirndls. Then we are talking about cars. Someone is always having a problem with a car. It offends us, how dependent we are upon them—these, the most intrusive insistence by the outside world that we can't persist alone in our idyll. Chantal describes living in New York with a car with a dead battery. She'd go out in a tight skirt and high heels and begin to push her aged VW bug into the street and instantly would have more help than she knew what to do with. (If at the time any of us noticed the sexist common denominator of these stories, we didn't verbalize it.) There follow more stories about New York, a distant colony of West Delphi.

Gradually the room fills with the presence of all the people we've been talking about—friends and family of those assembled, people connected to them. A neighbor whose father never forgave James Joyce for the way Joyce portrayed him in *Dubliners*. *Ulysses* is mentioned, thence the *Odyssey*, and Odysseus's long trip home. Ithaca, we agree, was probably much like West Delphi, minus the sea and the suitors. At some point, of course, the goddam idiots in Washington are brought up, and then the senator the philosopher's friend works for; the friend's father ran a Japanese internment camp in New Mexico during the Second World

War. It was he, in talking about these camps, who liked to mutter, "The poor goddamned human race," which the philosopher enjoys repeating. In the world the philosopher prefers to live in—which, for the nonce, we're all inhabiting—the apt phrase can assuage any cognitive dissonance. The senate seems to be present now as well, give or take ninety-nine of them. The president too, assuming we like him. We know everyone, actually. We are connected to everyone who matters.

The breeze blows in through the open windows, out of the soft dark, and we are the center of the world.

PART TWO

VIII

Genesis of the Delphic Style

We were young: most of us in our late twenties or early thirties, that undaunted time when anything seems possible and sometimes is. The philosopher was in his fifties but, despite his ritualistic bemoaning of the pass the world had come to, still possessed of that youthful sense that things could change for the better, once and for all. If people could simply come together in a congenial spot and solve the world's problems through talk. *What this village needs is a pub.* Violet Sleeper, though of an indeterminate age between sixty and seventy, was full of good-natured energy and pleased to be swept along on this tide in the affairs of newcomers. (Although being "swept along" is not an experience that Violet, whose schoolmarm sternness her former pupil Stanley Jewell never forgot, would have permitted had she not already stood at the helm of the ship and approved its direction.) We were all of us invigorated by a sense of reprieve. Adult life need not be, after all, a grim insipid business. It could be playful, full of camaraderie and wit. Rich in daily pleasures and ingenious plans for the future. And, if not strictly founders of the Republic, most other villagers didn't protest their enlistment as extras—or onlookers. After all, letting newcomers make damn fools of themselves has always been a spectator sport in this state.

Those of us recent residents, who'd grown up in several places, gone to college in another, worked in a third, a fourth, a fifth, and had formed our friendships based upon affinity, not vicinity—upon shared situations, temperaments, interests, work, and the like—suddenly found ourselves with friends and neighbors rolled into one. We not only shared a perspective on the world but occupied the same lovely corner of it. A collective love affair between people and place—there can be little that's more intoxicating than this. To begin with, it was the summer house feeling writ large, as if we were an extended family who had chosen this particular encampment to spend our holiday in—except it wasn't a holiday. Holiday had merged with the everyday, and we felt the need to commemorate this fusion by naming the tie that bound us, endowing ourselves with an army and a navy, promoting ourselves instantly to their highest ranks. If it didn't occur to us that the place was not there to serve as backdrop to our lively pageantry, we were not unusual for the era in this ecological blindness. If there were any dissatisfaction, it was only because we did not know in which direction to start marching.

So many of us were around so much of the time that there was a feeling of exemption from the daily grind, as if we had been paroled from the nine-to-five life to which the unfortunate rest of the world was sentenced. Everyone was always busy yet seemingly also at leisure. Especially in summer, with our ambitious gardens and elaborate repasts, we seemed to be leading the life of nineteenth-century squires—if those who'd lost their fortunes and had had to let the servants go.

Questions not infrequently asked of citizens of the Republic by diplomatic Envoys from Elsewhere have always been: But what do you *do* here? How do people make a living? Where do you *buy* things? How do you *survive*? (This is pre-Internet, recall, and even as of this writing reliable broadband is still unavailable in our neck of the woods.)[11] Gazing about them, seeing nothing but hills and trees, fields and cows, these visitors wonder, Where are the industry, the places of business, not to mention the shops and restaurants? (*What this village needs is a pub.*) Just as the protagonists of country house novels always have enough money to spare them from the nitty gritty of a job (and in these novels the people who keep the houses running smoothly rarely appear), especially in summer we newly minted citizens of the Republic could subscribe to the illusion that we did not really work for a living.

Violet, retired from teaching, supplemented her fixed income by selling her baked goods. It was rare to go into her house and not find her at the stove or the sink. Yet, unless she were in the very act of dipping doughnuts into hot oil or rolling out piecrust, she would invariably invite her visitors to sit down at her square oilcloth-covered table and have a cup of coffee.

---

11 *Neck* of the woods? Try to find out the origin of this peculiar phrase.

Not infrequently she'd offer a taste of what had just come from the oven.

Chantal taught French at the high school in Lancaster but in the summer was not teaching. Some summers she cooked at an inn in a nearby town, but much of the time she was working on the Church, giving it, even more than the Institute's living room, something of the feel of *la vieille France*, with the giant wardrobes she began to pick up at the salvage warehouses she and Swift frequented, the freestanding kitchen cupboards,[12] and the large floor-to-ceiling windows they had cut openings for, an unecclesiastical letting in of the light.

Chantal knew how to sew before she came to West Delphi, but in turning the church that had been a barn into a house she took on many tasks she'd never before confronted. If women used to be "churched," taken to church after childbirth to be resanctified, then Chantal was "womaning" the Church, hallowing the structure as a house for humans to inhabit. She thought nothing of taking apart a settee and reupholstering it, designing a bedroom with fanciful built-in beds beneath a pretty archway, so that visiting children would want to sleep in them. And all the while continuing to import French cuisine to the natives.

The place in progress, with its high ceilings, grand staircase framed in but not finished, heavy wooden unsanded floors, the mixture of delicate antiques and the inventive utilitarian—a telephone-cable spool served as the kitchen table—gave the whole a kind of squatter's elegance that was deeply comforting, as if this social arrangement could be altered whenever one wished. This was the feeling that pervaded the entire republic. Grown-up arrangements were, after all, arbitrary, and we need subscribe to them only so long as they suited our purpose.

Swift worked as a lawyer but kept banker's hours and spent much of his time shoring up the foundations of the Church and transforming its interior into a dwelling. In the room intended for their dining room he installed a curved ceiling of slim strips of wood that made it feel as if one were inside a rolltop desk. And, along with Chantal, he kept up their gigantic vegetable garden, tended their chickens and turkeys, and marshalled their dynasty of cats.

Next door to Chantal and Swift, Ben Metcalf was likewise busy with gardening, chicken-raising, and house repair, and various other more

---

12 Which, unlike built-ins, possess the additional virtue of not being taxable.

arcane projects. As has been previously noted, Ben set up the first satellite dish anyone had ever seen and, inspired by the philosopher, brewed beer and kept bees. After law school, instead of practicing, Ben had decided to work for the *Darby Sentinel*, and was thus relatively free to come and go—not to mention to hone his storytelling talents.

Otto, when he wasn't painting his wry and whimsical scenes of people and animals in rural settings, was fixing up the Schoolhouse—and later, when he'd bought it from Gilda, adding a porch, various outbuildings, and eventually a studio. The fact that he, like Swift and Chantal, was making a home of a building originally designed to serve as an institution nicely furthered one of the principles of the Republic: the subversion of stolid and utilitarian arrangements into livelier human uses.

Gilda worked in New York (doing what, we weren't sure: some executive function of some kind) but when we saw her—on weekends, and during the longer intervals of reprieve in the summer—she was, of course, not working.

Up on the hill the philosopher, furloughed from teaching, was in residence all summer. He tended his garden and his bees, mowed his lawn, made beer and wine and bread, played the stock market, complaining of the difficulty of acquiring up-to-the-moment information ("We're really out of the loop here."), read books, or simply sat in one of the white slatted wood lawn chairs and contemplated the universe. (The universe, being what it was, could require a lot of contemplation.)

Sasha, when she wasn't reading and writing and cooking and planting a flower garden, was making of the universe-contemplating a more lighthearted activity than it had been heretofore.

As has been noted, the philosopher's daughter, having thrown over the traces of corporate memo-typing, was reading the publisher's "slush pile" and working on a book.

Other residents longer in place were also around. The Jewells were in their barn or haying their fields. Lenny Hodge was attending to his animals or in the woods logging. Bucky Lefevre was in his trailer; his wife was across the road in the house, both of them keeping an eye on local traffic. The Meyers were retired. Michael Suskind, up on his hill, apparently lived off his trust fund. Marcia Silloway, an anesthesiologist, drove daily the hour to White River Junction, where she worked at the VA hospital, but this was an anomaly, a remnant of pre-Republic arrangements, and was dismissed from general consciousness. Marcia's husband had become the town clerk and so had to travel only three miles down the road to Center Delphi. Other people, who may have adhered to pre-Republic schedules, were simply politely made allowances for. It was thus possible to ascribe to the belief, however wishful and inaccurate, that everyone was available all the time. It seemed that, whatever immediate task might occupy center stage—baking bread, weeding the garden, mowing the lawn, sheetrocking a wall—there were always extras ready to emerge from the wings and add complication and intrigue to the scene. Like Socrates on his way to market, accosted by Alcibiades and thus forgetting that he'd been sent to pick up some cucumbers, the citizens of the Republic were united in feeling that nothing was more important than talk.

Besides by youth and conviviality, however, the birth of the Republic was assisted, as republics must be, by the midwife Imagination. For reasons best known to themselves, the gods had decided to toss a handful of passionate raconteurs into the pot of West Delphi and watch what happened. Individuals who were not only accomplished storytellers but crossed with cosmopolitan ease the border between the Country of Strict Fact and the Land of Embellishment.

Violet Sleeper had, for some years preceding the Republic's advent, written a weekly column for the *Lancaster Independent* chronicling the news from the township of Delphi.

> Merle and Jane Hatch held a family reunion. Present were . . .
>
> Weekend visitors of Mr. and Mrs. Bruleigh include their daughter, now living in Pittsburgh, and Mrs. Bruleigh's college roommate . . .
>
> Pvt. Jim Travis completed his basic training at Fort Dix, N.J., and is spending a few days with his parents, Ella and Reuben Travis, before reporting to . . .
>
> Mr. and Mrs. Myron Sidery and Miss Louise Welch were in Delphi on Tuesday to attend the funeral of Mr. Sidery's niece . . .
>
> The commencement speaker for the Lancaster Christian

School, Reverend Theobald Fenn, gave the sermon this last Sunday at the Delphi Bible Church . . .

Eddie and Edith Cobb spent Sunday afternoon with Violet Sleeper, and played several rounds of Yahtzee . . .

The news was largely confined to who visited whom when; if no one called her with news, Violet could furnish the column entirely from her own rosters. Then at some point, Ben, perhaps to relieve the tedium of covering the police beat in Darby, began to feed Violet material.

In the beginning his additions were scarcely noticeable. The columns simply got longer. He reported the movements of Otto and Gilda, Swift and Chantal, the inhabitants of the Threshold Institute. Of other, more recent citizens of the Republic: Gene and Diana Webb, Ivy and Dan Caulfield, Bill and Gladys Meyer. These differed little from Violet Sleeper's entries.

Otto Schwegler celebrated the opening of his one-man show at the Willowbrook Gallery in . . .

Andrew Mulcahy and Laurie Adler of New York City visited Chantal Meunier and Swift Newman for the weekend . . .

Stewart Silloway and friend of Boston spent last weekend with his father and wife, Jim and Marcia . . .

Gradually, however, other kinds of information began to filter in.

Gilda Francis drove her daughter Chloe to California, where she will begin her freshman year at . . . Chloe said she would miss West Delphi but would come back during vacations . . .

After the torrential downpour in Delphi last week, people have been back at work in their gardens. Sarah Jewell, for example, said that she can now walk in her garden without having mud stick to the bottoms of her shoes. "It was terrible," she said of the muddy conditions prevailing the week before.

> Otto Schwegler and young friend Leo Furness abandoned a trip to New York Thursday after noticing clouds of white smoke billowing out from under the hood of their early model Toyota station wagon. Leo filled the empty radiator by making hundreds of trips to a brook near the side of the interstate with a seven-ounce Coca-Cola bottle . . .
>
> Otto Schwegler received surprise Swiss visitors over the weekend, Anders and Sylvia Frisch . . . While the visit was a surprise to Otto, it was hardly a surprise to the rest of us in the village, who are becoming accustomed to seeing a parade of Swiss in and out of the Schoolhouse.
>
> Vernon and Phyllis Cleary came up for the weekend from Connecticut. Vernon mowed the lawn.

The writer no longer confines himself to paltry facts; he renders experience in detail; readers need not extrapolate how the people reported upon felt. Clauses have lengthened and been subordinated, as opposed to the string of independent ones characteristic of the Sleeper style. At the same time, the prose fairly pulsates with all that isn't said—the fact, for example, that Sarah Jewell punctuated the great majority of her sentences with "Terrible," in one form or another, in her hoarse, unmistakable voice, or that, concealed within the deadpan "Vernon mowed the lawn" is the fact that Mr. Cleary exercised continual vigilance over his lawn and was embroiled in a border dispute with Swift and Chantal because they did not keep theirs as militarily short as he thought they ought. This is a writer who knows his readers; they can be depended on to fill in the blanks.

Increasingly the column takes on the flavor of life in the village. The vital statistics of vegetable gardens are submitted, the lives of animals chronicled. Cars are mentioned with increasing frequency, since, as has been noted, the inhabitants are completely dependent upon them and, unlike with their houses, possess neither the ability nor the ambition to repair them.

> Gardens are growing, flowers are blooming, the brook is at the proper level for this time of year, and bears are leaving droppings on a few of the back roads . . .
>
> Chantal Meunier has planted a variety of French

vegetables, some with 140-day growing seasons . . . "Let's just call it an experiment," Chantal remarked.

Six households are raising chickens this summer. A total of 245 chickens are being raised, which is five times the human population of West Delphi. At last report Jim Silloway had 40 chickens, Otto Schwegler 55, Swift Newman 35, Chantal Meunier 35, Ben Metcalf 47, Gene and Diana Webb an undetermined number, and the Threshold Institute is debating the entire idea.

Violet Sleeper and Gladys Meyer went on their first summer tour of West Delphi Friday. Gladys drove the large Chevrolet sedan that is customarily used for this annual outing and Violet sat in the passenger seat. They first drove down the Lancaster Road from the Sleeper residence and turned left onto Mill Pond Road where they remarked on the advanced stage of the foliage and the abundance of wildflowers for this time of year . . .

An impromptu Labor Day barbecue was held on the Lower Forty just behind Bugtussle.[13] Several broilers were barbecued in full view of six fat chickens who were strutting about the yard. One neighbor said it was in poor taste to barbecue chicken in plain view of chickens who will one day share the same fate.

Swift Newman and Chantal Meunier of the Free Will Church went on the first of the season foliage tours Sunday afternoon. Just before sunset, they fired up their old gray Volvo and headed toward Michael Suskind's residence on the hill. The precise route of their short tour could be easily followed by observant village residents, since their Volvo hasn't had a muffler for nearly a month now.

The attentive reader will have observed that the prose has developed a subtle rhetorical flourish, as if what's been percolating beneath the surface has begun to boil over. The deadpan delivery no longer seems

13 One of Ben Metcalf's names for his residence. The etymology is obscure, but appears to derive from the name of one of his cats.

able to contain the exuberance of the writer, occasioned, for one, by the compositional freedom arising from being at one with his audience. (The freedom, perhaps too, of having no one to accept or reject his submissions. If the *Lancaster Independent*'s editors noticed a change in style and content, they were apparently indifferent to it or thought it of so little consequence as not to be worth remarking upon.)

The comically elevated language ("residence" for "house," "remarked on" for "talked about," "foliage tour" for "drive to look at leaves") not only deftly sets up for the return to the quotidian of "since their Volvo hasn't had a muffler for nearly a month now" at the end, but sounds an affectionately self-aggrandizing note as these residents become, in their own eyes at least, Someone. Here are the residents of West Delphi, experiencing a public celebration of their very existence on a weekly basis. How could they not, if not go so far as to *live* in a fashion that would make good copy, at least begin to think of their lives in these consecrating terms?

> The Meyers had a lawn sale Saturday and Sunday, the first of the year in this sleepy hamlet.[14]
>
> Stefan Nagel and Pieter Streuli, two renowned[15] Swiss artists, visited Otto Schwegler at the Schoolhouse for a weekend of relaxation. They spent much of their weekend strolling[16] about town in the Swiss fashion with their hands behind their backs.[17]
>
> Otto Schwegler got his two geese back from Louie Charbonneau who had been caring for them over the winter. The geese had been sitting on a dozen rotting eggs for weeks, a fact Otto discovered to his profound chagrin when one of the eggs dropped and broke near his foot.
>
> The Threshold Institute, a non-political philosophical and philanthropic organization, awarded its first ever distinguished service certificates to Ben Metcalf and Swift Newman for managing to complete law school against

14 Note use of "hamlet" for "village."

15 "Renowned"—says who?

16 "Strolling," not "walking."

17 Really?

> unbelievable odds. Said Katie Kramer, "We've never done this before."
>
> Vernon Cleary came up for the weekend with relatives from Haverhill and mowed his lawn.[18]

Violet didn't vet the columns before she sent them in to the *Independent*, though they continued to appear under her byline. She was paid by the column inch, so the longer the better, as far as she was concerned. And she enjoyed fielding the phone calls she received from inhabitants in other parts of the township of Delphi asking her, "Did that really happen?" "Well," said Violet, with an economy that many a French literary theorist has required volumes to achieve, "you never know."

As the weeks go by and the entries expand in length, the voice becomes increasingly oracular and embarks unashamedly upon the novelistic long view. A certain heightened, eschatological note can now be heard.

> Following the tremendously auspicious beginning to summer on Memorial Day weekend, a sleepy aura of magic has settled over West Delphi . . .
>
> Following Otto Schwegler's show, a host of well-wishers, amateur critics, and children too numerous to mention gathered at the Schoolhouse to congratulate the artist. In honor of the occasion, Gilda Francis, proprietress and hostess, rang the ancient school bell with the help of one of the children too numerous to mention. This jangling sound of a faded civilization frightened the geese, calves, rabbits, chickens, and woodchucks coexisting peacefully in the Schoolhouse yard. Some of the people too.
>
> The Great Zucchini Contest has dominated the intellectual and social life of the village for several weeks. It took less than a minute for the zucchini contest rules to be adopted by the Ad Hoc Committee for a Greater Zucchini Contest, but the repercussions are likely to be felt here for many generations.
>
> Threshold Institute scion Corky Kramer, who had veto

18 Note repetition of the Cleary lawn-mowing motif.

> power over the adopted rules, signed the four-page sheaf of papers into law seconds before the midnight deadline expired. There was a small ceremony commemorating the signature: a few snifters of brandy were passed around the book-lined library of the Institute, and the pen has been sent to Corsica where it will be permanently embedded in a special clear lava substance for preservation purposes.
>
> Said Kramer: "We have in mind a well-rounded zucchini. Extreme dimensions will not necessarily guarantee success. We have in mind the type of qualities that give wings to great thoughts and great ideas. This is a contest of the creative aesthetic, if you will."

Since the Great Zucchini Contest and its far-reaching significance will be dealt with in detail in a later chapter, we will pass over it here, noting only the tone of hyperbole apparently demanded by this momentous rivalry. In general the attentive reader will have recognized that not only do certain individuals begin regularly to appear in the column, themes have begun to recur. Or events recur, and become themes.

> A group of four Bulgarian tourists in a rented Rabbit[19] stopped in town briefly on Friday to ask directions. The foursome apparently got off the interstate in Lancaster to buy gas, and then one thing led to another and they ended up here, dusty, dazed, and confused.[20]
>
> The tourists decided to have a picnic on the town common (the piece of ground between the Thibeaults' and the road) since they had strayed to such a charming spot.
>
> Said one of the Bulgarians, a large woman who appeared to be in her late fifties, "This town is truly enchanting. It reminds me of Stara Zagora near my native Plovdiv."[21]

---

19 Note the alliteration's deft calling of attention to the superb implausibility of a "rented rabbit." (An early Volkswagen hatchback, for those who may not recall this incarnation.)

20 One may assume that it was not the Bulgarian tourists but the writer who is here referencing the well-known Led Zeppelin song.

21 These are real cities, contrary to the assumptions of many readers of this column when it was first published. (Presumably discovered in the same atlas that could not

> None of us who were present knew the meaning of either term, but we smiled at her and nodded agreeably.
>
> A group of joggers ran through town Tuesday and were not identified. Several village residents stopped their outdoor lawn work briefly as the runners passed and turned their heads slightly to follow their progress. There was scarcely any discussion of the incident.
>
> At dusk Saturday a station wagon bearing sightseers from a foreign jurisdiction drove callously up to the Threshold Institute gates, whether by design or inadvertence is not known. Three Threshold participants came to the side door of the main banquet hall and peered with childlike wonder into the ebbing translucence to see who had arrived. The car then backed into the driveway, turned around, and, as abruptly as it had come, departed. Shortly thereafter the twilight gave way to deepening night, the participants resumed their activity, and in the cobalt radiance of a moonless sky, the incident was forgotten.[22]

Like the lost balloonist, visitors happen by accident[23] upon West Delphi—whose location, it is true, is mismarked on maps more often than not (and now, years later, as has already been mentioned, remains mischievously elusive when "MapQuested" or "Google mapped")—and are astonished by the unusual "hamlet."

Moreover, a progression in the responses of the inhabitants to these straying visitors may be observed. In the first such incident (not quoted here), the descent of the lost balloonist, villagers "surged forth" to greet him; in the second, they "smiled and nodded agreeably" at the tourists; but by the third, "there was scarcely any discussion of the incident." After the fourth, it was "forgotten." What are we to make of this? Have these visits by outsiders become so frequent as to merit only the most perfunctory

---

locate "Meshdish.")

22 The poignant lyricism of "ebbing translucence and "cobalt . . . sky" is amplified by its being embedded in the mundane oddity of a car's driving into the yard and turning around, a combining of which tones—the lyrical and the quotidian, at which Metcalf is so markedly adept—also aptly describes the prevailing sensibility of the Republic.

23 "By accident"?

interest? So that their appearance in the columns has become a comic turn, like Alfred Hitchcock's cameo appearances in his own films—something to be noted, an occasion for self-congratulation at their perspicacity by the cognoscenti, and dismissed from memory? Yet it may be that there is more to be gleaned from these passages than their comic repetitiveness.

One may conjecture that in the beginning West Delphians *needed* the visitors to endow them with a sense of their own apartness and importance; but, as time passed, and they came to take these things for granted, like inhabitants of pilgrimage sites everywhere they learned to ignore the gawkers.

A cynical analyst might suspect a degree of exaggeration if not outright fabrication in these accounts, but a defter interpretation will locate in these paeans a tendency toward mythologizing (a subtle distinction perhaps lost on the aforementioned analyst), a giving of more than ordinary[24] importance to events, and wonder what occasioned it. We are not interested in journalistic ethics here, however: whether it be inappropriate to invent the color of a subject's socks or to put words in her mouth. The balloonists did descend; the Bulgarian tourists did stray; if the spartan facts were departed from they were nevertheless there to provide a foothold for climbing. If later the phalanx of German bicyclists or the busload of Hungarian sightseers who figured in the column were not strictly real,[25] their prototypes had been.

What's notable is how, in between the lines of these fanciful passages, may be discerned the very inception of the Republic. The genesis of the Republican "we"—a self-enclosed entity that must, in order to know itself, be looked upon by others, be seen by outsiders. We citizens-to-be required people who were not citizens to wonder about us, to admire us, to aspire to *be* us. The greater the numbers we could imagine looking with longing over our borders, the more unassailable we felt, the better able to go about our republic-building business.

24 "More than ordinary" is, admittedly, a problematic notion (How much is ordinary? How is it measured? Are the instruments reliable? And so on), but we shall, at least temporarily, glide smoothly over the knotty dilemma the phrase poses.

25 "Strictly real"—see preceding footnote.

IX

Further Investigations into the Delphic Style

Ben Metcalf, who wrote all the early *Gazette* entries, was the undisputed architect of the Delphic style. As has been mentioned, it was Ben who, looking for a house he could afford to buy, happened upon[26] West Delphi, and introduced his fellow law school classmate Swift and Swift's girlfriend, Chantal, to the republic-to-be. During that first winter, when the Church was as of yet uninhabitable, Chantal and Swift lived with Marcelle, a friend of Ben's, in a lightly heated farmhouse in an adjacent township. Here they met Reginald Snow (known to everyone as "Snowy"), whose family farm it was, and who, when younger, sang musicals to the family cows. This apparently parenthetical detail merits notice not only because it entered Delphic lore through Ben Metcalf's galvanizing rendering but because it serves as an excellent example of the inventive maneuvers that sprang up among these hills well before the advent of the Republic. Certain inhabitants of these private kingdoms, which topography begat, have long felt it incumbent upon them to proclaim their good fortune to all the world. If all the world be bovine, then what of that?

As for the Delphic style itself, Ben's impeccable command of tone, his unparalleled familiarity with the lives of those about whom he wrote, his broad knowledge of the world (Bulgarian towns, the hand position of Swiss walkers)—without these the column would not have developed in the direction it did, and he remained its foremost contributor. Even among these newly minted citizens who delighted in the idiosyncratic,

26 "Happened upon"? Hmm. We know what we think about *that*.

Ben was remarkable in never having lost a kind of childlike wonder at the things people did and said, and his astonishment was contagious. When he began a sentence "You know what X . . . " his audience, as with any tribe's essential storyteller, was rapt. It was he who initiated the tone of sublime irreverence and irreverent sublimity in which the columns are steeped.

After a time a number of entries were also contributed by the philosopher and his daughter, at which point the column began to appear under the aegis of the Threshold Institute News Cooperative: TINC. In his introduction to a collection of these compiled for the Institute's archives, the philosopher writes that

> as will be apparent, these reports, in violation of all accepted canons of the news industry, are a collage of facts, fiction, fantasies, and unabashed editorializing, all under the name of one correspondent . . .

(Still nominally "Violet Sleeper.")

> Stylometric experts at the Institute have beyond all doubt identified four different voices in the reports, and intelligence from other sources leads them to believe that at least one other individual had a hand in their composition. Readers must reach their own conclusions regarding the ethical implications of this astonishing revelation.

Leaving aside for the time being the introduction of terms of judgment ("violation," "all accepted canons," "unabashed editorializing," "ethical implications") into the column, let us remark upon this pluralizing of the narrators: formal narrative acknowledgment of the experience of belonging to the Republic. A republic founded by, and for, storytellers. Just as eighteenth-century-London coffeehouse discussions engendered the essays that engendered the English novel, the Republic's social encounters blossomed into prose.[27]

Rare indeed for writers today is the experience of knowing just who

27 And both groups of writers first made fiction behind the wizard's curtain of fact.

their readers are, and being able to gauge one's readers' reactions while in the act of writing is a heady experience, promoting bravura and expansiveness, and itself explains much about the Delphic style. Among other things, readers can be depended upon to know what the writer isn't saying. For readers to recognize the unsaid is like having their passports stamped: welcome home; you get it; you belong.

Yet even though the chronicles of Delphic activities seem to have arrived fully formed, like Athena through the forehead of Zeus, it turns out that there are literary precursors, even if the writers of the columns were unaware at the time that, like truffles and certain sought-after wild mushrooms, theirs is a tone and sensibility that springs up when the conditions are right. It may be found to some degree in every school newspaper, in every Alumni Notes, in the pseudo-village tone of *The New Yorker*'s Talk of the Town pieces. If you *went* there, if you're *from* there, you pick up the implications. If not—well, too bad for you—it's arch and inscrutable. In book form Mrs. Gaskell's *Cranford* (1853) and E. F. Benson's *Make Way for Lucia* series (1920–1939) offer two distinguished examples of what we might anachronistically call the Delphic style.[28]

As in the Delphic chronicles, what's most striking about these books is that, although they contain major and minor characters, the true protagonist is the community itself. Like us, they have turned their backs on the humorless larger republic of which theirs is a part and, intrepid settlers, have discovered a way of sustaining life in the rarefied atmosphere of jocularity. This is assisted by the circumstance that, unlike in novels in which romance drives the plot and provides the architecture (or, failing romance, self-realization), in both *Cranford* and the *Lucia* series, romance and self-interest are firmly subordinate to group equanimity. *Its* disruption furnishes the tension and its restoration the resolution. Even though marriages are contracted (something like the flu) and people die, the importance of such life-altering events is minimized.

> If a married couple come to settle in the town, somehow the gentleman disappears; he is either fairly frightened to death by being the only man in the Cranford evening

28 What connection may be drawn between this style and the nationalistic impulse—which is cause and which effect—is a non-tangential subject of this inquiry.

> parties, or he is accounted for by being with his regiment, his ship, or closely engaged in business all the week in the great neighboring commercial town of Drumble . . . In short, whatever does become of the gentlemen, they are not at Cranford. What could they do if they were there? The surgeon has his round of thirty miles, and sleeps at Cranford, but every man cannot be a surgeon. (*Cranford*, 5)

In *Lucia*, even when Lucia and her swain Georgie Pillson marry, it's a sexless liaison, a marriage of convenience and friendship, not passion. That women are in charge of these societies is the point only in that their being so relegates the drama of the sexes to the periphery and maintains such romantic drama as there is at an uncontagious level. Couples exist, but their stories are submerged in the story of the commonality. Passion, as Plato famously warned, is disruptive to republics, and no one has so far managed to write a domestic drama populated chiefly by men.

Distress, in these books, never rises above a certain level. We never see anyone weeping alone in despair. Such anguish as there is, is of the kind occasioned by the withholding of dinner invitations or the refusal to share a particularly succulent recipe for lobster. Even when Lucia and her rival Elizabeth Mapp are swept out to sea upon an upturned kitchen table and presumed dead, the mourning is mitigated by brouhahas occasioned by the carving of an appropriate memorial—the carver didn't leave enough room to make the letters of Elizabeth's name as large as Lucia's—and by the uncertainty of their heirs as to when and whether to lay claim to their inheritances.

Reading these books you feel that, really, nothing can be too grim. Life can be lived lightly, after all—or, at least, taken lightly, spoken of lightly, and this seems to be much the same thing. It's the difference between entertaining a dinner party with a witty account of a recent difficult experience and confiding to a close friend about the same event that one is near despair.

While the apparent permanent leisure of these village's fictional inhabitants cossets the reader's wish to enjoy the same, the books' deepest appeal is to that part of our nature that yearns not to be blamed for what we cannot help. To be known, accepted, and not taken to task for our petty foibles. We don't regularly commit cardinal sins, but maybe we reserve for ourselves the larger piece of cake, prevaricate when refusing a dinner invitation, pass on unkind comments about someone behind their backs.

Snob and social climber that Lucia is, desirous of being always at the center of everything, she remains likable not only because, unashamedly pursuing her ambitions, she suffers from no self-doubt, but because she doesn't hold their less savory qualities against other people. She secretly practices her part of piano duets and then pretends to Georgie that she is playing a new sonata for the first time. Fully aware of this, he is half irritated, half amused. It's a sign of their growing intimacy when he lets her know he's on to her, and when in turn she lets him know she knows he is.

Greater trust hath no friendship than this: you let someone see through your pretenses, and they don't censure you for them. It would be very hard to go on, day-to-day, did we not have that comfort to settle into, at least sometimes. Most often we relax our relentless efforts to disguise our vanities and insecurities, if we're lucky, only in the privacy of our own homes. Yet in West Delphi during the heyday of the Republic, as in the fictional Tilling, one could sing this refrain, this chorus of mutual liking, practically without ceasing.

And in West Delphi we went a step further. Not only did we tolerate one another's crochets, quirks, caprices, we actively celebrated them. We didn't suffer from fatal flaws, we were given to charming eccentricities. Our flaws *were* charming eccentricities. They merely provided a piquancy to the overall flavor of the mixture. What serendipity to have landed among like-minded people who recognized this.

Social life has naturally always required a certain amount of pretense, of dressing up and being someone other than one's at-home self. That's essentially its definition. In a small community, this is trickier to achieve and requires a certain amount of collusion by one's fellows. In the Lucia books, Elizabeth Mapp is the antagonist because, motivated by jealousy, she strives to expose Lucia's pretenses. She wants to bring things down to the brass tacks that Lucia prefers to keep obscured. Their rivalry keeps things hopping. Elizabeth wants to be the queen of Tilling that Lucia is, but in laying Lucia low, Elizabeth would also force things to an unmistakably personal level. Everyone else knows exactly what's going on, so the level of pretense is more along the lines of family charades: no one is expected to believe that Uncle Percy is really Napoleon or Aunt Gladys Joan of Arc. But to pretend that they are derived from all that is most generous in human affection.

Lucia ultimately triumphs for one supreme reason: she's more fun. Around her, everything matters more. She livens things up. She wants to be the life of the party and isn't ashamed to acknowledge it. If she does sometimes weary her guests by subjecting them to an excess of second-rate Beethoven, she makes up for it by her delightful schemes. To make a grand occasion out of everyday life is her great gift, and it is this that earns her the devotion of her fellow villagers.

While West Delphi had no one reigning monarch,[29] it had Otto and Gilda, Chantal and Swift, Ben, and the philosopher—all preeminent personalities, capable, each in their own way, of being the sun around whom other planets orbited. Yet instead of exerting competing gravitational fields, canceling out each other's pull, their attractions magically proved complementary. Any rivalry was purely good-natured[30] and understood to fuel the fires of patriotism. If some people are more emphatic, denser than others, they yet need to find the soil and nutrients that allow them to flourish.[31] These West Delphi supplied in abundance.

The two European newcomers carried with them, as earlier settlers did seeds, a long-established tradition of savoring daily life. A certain ceremony accompanied eating at the Church, Chantal having imported along with her recipes for cassoulet and tarte aux pommes the French habit of making of a meal more than itself, as if some kind of transubstantiation were occurring. (Transubstantiation, it should be noted, would decidedly *not* have been a concept sympathetic to the Free Will Baptist Church in which the building found its first incarnation.) From introducing better coffee to gathering us to feasts at long tables, the Europeans encouraged their somewhat more reticent and less socially bon-vivant American

29 Except, arguably, Violet Sleeper, whose reign, however, like those of most contemporary monarchs, served a largely symbolic—though nonetheless essential—purpose.

30 See Chapter XII and the discussion of the Great Zucchini Contest, for example.

31 The question, of course, remains (as it does about the state as a whole): were people already given to idiosyncrasy attracted to this clandestine republic by some secret signals in the territory or would anyone, given the nurturing magic of the place, have been transformed into a citizen?

neighbors to commemorate the pleasures of being in a place together, the extraordinary occasion of being in this particular place, West Delphi, with this particular group of people. Chantal's passionate habit of discovering controversy in the most quotidian of events, Otto's lively willingness to assist in embroidering everyone else's inspired lunacies—these, along with the philosopher's considering every dinner gathering an opportunity for elevated discourse, gave to Republic dinners the eventful character of summit meeting, cabalistic intrigue, and ritual celebration.

Yet neither Otto's nor Chantal's magnetism would have exercised its attraction without the corresponding draw of their companions', Gilda's and Swift's, ardent personalities: Gilda's celebratory enthusiasm and Swift's opinionated vehemence. Nor would any of these have sufficed had it not been for Ben Metcalf, whose genius for finding the transcendent in the everyday and the everyday in the transcendent first gave the Republic voice. Everyone's hands are all over the invisible constitution.

The implicit *we* in which the writers of the Delphic column could so snugly wrap themselves was also an actual first-person plural. That is, we did not speak solely as ourselves. Like the spring in the town's namesake, we bubbled up from our surroundings and—to the right hearer—became articulate. Our surroundings spoke through us. And, beneath the particulars, the predominant note one hears in the columns of the *Independent* is celebration. Pure, unfiltered joie de vivre.[32]

A new way of life has been discovered and demands documentation. The two writerly impulses—pleasure in what's there, supreme pleasure, amounting to veneration; and plaint, the longing for what isn't—that usually vie with each other have, here, magically made peace. The world may be going to hell in a handbasket, as the philosopher enjoyed remarking, but who can spend all one's time deploring this fact? Besides, it's traveling in that direction somewhere else. And your preoccupation with how to make the good life even better can scarcely be considered solipsistic when other people share it with you.

32 Certain Francophilic citizens of West Delphi have noted that this phrase appears to have no proper analog in English. These, however, are dangerous international waters into which this chronicler has no particular desire to plunge.

X

Annals of the Republic: Book the Fourth

There's a photograph, taken at a celebration of Violet's seventieth birthday, held at our house one fall, when I'd stayed on after the philosopher had departed for the teaching year. Violet sits at the head of the table, the cake before her, wearing her wig. Her hair was thinning and she often donned this metallic gray headdress to go out in. It was as if there were two Violet Sleepers: the familiar kitchen one, whom we visited, and the one who sallied forth into the world. In her helmet-like wig she looked ready for battle, anticipating spoils. Yet, seated at the head of the table with all these people standing around her, she looks so small; she's squinting, her drooping right eyelid held up by a kind of straight pin attached to her glasses. She looks vulnerable as well as commanding, an improbable combination—which, perhaps, contributed to her social success.

We used to marvel at how Violet got people to do things for her. Where some older people lapse into isolation and helplessness, Violet kept a retinue of minions busy. She was never outwardly coercive, yet we all found ourselves doing things for her we had not gone to her house expecting to do. Standing on a chair, I washed her ceiling for her, which had become dingy from woodsmoke. Her kitchen was always immaculate, its high-gloss white woodwork gleaming, her floor, which she swept and mopped on a daily basis, cleaner than most people's tables. My father put in her garden for her one spring. Jim Silloway stacked her wood. Chantal and Ben ran errands for her in town. Once Violet could no longer drive, Gladys Meyer took her on a weekly shopping trip. Other people did other things. And she knew just what was growing where. She would ask, "How's your garden?" and it wasn't an idle question. She knew—I don't know how she knew, but she knew—that we had a particular kind of rhubarb—green when mature, rather than red—growing below our house, which she thought made the best pies. She would remark upon its superior flavor every June and I'd check, and, sure enough, it would be ready. I'd bring her some. She'd act pleasantly surprised.

One might conclude, looking at the birthday photograph, that although we may have imagined we were a republic, we were in fact a monarchy. It's as if you were to take Queen Victoria and sit her down at the signing of the Declaration. The monarch might not wield official authority, but her presence would confer an endorsement, a benediction; a historian might not unreasonably assume that because Violet's departure coincided with the Republic's demise there was a causal connection.

Violet's rule, if rule it was, was subtle. Her laws were few, but immutable. Cleanliness, neighborliness, not speaking badly of people—these were the values she abided by, though never articulated. She never needed to. Her manner of behaving made it evident when she disapproved of someone. Silence, a pursed lip. Those unfortunates seemed to be people who, in one way or another, didn't keep things *in order*. I remember her incredulity when I told her that we had never washed the windows in our house. (My mother might have, but I didn't recall this.) Violet's windows, since her house stood at the very edge of the dirt road, from which cars churned up dust, had to be cleaned on an almost daily basis. I could see us, as clearly as if we were being invited into her never-used front room, entering in Violet's mind into the category of people for whom *an exception must be made*.

Compared to Violet's, several of the households in West Delphi were unkempt, some profoundly so. The Hodges' house listed to one side and you had to step across tilting, loose floorboards to make your way into their kitchen, which was piled high with unsorted possessions of all kinds. The Lefevres' place was a junkyard of old cars, pieces of machinery, an abandoned trailer pushed into the woods to make space for a new one. If you approached their house from the back, along the stream, you happened upon a most amazing sight: an entire bank of buried cars, compressed, one on top of the other, like the cities of Troy, from early to late models. It was a museum of cars and also a retaining wall, and, it was possible, part of a septic system; old cars have been used as holding tanks for sewage, and this would have been a high-rise among septic tanks, a multiplex, although rumor had it that the Lefevres' waste pipe emptied into the brook.

Lenny Hodge never said anything directly negative about Violet Sleeper, but he, like Violet, had a way of making it clear what he thought of people, and he thought that Violet was a holier-than-thou busybody. Stanley Jewell had a way of letting it come up in conversation that Violet had been a schoolteacher—*his* teacher—and his "*Oh* boy" if you asked him what she'd been like made it clear that no one who'd known her in that role ever quite forgot to be afraid of her. It may have been in the guise of eternal pupil that Stanley would do yard work for Violet and stack her wood. But he and Violet were also friends; they sat across from each other at the kitchen table, listening to the Red Sox games on the radio, Violet wearing her Red Sox cap.

We marveled at inveterate resentments. How could people be neighbors and dislike each other so much? There were difficult people, it was true, like Vernon Cleary, who was ferociously territorial about every blade of grass on his property line, or his sister Louella Sancerre, down the road in Pikesville, who had complained to the higher-ups because the postmistress gave people their mail at the post office, thus taking up valuable federal time. Louella had tried to prevent the fire department from putting out a fire in her brother's house and had to be bodily moved aside so the firemen could attempt to save it. (She subsequently sued the fire chief for assault.)

But these were anomalies, we figured; to all appearances people lived and let live. There seemed plenty of room to do this in a rural area of a rural state, and Violet had the born diplomat's way of letting other people speak her mind for her. I now recognize that she was unusual in being prejudiced in the way opposite to people who claim to be broad-minded but reveal, when confronted by actual human representatives of whatever group of people they are so broad-minded about, that in fact they are anything but. Violet's prejudices were firmly held, but actual individuals she came to know were always exceptions to these rules—though knowing them never seemed to alter the general proposition. These were simply *there*, immovable, like the pillars at Stonehenge, worth only so much speculation. There was what you thought—and then there was how you lived. If for some of us this was a tantalizing paradox, it didn't bother Violet.

Violet was also West Delphi's gatekeeper, its passport registry. People from all over the country who had second houses in Delphi made Violet's house their first stop when they arrived for their summer sojourn; they did not feel that they were really there until they had seen her. We didn't. For many years Violet had the only other key to our house. To visit her admitted us back into the kingdom.

In the birthday photograph, standing just behind Violet, are Swift and Chantal and me, all of us looking very young. This party for Violet occurred not long after my thirtieth birthday, which I had decided to commemorate by running the circuit from our house to Birchwood and then back around through the village, a distance of about six miles, three times my usual distance. It was a victorious feeling when, heading down the long slope that leads past the site where the old hotel once stood, I realized that I was going to be able to complete the run. I hadn't told anyone what I was planning to do, in case I failed to do it. But afterward I bragged, and Swift said, "I could do that." "No, you couldn't," I scoffed. "You don't even run." "I could," he said. "I'll bet you a bottle of scotch that you can't," I said. I was riding high off a bet on the presidential election that had won me a bottle of Laphroaig from my father, though I had not managed to collect it yet. "All right," Swift said, "but you're going to lose."

Chantal shook her head. "He's very strong," she warned me. As about so many things, Chantal spoke in the portentous way of people who have access to a domain of knowledge closed to the rest of us, but I dismissed this as exaggeration.

In order to keep Swift honest, I would have to run the loop again with him. There's a photo of the two of us, taken by Ben Metcalf, as we crest the slight rise that leads from the Church down past Ben's house. At that point I still had some hope that the final hill up to our house, so steep one is winded merely walking it, might vanquish Swift. But not much hope. He had run steadily, breathing no harder than I; evidently practice was not necessarily required for some endeavors.

Why was I surprised? I had made the circuit without having worked up to it. Clearly will was the determining factor here, not expertise: a character trait that, along with the desire to do something others considered foolhardy or—even more inspiring—impossible, many of the founders of the Republic apparently shared.

In the photo, next to Chantal stand Ivy and Dan Caulfield, a young couple who'd moved to West Delphi early on in the Republic and built a small ramshackle house on a hill up above the Jewells' farm. When they were expecting a baby, Chantal bought a rusty brass crib, painted it white, and filled it with fluffy bedding she'd sewn. It wasn't only that Chantal could accomplish any task she put her mind to—bake baguettes, skin rabbits, upholster furniture—she also took people under her wing. When Stella Swan left her abusive husband, she stayed with Chantal and Swift. I came by one morning and was surprised to find Stella sleepily rising from a bed they'd set up for her in their living room. Chantal's niece from France and Swift's from Wyoming came and stayed for extended periods. Chantal took them in hand. "You will get a lot from me," she told Swift's complaining niece, "but not if you whine." (The niece didn't.) Otto was the same. You never knew who might be staying in the Schoolhouse, or for how long. This involvement with other people's lives, so different from the cooler, hands-off attitudes not only of my parents but of most people I knew—was it idiosyncratic? Particular, coincidentally, to Otto and Chantal, who hadn't known each other before West Delphi brought them together? Was it European—a continent not so obsessed by self-reliance as the capitalistic forward-march?

Good fences apparently did not make good neighbors, in their view. People have always helped each other, in these backwoods. If you skid off the road the first car to come by will stop and help you; people depend on each other inextricably. But practical assistance is not the same as emotional involvement; historically privacy has been resolutely respected. You may know everything there is to know about your neighbors but you don't discuss other people's business. The raised eyebrow, the barely audible "mmhmm"—these are all the comment required. Not to be one's brother's keeper, however, does not seem to have been a commandment that the citizens of the Republic wholeheartedly embraced.

Next to the Caulfields sit John and Martha Flanders, who'd bought the Averys' ranch house, the one the Averys built after they sold their farm. When the old house's contents were auctioned off, I bought a wooden ironing board that Randall Avery had made for Shirley soon after they were married. Over the years I've refused several offers for it by antique-hunters and "primitive" aficionados.

At the time the photo was taken, Martha Flanders was already suffering from the cancer that would kill her not very long after, and Sarah Jewell, who had become friendly with her, has an arm protectively around her. Hiram stands next to Sarah. Otto and Gilda were in New York. Ben Metcalf was taking the picture.

Except for me, not a single one of these people remains in West Delphi. The Flanderses, the Jewells, and Violet Sleeper are dead. The Caulfields divorced and moved away. Swift and Chantal moved away and divorced. Ben moved to Lancaster. Even the dining room is no longer there, since this event preceded the philosopher's inspiration about the pantry window that turned the front room into the dining room.

It's not a simple thing to look at this photograph, it turns out. Like the runner who bore the news of the Greeks' defeat at Thermopylae, how do you even begin, when the people who experienced it with you are gone? It's as if several radio stations are coming in on the same bandwidth: too many different feelings jockeying for supremacy. Nostalgia for our youth; regret for the loss of so many of the participants, through death or departure; vertigo, as I try to keep in focus the way I saw the Republic then compared to how I see it now, over three decades later. Regret, also, for the loss of the single vision I once had, when I couldn't imagine, as most citizens of most newly founded republics cannot, that it could ever decline, let alone cease to exist. How could we, then, have been expected to know not only that *all* republics are imaginary, their charters fiction, but that no republic has yet been invented that can withstand both the disruptions of individual passion and the indifference of its citizens?

XI

The End of Freya's Reign: Part the Second

It is now the third summer of the reign of our beloved Freya and here that my story truly begins. We have had a spring unusually mild for our northern latitude: lilies of the valley appeared when snow still lay on the ground, and the dandelion and apple and cherry bloomed several weeks early. Already we have been producing so much honey that we've had to shove drones out of the hive to make room for it. Exiled, they fly around pitifully, sounding so ferocious, although as everyone knows a drone is as dangerous as a piece of milkweed fluff. Without the guidance of the workers they keep bumping into the hive and the younger workers, out taking their orientation flights, laugh at the hapless drones and call them bumblebees. Ignorant June bugs, I heard them taunting them, until their instructor ordered them to stop. Even if the drones do seem useless and idiotic (and here the instructor couldn't suppress a chuckle herself, as two of the drones collided in midair, stunned each other, and fell to earth, buzzing like deerflies), if it weren't for the drones, way back when, none of those cheeky workers would have been there. "We must always bear in mind," the instructor said, "that any drone could make history." (Here again she had to hold back a grin as she scolded two young workers who were tickling an old fat drone who had rolled onto his back and was waving his legs in the air, unable to right himself.) "We must always bear in mind," she said, "that each drone is the potential father of a race."

Soon, however, these young bees—I, Honeysuckle the Tenth, among them—were out with our elders packing pollen in our sacks: the clover, the basswood, the blossoming pea. Soon we will harvest the daisy, the purple vetch and black-eyed Susan, aster and Queen Anne's lace. Conditions in the hive, however, are not good. Every possible bit of storage has been used up and workers are being turned away with all but the richest pollen. Naturally this does nothing for morale. Wasps, hornets, and foreign bees sense the unrest and hover near. The hive has not been invaded since before Radegund's time, when Queen Veronica died without a successor and wild bees killed the guards and stole all the honey from the hive.

But suddenly this summer, just when everyone despaired, the beekeeper is back in his big yellow hive, which stands up the hill from our hive in a grove of maple trees. (On occasion we harvest the maple blossoms, but they are not our favorite, and this year we didn't bother with them.) Yet something is amiss. By now, Queen Freya says, the beekeeper should have put on the extra story for the honey, but not only has he neglected to do that, although he comes every day to sit and look at the hive as he always has, he seems not to notice what goes on: the drones buzzing on the ground, the workers being turned away with sacks full of pollen.

Perhaps he is ill, the queen has suggested; there are diseases that can kill off entire populations of bees, though our hive has fortunately been spared these ravages. Perhaps the beekeeper is suffering from a beekeeper's version of these. On my trips to collect pollen from the daylily and bee balm that have begun to bloom near the beekeeper's hive, I sometimes pause a moment in my labors to look into one of the openings. Sometimes I have seen the beekeeper, sitting still, doing nothing that I could see, and I wonder about him—or her. I don't know. Is the beekeeper a queen without a brood, a worker without a queen, or a drone with no purpose in life? How does a beekeeper survive, alone in a hive? There are thousands of bees in a colony and we would die very quickly on our own. Though each of us makes her (once in a great while his) contribution, more important is the hive as a whole. Each of us workers lives only a few weeks, and most drones last less than that; only the queen endures from year to year.

In previous summers, according to Honeysuckles Fourth through Ninth, there have been other beekeepers in the hive. Never many, only one or two staying there, but beekeepers from the valley used to visit, bringing honey with them or accepting gifts of pollen from our beekeeper. Or perhaps it wasn't honey—we could not tell. Their customs, because we do not understand them, seem strange to us. How is it that beekeepers do not recognize beekeepers from other hives as invaders and drive them off?

Could the big yellow hive in which the beekeeper lives be not a hive at all but a cell, and the place of many hives, about which I have only heard, be in fact a collection of cells, and all of them constructed in a great hive so immense that our small eyes cannot see it?

I have asked others what they think of this matter—if, for instance, it be conceivable that the beekeepers themselves do not know the answer to these questions. I have attempted to imagine what it would be like not to know the difference between a cell and a hive, but the other forager bees find me foolish to think so much about the beekeeper. "Honeysuckle, there's work to be done!" they scold me. "What are beekeepers to us?" my fellows scoff.

"More than you think," Queen Freya said when this conversation was reported to her. But beyond reminding us that the beekeeper set up our hive and installed both Queen Veronica and Queen Freya's own predecessor, Queen Radegund, upon their thrones, she seemed unsure of the answers to these questions. Perhaps it is because of the overcrowding—no one can think. "There's work to be done!" my comrades exclaim, but that's just it. We work and we work, bring in load after load of nectar and pollen, but because there is no room to store them in the hive, to what avail is our labor?

Already it is rumored that the nurse bees are feeding royal jelly to some of the larvae, nurturing a new queen to lead a swarm away from our overcrowded hive. I was shocked to hear this; when I worked as a nurse bee (each of us must do every job in the hive, one after the other), such a thought never entered my mind. But maybe that is because, when I was a nurse bee, the hive was not yet so overcrowded. Perhaps I, too, wishing to make room, would have fed the royal jelly to larvae and grown a new queen. I never thought that such a thing could happen in my lifetime and I do not know if I wish to live to see it.

It seems to me that the best course of action would be to appoint one of us to watch the beekeeper, to observe him in his hive as he has us in ours. I know by now, however, that any such venture will be up to me. Older, more experienced workers, like Balm-of-Gilead and the venerable Golden Rod, would be more suited to the task than I. But to suggest such a thing would incur their ridicule or wrath. "We do the jobs set out for us, Honeysuckle," they would say, "and that is that." We ripen from larvae into workers, we strive all our lives for the good of the hive, and then we die. Nothing to regret in that—so have we lived for centuries, and so I hope shall we continue to. Yet sometimes, after all, we are called to extraordinary tasks to defend our hive against invaders, to venture off into unknown territories in fealty to a new, untried queen. What I am about to do might be a task to which no one has yet been called—sentry to the beekeeper—and I, Honeysuckle the Tenth, merely one in a long line of such sentries. This may prove a job as necessary to our survival as any other. I feel sure that Queen Freya, dared I tell her these thoughts, would give me her blessing.

XII

Annals of the Republic: Book the Fifth

Certain historians mark the zenith of the Republic by West Delphi's first Fourth of July parade. Others cite the Great Zucchini Contest. Still others, the discovery of a new subatomic particle at the Threshold Institute. While it may be to quibble too hair-splittingly to attempt to designate as definitive *one* among these three momentous occasions—all, as will be seen, are events of profound and far-reaching significance—it is perhaps worth noting that the reports can reliably be ascribed to three distinct writers. It is not impossible, therefore, that each vested their interest in, threw their weight behind the particular event upon which they reported. Perhaps, even—and this is where any objective appraisal of the Republic of West Delphi threatens to founder—these reporters' participation in, even investigation of these events cannot be separated from their reportage of them; we may go so far as to suspect that the knowledge that they would be reported is a good part of what engendered the events in the first place. But let us take a short detour for

> A Disquisition Upon Critics
>
> A critic, it bears reminding ourselves, is also a person. A critic is a person who wishes to seem *not* to be a person, but a thinking consciousness, a pure objectivity. Such a being takes care not to reveal identifying qualities—background, likes and dislikes, etc. It therefore becomes the job of subsequent critics, writing upon the same subject, to attempt to ferret these out—in short, to figure out what the

> critic is *not* telling us. Criticism is thus, by its very nature, shot through with subterfuge. We simply point this out.

Leaving aside the question as to which event delineates the acme, the apex, the apogee of the Republic—that moment when the roller coaster car pauses, a tiny eternity, before plunging down the slope—we will simply examine each in turn and perhaps a hierarchy of significance will emerge. Certainly the lofty rhetoric of the reportage makes clear how importantly all figured in the life of the Republic.

> West Delphians streamed from their farms, country homes, remodeled churches and schoolhouses, chalets, camps, and tents, harkening to the call. The throng gathered at Windblown Acres where the parade started when the blue ribbon was cut by Violet Sleeper, resplendent in her colonial cap and gown.
>
> The marchers sallied forth led by the W. Delphi Independence Day Reunited Band . . .

. . . Which included a saxophone, two guitarists, drums, accordion, fife, washboard and spoons, rhumba sticks, tambourine, and a large section of kazoos.

> The eminent town professor, director of the Threshold Institute, dashing in his Mexican attire,[33] sauntered by with the huge Institute banner . . . Ivy and Dan Caulfield descended from the hills on their beribboned motorcycle . . . John and Martha Flanders proudly marched with their well-behaved dogs.
>
> Daintily propelling her custom-made, personalized wheelbarrow, full to the brim with flowers, Gladys Meyer was oblivious to everything but the beauty of the occasion . . . Even Swift Newman left his thriving 9-1/2-acre vegetable garden long enough to join in the revelry . . . The Jewell cows halted the chewing of cud as they looked

33 A poncho he had acquired during a sabbatical spent in the state of Guanajuato.

> wide-eyed at the joyous crowd trooping past their once peaceful pasture . . . Resident frogs of Free Will Pond, alerted to the occasion, added their croaks to the din.

Otto played "When the Saints Go Marching In" on his saxophone. Leo Furness accompanied him on a drum. Andrew Zvezda, seated in a wagon, played old Russian folk songs on his accordion, while Michael Suskind ran back and forth with his guitar, trying to find out what key they were playing in.

A visiting couple leading their dogs complained that the parade was not well organized, but another visitor offered appreciative remarks, employing such terms as "laid-back," "cool," and "mellow."

The only flag in town (of the greater Republic) dated from 1910. Violet Sleeper considered borrowing one from the cemetery but feared that this might be sacrilegious.

No one stayed home. Stanley Jewell, it is true, was haying, but he "stopped his tractor, not to miss the amazing spectacle." Even the animals participated. Cows gawked. Dogs marched. Frogs croaked. Nature itself, it seems, was complicit.

Unlike in most communities, no one lined the parade route. Marchers and viewers were one. Violet Sleeper, apparently the village matriarch,[34] was unable to march, but after cutting the ribbon (*op. cit.*) she "viewed the parade from her wayside porch and waxed [*sic*] encouragement for the long march ahead . . . The colors were dipped in deference [to her]."[35]

It could, of course, be debated whether a parade is, in fact, a parade if there be no spectators. Although the *Lancaster Independent* records that a "score of photographers clicked the irrepressible scenes into

---

34 See Boggs & Kettle, 97 & ff., as to whether the Republic of West Delphi should properly be considered a matriarchy or a patriarchy—or some other -archy heretofore unidentified.

35 See Fling, 192 & ff., for a discussion of the interesting and idiosyncratic role played by V. Sleeper in the founding of the Republic. Fling is particularly sound in elucidating the contribution made by Sleeper's baking expertise, incidentally providing a—perhaps inadvertently—thrilling account of the chocolate zucchini cake theft from Sleeper's outdoor freezer immediately following her demise. No charges were ever levied, but many villagers felt fairly certain that they knew who it was, said suspect's indefatigability in pursuing sweet somethings being well known.

history," eyewitness reports suggest that, post-click, said photographers themselves formed part of the spectacle.[36]

Its route? To the end of the village and back. That is, it set off from Violet Sleeper's "Windblown Acres," dipped down past the Schoolhouse, the Meyers' house, and the Jewell Farm, at the Webbs' took a sharp left onto Mill Street.[37] Hence the parade proceeded past the steeple-less Free Will Baptist Church (in which designation an oxymoron might be spied lurking); the former Dance Hall, now Vernon Cleary's locked and shuttered but impeccably mowed residence; Benjamin Metcalf's snug cottage, Bugtussle; across the Iron Bridge—upon which marchers signally paused to gaze down at the Waterfall, former site of the grist mill from which Mill Street took its name—then on past Lefevre Hollow; up to the Beaver Pond;[38] and finally to the yellow house, unoccupied, owned by two retired schoolteachers from Connecticut who hardly ever came up, who were always referred to as the "Carter girls."[39] Thereupon the parade made an about-face and returned back whence it had come.

36 As we have previously noted, to be simultaneously observer and participant well describes the excitable state of mind in which West Delphians luxuriated.

37 This is the name, as previously noted, that West Delphi resident Benjamin Metcalf gave to an as yet unnamed road in order to provide his residence with a number, without which he had difficulty placing wholesale orders under the name of Delphi Industries; for an in-depth discussion of the Republic's preponderance of "imaginary" institutions and organizations see Squander, 270 & ff.

38 Not yet Pirate Harbor, as it came to be known some years later after the mysterious appearance of a small, handmade, wooden, rather illicit-looking ship upon its waters. Built, it was learned, by a resident whom no one had met and whose identity was serendipitously (?) discovered when the present writer, in falling into conversation with the proprietor of a chocolate shop in the state's largest city—a shop which she had heretofore never frequented—found that the proprietor's father coincidentally (??) owned land in West Delphi. After the requisite number of exclamations of astonishment, further questions ensued. Coordinates were given. "But that's—did he put that boat there?" "Oh, yes, he built it," said his son, as if there were nothing unusual about it. As—of course—there wasn't. Not in West Delphi. To which place the shipbuilder had been called by the Delphic winds, there to construct his particular ark.

39 For the tendency of names to persist past the tenure of those for whom entities were named, see Sprog and Whittier, 77-84. Their suggestion that the inability of some residents to "move on"—that is, to cease to refer to the "Carter girls'" residence as the "Carter girls'" even long after it had been sold—makes a not insignificant contribution to the tendency of the Republic's citizens to cling to a halcyon era that never in fact truly existed is ingenious if ultimately unfruitful.

> Following the first—since about 1880—and best-ever parade, a bountiful repast provided by the international cooks of West Delphi awaited in the Schoolhouse garden, whilst a minstrel strolled. At dusk there was a noisy but thrilling display of fireworks after which an almost reverent hush seemed to settle. In the wee hours . . . somebody dreamed that Thomas Jefferson and his peers were mightily pleased.[40]

And thus concluded the first Independence Day in the Republic of West Delphi.

The discerning reader will at once have noted a paradox at the heart of this event. Officially—it was July Fourth—the parade commemorated the independence of the colonies (which became the greater republic) from Great Britain. Yet—and not only because Vermont was not one of the original thirteen—it was evident to all concerned that it was not celebration of this bygone event that so animated the proceedings. One may safely say that it was their own independence that West Delphians celebrated, using the ostensibly more significant Independence Day as cover.[41] No Fourth of July parade, in the experience of any of the participants, had ever been so enthusiastically, joyously, and cacophonously performed.

Later on in that same momentous summer ensued what came to be known as the Great Zucchini Contest. Its rules are outlined in the Threshold Institute's Bulletin 683, referencing Contract 7250, but it is to be doubted whether Bulletins 1–682 and Contracts 1–7249 ever crossed the threshold into corporeal existence. Certainly they are not extant.

---

40 This last line provides us with a substantive clue. The writer, in both his rhetoric and his allusion to a founding father, makes evident the exalted regard in which the citizens held their republic. But the line is drenched in ambiguity. First, were "Jefferson and his peers" "pleased" because their Republic was being celebrated or because they recognized the incipience of another, perhaps purer incarnation of what they'd had in mind? And, finally, who is this "somebody"—or, might we venture to say, "Somebody"?

41 As noted in Quash & Wining, 122 & ff., there was, from the inception of the Republic, an anxiety about being spied upon that suggests that its founders were well aware of the seditious nature of their enterprise. Also see Whiff, 47 & ff., whose analysis of the high mineral content of West Delphi's drinking water and its possible causative relationship to the founding of the Republic is thought-provoking if fundamentally unsound.

Perhaps a numerologist could derive significance from the numbers of the ones that remain; this researcher confesses to not only an incapacity but a profound lack of interest in such a line of inquiry.

What is telling, however, is the amount of pure candlepower brought to bear on this matter. An entire think tank of fellows appears to have been convened to probe and ponder not only the requisite determinants for the winner but the very nature of the contest itself.

As several resident Fellows were quick to point out, the phrase could be taken to mean either "a *great contest* in, on, or about zucchini," or "a contest for or about the *great zucchini*." Though Institute researchers could find nothing in the traditional zucchini literature of the Western world that would clarify this ambiguity, and, indeed, could find no evidence that any other human community has ever been foolish enough to stage such a contest, the Fellows approached the problem with characteristic zeal and in a spirit of cool scientific detachment.

After heated discussion it was decided that, given the size of West Delphi, the contest itself could not be great but was, in fact, a "piddling contest to select the greatest zucchini." Thereupon the Fellows got to work and established six criteria with percentages: "weight (15%); length (15%); girth (15%); color, sheen, general complexion (15%); volume and density (20%), as determined by the said Mrs. Sleeper using the Archimedean water replacement method; and shapeliness and style (20%), sometimes known as 'flair,' 'pizzazz,' 'éclat,' and 'class.'" At the end of the contest, the rules go on to state, the judge will "integrate the results, divide the result for each entry by the square root of the average zucchini submitted, and immediately post the name of the winner on her porch." As a warning it is noted that if the "natural state of the zucchini submitted for judging has been altered in any way by the addition of lead, heavy water, quicksilver, shoe polish, floor polish, shellac, paint, or ribbons," the judge may "disqualify that zucchini and severely reprimand the contestant."

It is perhaps difficult for those of us living in a later era to understand the passions, indeed, the near-religious fervor, that fueled the contest. Those who have never marveled at the size attained by zucchini or lived in a tiny, isolated community will likely make the mistake of thinking either that such a contest was conducted tongue-in-cheek or that the inhabitants had too much time on their hands, or both. A mistake, it must be confessed, into which this researcher nearly fell. However.

It first should be noted that it is very difficult for any group of people to act satirically over an extended period of time. Such bursts of *taking lightly* cannot be sustained for very long. It runs contrary to human nature, which cannot continue indefinitely without wanting to know the point of things, or the benefit to self. This is not to deny that a certain satirical tone underlies the promulgation of the contest rules. For example, the writer (the document is signed by the president of the Institute, and it is to be supposed was drafted by him) at one point seems to compare a zucchini to both Abraham Lincoln and Fatty Arbuckle,[42] yet just as one is about to assume that none of this could be meant seriously, it is noted that a "recalcitrant Fellow who stubbornly insisted that there is no way in which zucchini can be great has since been defrocked by Institute officials." Tempers, clearly, ran high.

The account of the signing of the document, published only a few days later in the *Lancaster Independent*, makes clear the gravity of the proceedings. We refer to a passage *op. cit.*

> . . . the repercussions are likely to be felt here for many generations . . .
> . . . small ceremony commemorating the signature . . .
> . . . the pen has been sent to Corsica where it will be permanently embedded in a special clear lava substance for preservation purposes.

Scrog (in *Social Significance of the Lesser Squashes*) and Krupinger (in *Vegetables in War and Peace*) are both persuasive in the readings of the aforesaid documents as satire, and yet, risking the accusation of loss of objectivity (and the forfeiting of bribery in the form of delightful dinners prepared by West Delphians), this researcher will go out on a limb and say that they are mistaken. Just plain wrong. They confound tone and substance and mistake gaiety for lack of seriousness. In support of this bold assertion the researcher need only cite the following.

---

42 We note the recurrence of this name in the Chronicles yet cannot account for it. Roscoe "Fatty" Arbuckle was a silent screen star of the 1910s, but as to his iconic significance to the director of the Threshold Institute, we can but speculate.

This particular manifestation of the Virgin arose in another part of the world entirely. The statue holds aloft what is clearly a "great zucchini;" garlanded about her feet are other zucchini, intertwined with what appear to be oak leaves. Krupinger has apparently not run across this evidence of a zucchini-worshipping cult; Scrog notes it but interprets the piled-up zucchini at the feet of the Virgin as suggesting a pyre: the leaves, flames—the implication being that she is on the way to being immolated; the smiles on the faces of the bearers are not in fact expressions of rapture and pride in being chosen, but sadistic, anticipatory grins.

OUR LADY OF THE LARGE ZUCCHINI AT THE BLESSING OF THE ZUKES

While it is true that a strain of resentment against the all too rapidly growing and seemingly unkillable vegetable can be traced throughout its history (to wit, the "Great Zucchini Terrorist," as of yet still at large in a community not far from West Delphi, who preyed upon parked cars, trustingly left unlocked: when the drivers returned, it was to find the front passenger seat full to spilling with the dark-green cucurbit),[43] it need hardly be said that when any entity, be it animal, vegetable, or mineral, evinces such power of reproduction and multiplication, it is inevitable that it arouse hostility among those less prolific. That the zucchini has served as a symbol of fertility throughout history and been celebrated as such is simply not open to question. It is the considered opinion of the present writer that the light tone misread as satire by writers *op. cit.* is in fact metaphorical and that what is being talked about is *something else altogether*.

It is well known that writers suffering under totalitarian regimes have resorted to metaphor with great success as a kind of verbal portmanteau to smuggle across their ideas beneath the very nose of censoring officialdom.

---

43 For a fascinating and exhaustive discussion of the implications of the zucchini's being left in the front instead of the back seat, and on the passenger's instead of the driver's side, see Wilson-Wiggins, 372 & ff.

(Officialdom, as is also known, being tone-deaf to allusion, metaphor, syllogism, and the like.) The same method, beyond any doubt, is being employed here. (And *here*.) But who, a reader may well ask, is being oppressed and what is being smuggled across?

Let us set aside the first half of the question for the time being and concentrate on the second.

It was not, as is commonly supposed, an *apple* with which Satan tempted Eve, but a cucurbit, a squash, *most likely an ancestor of the common zucchini* [my emphasis], the original Hebrew mistranslated by a Greek, the error perpetuated by Latin writers and so on into the King James . . . (Higginbotham & Spleen, 46)[44]

The preponderance of the evidence is—well, preponderant. Need the implications be spelled out?

Well, apparently. If the Great Zucchini Contest be understood not as a competition to grow the biggest dark-green rather tasteless summer squash (the bigger it is, the less tasty it becomes; hence the necessity for such waste-not, want-not recipes as zucchini bread, chocolate zucchini cake, etc.) but to lay the greatest claim to the *knowledge of good and evil*, which the so-called *apple* represents, then things look a little different, don't they? What is being contested is *no less than the claim to understand the legacy of the Fall* better than the next fellow.[45] And the zucchini, held aloft by the Virgin on its (their?) way to being burned at the stake, takes on a rather more sinister cast, does it not?

In choosing among the entries, Violet Sleeper thus attains a mythological stature. Something like Paris deciding among the three goddesses, who promised him (respectively) power, wisdom, and love, Violet Sleeper had to decide among the five entries and in her sagacity may well have prevented another Trojan War by splitting the prize between Gladys

44 Numerous writers beyond those cited here have pointed out that apples were not known in the area in which the Bible was written at the time it was written. In the book of Genesis, the fruit of which Eve eats is not named. The fruit has been variously thought to be a fig, a pear, and a pomegranate, among other things.

45 That is, not so much what happened after we'd discovered what the deity wished to keep from us, but, in Delphic terms, why, being exiled from the garden of the larger republic, citizens were driven to the lengths of creating yet another republic of their own. "Getting back to the garden" seems to have been an injunction that they were at first content to interpret literally—and then not. To ferret out what, precisely, they wished to achieve, is, of course, a central aim of the present inquiry.

Meyer's "redoubtable Italian Stallion" and Otto Schwegler's "unforgettable Slender Lady."[46] Despite the objection by the president of the Institute that the "rules and procedures of the contest were blithely disregarded" and "judgment was restricted to the most simplistic quantitative levels," and his expression of regret that "Institute officials can only dream of the day when a more reflective attitude will pervade this earthbound village,"[47] Violet Sleeper is to be credited with having shown a diplomacy by which Paris could well have profited. Of the winners Violet is said to have said, "They are both such handsome vegetables."

Ultimate and, to the mind of this researcher, incontrovertible evidence for the sub-rosa significance of the Great Zucchini Contest, zucchini in general, the Fourth of July parade, and in fact for the entire Republic of West Delphi is to be found in the press release put out soon after by the Threshold Institute announcing its discovery of a new subatomic particle whose nature explains nearly everything that had to date and would, henceforth, occur in this oracular hill town. Because of its overweening significance, the article reporting the discovery is here given in its entirety.

The Discovery

> Researchers at the Institute, that mysterious metaphysical organization devoted to the study of threshold phenomena, have recently announced the discovery of a new subatomic particle, the "ti," or "ti-particle," t.i. of course being the acronym of "Threshold Institute."

When last interviewed, the researchers could hardly contain their excitement about their discovery. In the words of one of the researchers, it happened this way: "We were just sitting around, reading reports about baryons, leptons, kaons, quarks, and so forth, and, frankly, we were getting a little tired of it. Then suddenly someone said, 'Hey, what about that . . . well . . . thing . . . item . . . whatever . . . we were noticing the other day—you can't see it, right?'"

46 Which pair, the present writer would be remiss in not imagining, rode off together into a vegetable sunset, thereafter to . . . well, the faculties falter at furnishing an appropriate finale to this sentence.

47 The Institute's entry, we must, in the spirit of full disclosure, point out, did not merit even an honorable mention.

That's how the ti-particle came into being. In the researcher's own words: "It just sort of happened."

"Wobble"

When asked to describe this new particle, the researchers cited such characteristics as "forthrightness," "wobble," "implacability," and "rectitude," emphasizing—for those of us unfamiliar with the language of particle physics—that these terms do not mean what they commonly mean. The researchers admit that this is confusing, but have no explanation for why this is so. *It even appears that* any *word in the language, when applied to the ti-particle, will possess a new and extraordinary meaning.*[48] Thus when at the Threshold Institute a group of researchers is overheard discussing the "laxity," "ridiculousness," and "vicissitude" of a ti-particle, they mean nothing even close to what one might imagine they mean.

Unlike the particles studied in physics laboratories, which require particle accelerators costing billions of dollars in order to be researched, the ti-particle requires no such elaborate machinery. It can be "observed" whenever any two people are together and thinking about it. This confluence, you might even say, *produces* the ti-particle.

Also unlike other subatomic particles, some of which are often labeled "exotic," such as the lambda and the xi, the ti-particle is a very homey particle, and the researchers are amazed that no one has discovered it before. They say that, once noticed, it can never be forgotten.

The "it-particle"

The only other particle ever identified at the Threshold Institute was discovered on Sept. 17, 1979, at approximately 4:30 p.m. The sun had sunk quite a ways towards the horizon and everything looked especially bright in that late-afternoon way that is so moving and

48 This chronicler's emphasis.

the researchers were just sitting around on the front lawn of the Institute when this particle, which they called only "it"—and later the "it-particle"—hove into view, or appeared, or whatever it is a particle does to make itself known. The it-particle, however, has never been seen since. The researchers speak of the lost it-particle in sad and reverent tones. They particularly mourn the fact that they will never be able to provoke the interaction of the it-particle and the ti-particle and observe the results.

When asked if they feel that the discovery of the ti-particle may prove beneficial to mankind in any way, the researchers shrug and smile. They know, they explain, but they can't say.

XIII

Annals of the Republic: Book the Sixth

As summer turns to fall and fall to winter, the tone of the *Independent*'s columns grows wistful. Something seems to be missing, even if the reporter does not know what.

This has been a week of rain, damp feelings, restlessness, upheaval, slow-growing gardens, and visitors.

Small villages, even special ones like W. Delphi, must come to terms with life's imponderables: with love and age, youth and war. Yes . . . even W. Delphi must go through periodic ablutions at the fountainhead of truth, said a wizened old sage who passed through town on the back of a weary workhorse Wednesday at dusk . . .

By the end of the week some inhabitants were seen poised at our southernmost boundary, hands shielding their eyes, anxiously peering into the near future for the arrival of the next week. "Here it comes!" said one resident with a rarefied blend of joy, anxiety, and awe in her voice.

And:

Four days of rain followed by four days of chilly weather got the notion of summer out of most people's minds pretty quickly this week. Predawn mantles of woodsmoke hung over the village nearly every morning, replacing the croissant-like layers of mist that had been here the week

> before.
>
> Small eddies of conversation swept about town; people spoke of weather mostly . . . One resident, huddled against the morning chill in the embrace of a shawl, asked rather incredulously, looking up at the sky, "Can this really be it?"
>
> Many of the summer people have gone, leaving boarded, dark houses where once there was dancing and the sounds of children . . .

As if in sympathy with the weather, Stefan Nagel, one of Otto's visitors, could no longer "stroll about with his hands behind his back in the Swiss fashion" because on this occasion he "had a broken leg and each time he would attempt to walk that way, he fell off his crutches onto the ground. It was a sad and unusual sight."

Gilda, back at work in New York, came up only a couple of times a month, and the *Independent* noted that the "cyclical nature of her visits is a source of much local interest." Mark Silloway spent a week with his parents but then returned to his home in Massachusetts. The Threshold Institute had decamped to its winter headquarters farther south. Bill and Gladys Meyer left to spend a week in Ontario. The present writer spent a week in Boston. There is much leaving, little arriving. There is continual preparation for cold weather. Gardens are taken in, remodeling jobs completed. Swift finishes replacing the sills of the Church and insulates around the foundation in "commemoration of Vermont's button-up week." Ben Metcalf insulates his attic. Violet Sleeper is "busy as a squirrel putting up food for the winter. Her most unusual product so far is beet jelly that 'doesn't taste like beets at all.'" A certain lassitude and feeling of helplessness, however, are evident.

> Winter officially arrived in the village on Oct. 14. Frost was reported a foot deep on some windshields. The Schoolhouse geese, Hansel and Gretel, were heard to complain bitterly about the north wind that came up on the evening of the 13th . . .
>
> All of W. Delphi has been wondering what to do about the fact that Ben Metcalf has had no water running to his

> kitchen sink since last Christmas. It was known that Ben was using his bathtub as his sink. In response to inquiries about the matter, Ben replied nonchalantly, "Why bother? It will just freeze next winter."
>
> Delusion (lending authority to those historians who ascribe all of human history to the influence of climate) seems to be on the increase. Swift and Chantal announce that they have made plane reservations for themselves and for Koshon [sic] to go to Paris the week of Nov. 1. They said they will give Koshon a tour of the Louvre and let him drink water from the Seine . . .[49]

Wayfarers continue to wander into the village—"several dozen hikers who had strayed from their trek along the Appalachian Trail came into W. Delphi Friday evening"—but their appearance is routine by now and greeted with little interest and enthusiasm. Even an astonished and appreciative audience (the hikers decide to stay for several days) can no longer comfort the West Delphians for the loss of other citizens.

> Gone with the hot wind of summer are numerous fair-weather residents. They began their exodus in fitful trickles with the first autumn color that showed on the trees. The flow increased steadily as autumn progressed.
>
> Like a lone schooner headed for the icebound North Sea, the village has been stripped to its skeletal bare-bones winter crew.

Given the double-edged "fair-weather," one may safely say that the West Delphians (at least, the chroniclers) who have not left feel left

49 One researcher went so far as to travel to Turkey, in search of a "Monsieur Cochon" who had reportedly "gone to Istanbul to retire to the Sea of Tranquility," only to learn, once there, that "Cochon" is French for "pig," which, had the researcher had the terrifying Mademoiselle Artichaud for first-, second-, and third-year French, they might have known and thus been spared an expensive and exhausting journey. Equally, this knowledge might have gone some way toward clarifying the circumstance in question, namely, the reluctance by said pig's owner to acknowledge the fact that said pig had been turned into bacon.

behind. It is too small and tenuous a community for the loss of any one person not to figure prominently.

Other fall departures included the Carter girls, the Meyers, and the Thibeaults, who now winter in Florida.

Finally even Otto is gone, at the White River Junction bus tearfully (if ambiguously) extending "gratitude to the scores of chickens, cows, ducks, and geese who have made my five months here memorable." Said Violet Sleeper with characteristic understatement, "We will miss him."

Given the dearth of people, animals begin to figure more prominently in the annals.

There are still many, many rabbits, whose long ears tend suddenly to rise up out of the tall grass when one is walking by. Swift killed his last twenty chickens recently. After witnessing the slaughter, his three turkeys left home. They are now to be seen pacing disconsolately up and down Mill Street, asking passersby for asylum.

A rather flippant black-and-white cat wandered into village territory and spent two nights with local cats before departing.

One can feel the days shortening, the temperature dropping, as the remaining citizens attempt figuratively to batten down the hatches. Yet, as if their anxiety cannot be contained, there begin to be reports of shadowy figures creeping about the village.

Several observers have reported seeing black-robed figures moving furtively in the woods and brush hereabouts. They have been seen turning over rocks, looking under mushrooms, poking their noses into hollow trees, peering behind bushes, glancing apprehensively over their shoulders.

It is worth pausing to read this entry more closely. Note, one, the anonymity of the "several observers," and the vagueness—no number, no size—of the "black-robed figures." To begin with, these figures' "moving furtively" might suggest threatening motives, and yet, as we read further, we see that they, themselves, are in fact "looking," "peering," "poking their noses into," all while "glancing apprehensively over their shoulders." Could it be that these figures are the unconscious projections of the residents themselves? A paradoxical amalgamation of the wished-for outsiders who are consumed with interest about them and that part of themselves that is *afraid* of being seen, and found out—whatever that may signify to their unconscious minds? As if in corroboration of this interpretation, the paragraph continues:

At first it seemed to our observers that they were merely some more of the many speculators hunting elusive truffles or ginseng. These one may stumble upon at almost any time, even when the berries are ripe, but these hunters are normally forthcoming in their answers to questions like "What are you doing here?" and do not look furtively over their shoulders. So far as can be determined at this point the black-robed figures recently detected have more sinister motives. One reporter said he could hear them muttering something like "I wanna find a cult! I wanna find a cult!" or words similar to that.[50]

To deflect suspicion, one villager suggested that the black-robed figures might have been Jehovah's Witnesses, but this could not be confirmed.[51]

Furthermore, suspicious visitations increase in frequency and dramatic import.

Several villagers have heard and seen a helicopter flying low over town lately. There has been tremendous speculation over just who it is or why it has been flying so low. Some think it is the FBI looking for crime. Others believe it may be agents from the Soviet embassy in Washington looking for signs of Violet Sleeper's beet jelly production factory.

As if recognizing that they need to affirm strategic alliances, several West Delphians paid a visit to Otto . . . in New York City and were happy to find him generally in good health and spirits, if looking a bit hungry for Violet Sleeper's chocolate zucchini cake. The sojourn terminated rather dramatically, however, when Otto was called home to march behind his country's flag: Switzerland had declared war on Liechtenstein. . .

Sadly, no news has yet reached West Delphi from the front. Fellow

50 Swivell and Towt, in West Delphi: Oracle or Ostrich?, not so subtly suggest that the Republic itself might be considered a cult.

51 This group bore a complicated significance in the life of the Republic—representatives, as they are, of a system of belief they see it as their mission to promulgate—e.g., the philosopher's and Otto's competitive boasts as to who had contrived the best means of deflecting these particular visitors: the philosopher, by keeping them waiting in his woodshed one rainy day, or Otto, by inviting them in and keeping them talking for over an hour as he explained to them the wrongheadedness of their attempts to convert him. Did West Delphians fear conversion or did they, rather, hear in the JWs' proselytizing an uncomfortable echo of their own empire-building ambitions, now being held up to them in flagrant relief?

citizens are a little worried: accustomed to the rank of general in the West Delphi army, will Otto, a mere private in the Swiss forces, be able to follow orders?

The attempt to impose a village sensibility, a Delphic worldview upon events, is as transparent as it is transitory. In the expansive days of summer, it was easy to believe that all the world thought Delphi important, but in the darkening days leading up to the winter solstice it was almost impossible to believe that anyone at all did—thus, perhaps, the appearance of further "signs" affirming West Delphi's consequence appearing in the *Independent*.

> The Strategic Air Command flew over West Delphi recently but whether this had to do with the loan of a West Delphian general to the Swiss army or with Violet Sleeper's infamous beet jelly was unclear.

Though here we hear self-importance combining, rather unusually, with an insouciant admission of ignorance, a kind of cosmic shrug.

> There are occasional brief attempts to fan the embers of social activity. Chantal organized an impromptu dessert party, which caused various residents and nonresidents to bake pies, but one senses that the festival atmosphere is half-hearted, simulated rather than felt.

> There was not a great deal of Halloween activity in West Delphi this year. Several villagers confused the date and were all ready for witches and goblins to knock on the door on Saturday night instead of Sunday. When none appeared, they were bewildered and ate the treats themselves.

Reports of the activities of the missing sometimes trickle in.

> Katie Kramer, W. Delphi's ambassador at large, has sent a weighty "State of W. Delphi" message from her winter embassy in Santa Fe, concluding with some alarm that few

people in the larger civilized world have heard of us.

She writes: "Everyone I speak to about W. Delphi says, 'But what is it? And how come if you're an ambassador, you have to waitress for a living?'"

This is a question that she too is trying to answer.

One finds a new theme now broached in the chronicles—the attempt to lure industry to West Delphi—clearly in the hope that this might allow those who were currently traveling elsewhere to earn a living to settle in the village year-round.

> Since beets, in various forms, is the national dish of the Soviet Union and some Balkan states, there has been talk of selling the recipe to the Russians. Violet Sleeper has been engaged in sensitive trade talks with the US State Department this month. The question concerns the extent to which beet jelly can be considered a weapon, and hence subject to the American–Soviet arms embargo.

If the sale is approved, the deal could mean hundreds of new jobs for this village of 41. Most probably we would have to work overtime to fill all the orders.

> The Threshold Institute has begun a full-scale analysis of Fred Frumpkin's[52] eagerly awaited machine that makes coffee stirrers from old barnwood. It arrived FOB from Tokyo Thursday.
>
> "It's a fantastic idea," said one Institute source. "Simply fantastic."
>
> The Institute agreed to take the Frumpkin case because of the vast economic potential for the village this machine holds. The source also confirmed that the coffee stirrer

52 Expecting "Fred Frumpkin" to, like Fatty Arbuckle, actually exist, the author has so far been disappointed in her researches.

> project is the first tangible endeavor undertaken by the Institute in 25 years. Ordinarily only projects of ethereal or subliminal content are considered.

The real news of the week was discussion of the soon-to-come W. Delphi hydroelectric substation on the Delphi Brook just east of the village.

> Approval was granted April 15 by the proper authorities (as if from heaven) and people have been busy planning what to do with the 50 kV of electricity the station will generate when it comes on line . . . One popular notion making the rounds is construction of a 50 kV lighthouse to act as a beacon to West Delphians returning to the village late at night.
>
> Another is to install electric heating elements under all four miles of village roads to eliminate frequent winter icing conditions.
>
> "Our roads would be like giant hot plates," one bubbling resident effused. "We could keep our buns warm on the road and perhaps keep dinner warm too."
>
> Several people are already planning to move their houses closer to (and even on top of) the roads to lower heating bills—in the event the plan should move forward from the shadowy realm of speculation to the clear light of reality.

Never, it seems, does an idea take hold of the Delphic imagination but it is at once expanded to its outer limits. Whether this interpretation of the categorical imperative was one that West Delphians harbored before coming to West Delphi or whether the influence of the place brought it about is, of course, a fundamental question that was doubtless addressed at one of the Republic's many philosophical congresses but of whose resolution, alas, no record, to date, has surfaced.

In civilian affairs, the chief concern of villagers remains transportation.

As there appears to be no getting away from freezing rain and mud (not to mention cars that go bump in the night and then stop), it was decided that construction must soon commence on a subway system linking West Delphi with the outside world. The Lancaster branch will be begun first. A special express will whisk villagers to the metropolis in two shakes of a pig's tail. (This length of time was said by experts in the Chronology Division of the Threshold Institute to be longer than "in the wink of an eye" but shorter than "once in a blue moon.") There will also be a local, which will stop at East Delphi, South Delphi, Whittiers' Store, and the Iron Bridge.

A hopefulness, however, underlies these wishful prognostications. One notes that, from proposing ways that the world might come to them, West Delphians have begun to think of ways in which they might go to the world. To be frustrated, it is true, by mud season, that fifth Vermont season for which, to the knowledge of this annalist, there is no term in any other language.[53] It is a season that has led more than one resident to the conviction that the poet T. S. Eliot could not have written the magisterial first line of *The Wasteland*—"April is the cruelest month"—without having spent a mud season in West Delphi.

But even mud season, as the book of Ecclesiastes too would have pointed out, had its author known about it, must end sometime, and a note of tremulous joy begins to trill forth from the columns' prose.

A cold January and early February have chilled but not entirely dampened the spirits of West Delphians. Activities reflecting optimism and hope for an early spring abound. Indoor planting, for example, has begun for some gardeners, particularly of hard-to-grow items like leeks, Brussels sprouts, and kidney beans.

Other village residents have been wearing green-tinted sunglasses, preparing for the greener summer days ahead. Others have been readying sugar equipment for the first sap run.

As the frost continued to ooze its way relentlessly out of the earth, expectations filled our valley this rainy week in small waves of dreams and silences.

---

53 Research has dredged up the existence of a French existentialist play, La Saison de la Boue, whose author, Gaston Comme-Il-Faut, is believed by a number of critics to be a pen name for Arthur Rimbaud, author of ***Une Saison en Enfer***.

Spring came briefly to West Delphi a couple of weeks ago, then vanished. Visitors have followed suit. General Schwegler arrived at last to inspect his troops and found them a little lethargic, although their spirits rose (as souls to heaven) at the sight of their long-lost commanding officer. General Schwegler was accompanied by his aide-de-camp, General Furness, who often apologizes to inanimate objects for his own animate state, saying, for example, to a music box that seemed to react negatively to him, "Well, pardon me for living!" This valuable saying has real threshold potential, and researchers at the Institute are now studying it thoroughly.

By village acclaim, Saturday, April 25, was the end of winter. On that day, most of the snow had gone; the danger of flooding from Free Will Pond had passed, and several village cats had once again taken to sleeping under parked automobiles during the hottest part of the day.

Of course there was little green to be observed anywhere, but vigilant persons, by peering under rocks, logs, or pieces of bark, saw those pale white shoots of summer working their way toward the sunlight.

By week's ebb, fiddlehead ferns everywhere had unrolled their green snaillike noggins, Persian lilacs had opened into full blossom. Corky Kramer had aired out the musty halls of the Threshold Institute and settled in for the summer . . . Garden planting has been concluded just about everywhere.

At long last it is early summer, like an opal in Venice. We listen to the monks sing vespers in San Giorgio Maggiore. Ah life, ah Delphi!

There is rhapsody again, yes, but does one not hear, as well, the muffled bass note of a self-consciousness that has not been there before? No longer is it all quite so new, quite so innocent. In a subsequent entry, this note increases in volume.

An endless week of dreary rain and foggy nights has been followed pleasantly this time around by soft green summer days. Children returned to village swimming holes and once again W. Delphi was fit to be a *Saturday Evening Post* cover.

Everyone commented on the delicate mist that began to collect in the low valleys each evening toward sunset. Small groups of inhabitants gathered quietly to watch the earth in such rare repose. One observed that the scene looked a bit like a Dessert Farm breakfasts' cream commercial, which was filmed on the moors in Cornwall, winning several British awards.

What can account for the introduction of this new sardonic instrument to the ensemble? This note of disaffection—is it a sign of foreboding? A recognition, however subliminal as of yet, of the beginning of the end? Does the wry comparison of bucolic bliss to cynically euphemistic commercial landscapes signal disillusion, an awareness that, after all, West Delphi is not alone in finding itself paradise on earth?

XIV

The End of Freya's Reign: Part the Third

At first it felt peculiar to me to shirk my duties as forager, and I continually had to remind myself that the pollen I carried back to the hive could not be put to use. It even began to seem to me that others were of the same mind. I saw workers flying purposefully off on reconnoitering flights, but when they returned, their dances gave strange directions. I could not follow them. No one could. We could no longer interpret each other's warnings.

I came to know the beekeeper's customs. He did not rise at first light, as do we, but lingered in a cell on the upper tier of his hive like a nursling. Then, when he did arise, he descended to a cell on the lower tier and prepared his nourishment. I say "he" only because I have recently learned that the beekeeper is male, but at the time I thought of him as "it," or, more often, "she," since he performed a worker's functions. I did not know that beekeepers have no queens or drones; all may be workers, male and female. At times the male becomes a drone and the female a queen. It is a world I do not begin to understand, nor do I know that I wish to.

I flew from opening to opening, and when the beekeeper emerged from the hive I followed him. In a piece of ground not far from our hive he pulled up some plants but left others. I did not understand what purpose this activity served until one day, upon extracting a red root from the soil, the beekeeper, after cleaning the dirt from it, opened his mouth and put it in.

Food! I wanted to tell everyone. Beekeepers eat food from the ground! They are collectors, as we are. (Thieves, some say, who think it wrong for beekeepers to take honey from our hives. But these are wild, untutored bees, as Queen Freya explained to us, who do not understand the importance of beekeepers to hives like ours.) I flew back to the hive and inscribed my information in the air, but no one paid the least attention to me. Those who noticed me at all were simply irritated. "Oh, Honeysuckle, is it about the beekeeper again? Let it alone. There is no help to come from that quarter." But I couldn't believe that my watching would prove fruitless. Why would I, the eleventh Honeysuckle, have been called to the task if it had no use?

For a long time, however, I have been guilty of an error of judgment: I have looked upon the beekeeper as if he were a bee, and attempted to ascertain the purpose of his actions. I did not understand—I am yet so far from understanding—that any being, of any species, might engage in a task that has no use, that does not serve the greater good. So much have I to learn! So much! And I cannot say that I am glad to have learned what I have. I do not know of what use my knowledge will be. The other workers are not interested. Even if there should be a Honeysuckle the Twelfth, and I could impart my knowledge to her, what would be the use of what I know? Will it help us to survive?

There came a day, nevertheless, when it seemed to me that I understood the beekeeper's thoughts. Perhaps, just as he came to understand the workings of our hive through his watching, I came to understand him. And then I was astonished, because his thoughts were bee thoughts (or, perhaps, these were those thoughts of his to which I, a bee, had access).

And how foolish and disorganized the world of beekeepers appeared to me! Had they always been thus or had something happened? This beekeeper and those who visited his hive behaved like a swarm who had lost their queen and had forgotten how to nurture another. The beekeeper could act as a drone, but not a nurse bee, and apparently could not join forces with other bees and find nurse bees among them. If only I could warn him—I, Honeysuckle the Eleventh, of the fourth tier of the north side—but alas, being privy to the beekeeper's thoughts, I understood their weakness. Once beekeepers had interpreted the messages of the world just as all living things must in order to survive. But what I did not know was whether beekeepers had lost their ability because they had lost their queen or whether they had lost their queen because they no longer understood the world and their place in it.

I began to understand, however, that, just as Queen Freya had said, our world is not separate from the beekeepers', despite what so many in the hive now murmur. "What have beekeepers to do with us, Honeysuckle?" The question reverberates in my mind. The overcrowding has distorted their thinking. "Everything!" I want to reply, but who will listen? Besides, they will object, beekeepers did not engender us; they did not endow us with our tasks in the world. These naysayers have forgotten that beekeepers have built hives for us and invited us into them and thus have the power to destroy them and us. I do not know in what way, but I have become convinced of this fact. I longed to speak to Queen Freya of this; surely she would know what to do, but I dared not seek an audience. (For the rest of my days—few though they be—I shall castigate myself for my cowardice in this.) And I cannot impart my fears to the other workers for they would then regard the beekeeper as an invader, and instead of flying heedlessly over him as he sits beside the hive, they would sting him and wish to kill him, to cover him and all other beekeepers with resin so they cannot infect the greater hive, in which we all live, with their malevolent purpose.

As I have watched the beekeeper, however, I have begun to suspect something further: that he knows all this as well. He understands that beekeepers are to blame for the dangers besetting our hive—terrible things that can destroy us more quickly than a harsh winter. And moreover that, without us, the beekeepers themselves cannot survive.

And yet, just as am I with our hive, he is helpless to prevent the destruction. I have come to understand the despondent and disconsolate way in which he sits and watches us, or gazes across the field full of wildflowers. *Nothing to be done,* he is thinking. *Nothing to be done.* Because I have a worker's nature, hopeful and industrious, at first I found this attitude of dejection repugnant. Yet, because I have observed the beekeeper so carefully for so long, I have come to be not unsympathetic to his distress. After all, have not I—and the Honeysuckles before me—suffered from the same plight? We know that which we can do nothing about, and no one wishes to listen to us.

However, I have little time to contemplate my new understanding. Only recently, a new calamity has befallen our hive. A queen was hatched, Gloriamundi the First, and she led a swarm away from the colony on the first day that workers returned with aster pollen. Freya tried to prevent her, but there was nothing she could do. Too many workers, fed up with the pointlessness of their labors, cast in their lot with Gloriamundi and took flight, even though they did not know where she was leading them, nor, I suspect, did she. How is it that the beekeeper does not recognize what he needs to do to help us? Is his mind too preoccupied by the world we cannot see to notice the catastrophe occurring in his own garden?

After this our beloved Queen Freya fell into despair, and it was easy for the next challenger raised by the perfidious nurse bees (I am sorry, but I must speak my mind: I do not believe that it was necessary to raise a new queen; we should all have rallied to Freya's support, and perhaps what next befell us might have been avoided)—as I say, it was easy for the next challenger to overcome our weakened queen.

I have not long now to record our history; I too am failing. It is perhaps only because I have spent those long intervals in observation of the beekeeper that I have been spared as quick and drastic a death as the rest of the workers. Indeed, I do not know what befell them. Soon after Freya, made frail by despair, was killed by the glistening Pallourdia, workers began to die. They set off on foraging flights and did not return. Or, if they did, it was without pollen, and shortly thereafter they collapsed. Now there are not enough workers to clear the dead ones from the hive. The end is only a matter of time.

We have heard rumors, of course, of diseases that can lay waste to an entire hive. And there are other ways in which a hive can be destroyed. It can be attacked by bears—something like beekeepers but with more hair, and as happy to eat *us* as the honey we make—or we can starve during the winter. But this is something else again, a terrible new plague that, it is rumored, has been killing hives far and wide, and which even the beekeepers, it is said, do not understand, although some beekeepers believe that it is their own behavior that has brought this ruination down upon us.

But why? Why? What could the beekeepers have done that could affect us so terribly?

Alas, I am afraid that I, the last of the Honeysuckles, will never learn the answer to that question. *Our* beekeeper, however, I suspect, knows. Hence his despair. *We are doomed*, he murmurs. *We are doomed and we have doomed all living things.*

My last sight in this world, as I alight upon our entryway, too feeble for further flight, is of the beekeeper, seated on the stump where so often, in happier times, he sat to observe us at our work, now gazing at our dying hive.

XV

Interlude Two: Winter

When anyone comes down the road, the dog barks first and then the curtain is drawn back from the two sides of the window at once, like hair pulled by hands away from a face. The two seemingly enormous heads bend forward, almost to touching, and look out. It's a ritual, almost ceremonial motion. Together the heads fill the window and knowing the bulk of the bodies to which they are attached makes it tempting to think of them as gorgons' heads, their snakes temporarily transformed into frowsy curls. This is what someone with a literary imagination and little direct knowledge of the people in question, coming down the road in a car or on foot, turning right into the driveway that leads to the Threshold Institute, might imagine. What, for their part, are they thinking? When the curtain falls back and they face each other again—over a game of cards, leafing through magazines, or doing nothing at all?

They are mother and daughter, or two sisters, or possibly not related at all. There are so many people in the Lefevre household that it is never clear to anyone outside it who is living in the house at any given time. Violet Sleeper can recite the children's names in order, she had them all in school, but no one else knows them except possibly Stanley Jewell, who is friendly with Patty. The children now have children and these come out of the house in twos and threes. Then someone from inside yells something and they go back in. The women scarcely ever come out.

Is it the same two who look out to see who's coming, or do all the women take turns keeping their vigil? The same vigil Violet keeps, turning aside from a conversation at her kitchen table to look sideways out the window whenever a car passes. If she recognizes the car, she often knows where whoever it is is going and even why.

After the dog barks and the curtain is let fall, Bucky Lefevre opens the door of the trailer he lives in across the road from the house and walks out into the road to stare meaningfully at whoever is passing by. If it's someone he recognizes he yells, "Shut up, you gawddam hound, or I'll shoot the gawddam muzzle off your head!" Then he salutes the passerby—if in a car—with a raise of the gun he generally carries out of the trailer with him and yells, "Gawddam no-good dog!" If the person is on foot, he salutes similarly but adds further details. "That's a purebred, you know. Damn hard to keep clean. Come here, Brownie. What d'you think of this weather we're havin'? Ain't it awful? Come here, Brownie. Gawddam no-good dog!"

Bucky is separated from his wife, Grace. He moved out of the house and across the road into a trailer that is ragged around its bottom edge from salt rust. The reason some assert that this is a welfare scam is because, living separately, Bucky and Grace can get two checks; yet Bucky runs an electric cord across the road to the house and sometimes Grace is to be seen bringing him food across, and no one really knows the truth of the matter.

Bucky can no longer work because of his heart. Because the television is always on in the trailer, a blue glow emanates through its small high windows—an underwater world, or the world you glimpse if you poke a hole in deep snow on a bright day—and Bucky spends so much time in there that the blueness, it seems, has rubbed off on him. But when he comes out he's a grayish white, the color margarine was in the war before the packet of coloring was mixed into it. Or else he's red with drink, or from the exertion of yelling. "Gawddam ticker," he often says, shaking his head and patting his chest. "I never know what she'll do."

Because he never knows, the doctor has given him capsules of nitroglycerin to carry with him. If he feels an attack coming on he takes one and lies down wherever he happens to be—like the afternoon the philosopher came upon him lying in his driveway. He offered to drive Bucky back down the hill but Bucky just looked up from where he lay flat on his back in the grassy median, his .22 at his side, and said, "Gawddam ticker. I take a ride today, she'll think she can get away with this all the time."

The philosopher likes telling this story, with a kind of marveling respect for Bucky, whom he likes. In some way they have taken each other's measure and not found the other wanting. The philosopher, either in spite of or because of being a philosopher, never patronizes—not anyone without intellectual pretensions, anyway. He knows what hard work is—seventy-five cents a day working in the celery fields. Tobacco Road, he calls the Lefevre compound, after Erskine Caldwell's Depression-era novel. He shakes his head at their accumulated junk and deplores their burning their trash—a pile often smoldering beside the trailer, giving off an acrid-smelling smoke—instead of taking it to the dump as they're supposed to, but he would never think of reporting them.

Maybe because of this, or because the philosopher doesn't object to Bucky and his sons hunting "woodchuck" on his land, whatever the season, in return Bucky has taken it on himself to stand sentry; cars have to turn pretty fast down the road to get by him. Recently Bucky's son-in-law, also seemingly separated from his wife, parked a lavender school bus outside the house. It has curtains. He doesn't work either. Except when he's eating, he sits in the driver's seat and waits for people to walk by. When they do, he reaches over to the crank and opens the door to say hello. Once, when the philosopher's daughter was stymied by the recalcitrance of an editor in completing her editing of a manuscript, Bucky proposed that he and his son-in-law fire up the bus and drive down to New York City and *take care of that woman*. It was tempting. The vision of that lavender bus pulling up on the East Fifties sidewalk and Bucky with his rifle trying to get in the elevator to head up to the fiftieth floor proved a cheering tonic. *Gawddam no-good editors.*

Bucky claimed to possess some unusual talents. He could conduct electricity, he said. Hold a light bulb in one hand, insert the other into a light socket, and the bulb would light up. He exercised such fascination upon women, he said, that all he had to do was fix his eye upon them, say one word, and they'd be sound asleep. He had enemies—why, it wasn't clear. He carried on one long-standing feud with a family in an adjacent town notable for conducting long-standing feuds. This family's revenge for slights and injuries was reputedly swift and inexorable. Once, angered by something that had occurred at a gas station in Lancaster, they attached the gas hose firmly to their truck and pulled away sharply, wrenching the gas pump off its foundation. One day they came and rammed Bucky's trailer with a truck. "Gawddam sons of bitches," he said, showing the crease in the metal they'd made.

People in sparsely unpopulated areas are prone to suspicion. Merle Magoon always darkly hinted that setting aside land for national parks was a Communist land grab, and in his declining years maintained that regiments were ready to march down into Vermont from Canada. I mentioned to Merle Jr. what his dad thought. "He knows more'n I do," Merle said.

But such was Merle Sr.'s air of knowing whereof he spoke and of such long duration my habit of trusting him absolutely that I was never sure he wasn't right, that he knew something, less through unspecified sources, than because he just *knew*. There's no question that people who've lived here a long time know something that people who haven't just don't.

I feel the same way about Dexter Tapper that I did about Merle. Dex's main house is in Darby, but at the end of the road that passes my house he has a cabin that he checks up on almost daily. He's let me know he has foiled everyone from investigators after a rare kind of jack-in-the-pulpit to the state police, planning to arrest him after he warned these same investigators off with a gun. He's one of three people I know who claims to have seen catamount: two young ones, cavorting one early morning on the golf course over in Riverby. Dex had stopped his truck to watch them when the local game warden happened to pull up beside him, climb out of his cruiser, stand beside Dex, and contemplate the cubs for a moment, and then said to him, "They don't exist."

Whether the specifics of these stories are strictly accurate does not much interest me. The "strict truth" is just that—too strict. There's a lot you can understand if you allow stories a little leeway.

In the field in front of the philosopher's house, Stanley Jewell is baling hay. It's the second cut, the last this year. He has a radio duct-taped to the hood of the tractor, and the music crackles across the field. He looks behind the tractor as he drives. At regular intervals bales are excreted until the whole field is punctuated by the rectangular droppings, as if in preparation for an equestrian jump course or a game played by giants in which the bales will serve as mah-jongg tiles, or dominoes. They look wonderful lying about like that, on the shorn tawny field, in their compactness: loitering with such intent that it's hard to believe they await apotheosis solely in a cow's munching.

Stanley pulls the baler back down to the village and returns with his wagon. The philosopher's younger daughter and her friends who are visiting help load it, then return to the house and sprawl about the living room, scattering hay all over the rug that the philosopher has just vacuumed.

"All over my clean house," he complains.

"We've been *haying*," his daughter says.

"Will your friends be staying for dinner?" the philosopher asks. "It's fine if they do, I'd just like to know."

"I really don't know, Dad. Don't worry about us."

"I'm not worried."

"You sound worried to me."

"Oh, I give up," he says.

While they were out haying (playing farmer, he mutters) he made a casserole but now learns that with the exception of one person they will not eat it because it has meat in it. Nor will they eat the salad because it is made with the wrong kind of lettuce—politically, not gastronomically, incorrect. The philosopher tries to be tolerant of this activism—in principle he agrees with them, but it is the principle he would prefer to discuss and he is not always successful in raising the level of discussion to the higher plane on which he prefers to converse.

"Reinventing the wheel," he mutters. Being around young people as much as he is, he encounters a lot of that.

Stanley Jewell, his wagon so loaded it looks as if it couldn't turn a corner without toppling over, drives down the hill and past Bucky's trailer. Bucky comes out, eating something out of a tin.

"What's that?" Stanley asks.

"Octopus," says Bucky, "care to try a bite?"

"Ookey—no thank *you*," says Stanley. A dog runs over and yaps at the tractor. "Gawddam dogs," Bucky says, "never shut up."

"I've noticed that," says Stanley.

Stanley is wryness personified, yet there's no mean-spiritedness in him; he's cheerful and laughs generously at other people's jokes. He would agree with the philosopher—the world's going to hell in a handbasket—and his humor is the kind that arises in part from that essential disillusionment. There are forces outside West Delphi that cannot be understood by any rational person as working to any purpose other than to make ordinary law-abiding citizens' lives difficult. The bureaucracy, the red tape, the money every little damn thing now costs. The ineptness of those in charge of lightening the load—whether these be the town officers, the state legislature, or the clowns down in Washington. Look what the town put in the General Fund! Ought to demote *that* general! Make him a buck private! The outrageous salaries teachers earn and the kids can't even *read*. Every year there's a promise to do something about the property taxes but those monkeys in Montpelier never do a goddam thing. All talk. Instead tell people how to run their lives. Forbid this, mandate that. Tax everyone to death. Bring in fisher cats. Talking about bringing in wolves. Wolves! Have they *no* sense?

West Delphians—Vermonters—resist regulations on principle. Let common sense and the rule of not interfering with your neighbor's right to make an idiot of himself run things. Conversation runs on complaint—whether about the preternatural ability of tax listers to smell when you're putting up an addition; the roads (too icy, too muddy, too rutted); or the abundance of mosquitoes this year, who should have known better and stayed in Connecticut, goddam flatlanders.

This is a way of engaging the world that the philosopher finds congenial. It's a state of mind that doesn't want to tempt fate by indulging in too much satisfaction. Things may be all right—no, not so bad—but there's always room for improvement. The television brings the news into your living room and afterward it's hard to get it out, to be clear about where West Delphi's borders are or how heavily the world is bleeding into it. "Terrible, that's *terrible*!" repeats Sarah Jewell, appalled by what she's heard. Lenny Hodge insists that his large dog wait with his children at the end of his road for the school bus so they won't be kidnapped, because you never know what no-good skunks might be roaming around. Reputedly, Stanley Jewell is nervous about the Russians invading, and at one point some citizens of the Republic thought it would be funny to put up a sign at the entrance to West Delphi reading WELCOME, TOVARICH, but then realized that it wouldn't be.

In the fall the summer people leave and the village starts getting ready for the winter. Late vegetables are brought in—squash and pumpkins. Apples are picked; applesauce and cider are made. Firewood's been stacked. Lawn mowers are put away, praise the lord. Leaf peepers come up in busloads from down yonder but rarely find their way to West Delphi unless they be the Bulgarian tourists of Ben Metcalf's imagination.

The hayed fields have turned green again; the unhayed sections are golden and billow when a wind comes up. The motion is so eloquent that you'd have to be senseless to believe that weather isn't a language. The leaves are turning: first yellows, then oranges, then reds and purples, then all together. The radio gives "foliage reports," one of the odder things to listen to, as if we were shut up in cellars and couldn't look out the window and see for ourselves. As the leaves drift down—some days a few; some days, when there's a strong wind, many at a time—a stillness begins to descend, although that's a figure of speech. More accurately, it reveals itself. Something hidden has now been made plain. This feeling has its objective correlative in the fact that houses that were invisible when the leaves were on the trees can now be seen. The pine plantations are dark-green patches across the gray-brown hills. The lay of the land is clear.

This year I've stayed on after my father's gone back south to teach. I haven't yet closed off the upstairs, as I'll need to do when it gets colder, and the house feels large and empty. Haunted by its empty bedrooms, my father's especially. For many years two single unmatching beds stood in this room, one larger than the other, as if in preparation for Goldilocks's trying them out. The blue-painted one with the smaller headboard was my mother's, but aside from this there's nothing in the house I know she liked: no favorite chair, no paintings, no dishes. Most of the furniture was bought at an auction the first summer we owned the house: two hundred dollars for a truckload that included five beds, several dressers, two stuffed rocking chairs, a wicker couch, and the massive dining room table, china cabinet, and chairs, heavy Victorian-era reconstructions. After that nothing was added for years. I am sure there would have been arguments had she wanted to acquire anything else, since one fight at another house, occasioned by her desire to buy a sewing machine, lasted three days. Throughout which they spent the entire time in my father's study, emerging occasionally only for something to eat, like busy board members.

Everywhere I look in the house, something reminds me of my father. The chair he sat in beside the woodstove, the end table he made for my grandmother, the trompe l'oeil cardboard Acoma Pueblo pot a former student gave him. The drawer where he kept his pipes, still redolent years after he stopped smoking them. The photograph of the little girl holding balloons he took during a fiesta in Mexico, one winter after he'd retired and had to migrate somewhere each year when the unwinterized house grew uninhabitable. The muted colors of bare trees and hillsides in the painting by the wife of the Swiss harpsichordist he hired to teach for a semester when he was dean at the college. The Ukrainian Easter egg painted by another student, in whose family this craft was a handed-down skill. The dishes he redeemed Green Stamps for. The postcard of Ezra Pound contemplating the grave of James Joyce in Zurich.

And the books—most all of which we left in the house after his death, and to remove which would be to banish his spirit once and for all from the place. They are as familiar to me and my brother and sister as anything in life: the fawn-brown Harvard classics, the darker-brown Cambridge Shakespeare, the sea green Heinemann Plato, the pale-turquoise Thucydides, the crimson Dostoevsky.

Especially after he retired and lived there much of the year, he filled the house: not only his books and papers, but his wine-making equipment, his tools and old clothes. And it was full of his sounds. It had memorized them, it seemed: the creak of the stuffed rocker in the living room just below my room as he got up, signaling his ascent to sleep; the short walk to the downstairs bathroom, the closing, then shortly after, the opening of the bathroom door; the approach through the front room; the scale of thuds mounting the stairs; the level tread down the hallway toward his room; the brief pause as he flicked off the hallway light; then the door to his room closing, the creak of the bed, then quiet. He had a heavy tread, so there was a slightly ogreish quality to the mounting and descending steps, and as I got older I began to wait for them with a certain amount of dread. Being both an insomniac and a morning person, I couldn't fall asleep if someone else were still up in that sound-porous house, and in the morning I liked to write in an armchair in the sweet early quiet of the living room, listening to the birds through the open windows, and I experienced that horror particular to interrupted writers if I heard the footfalls and drawer-creaking upstairs before I had reached the end of whatever I was trying to reach. The two separate protesting squeaks of the dresser drawers being opened: the one in the smaller dresser, where he kept his T-shirts and boxers; the second in the white built-in drawers, where he kept his socks. Those hallowed, oft-extolled socks!—the green army ones he'd had since the forties, which had never worn out. He'd be damned if he could figure out what they were made of. (A remark implying multifarious conspiracies: the army's monopoly of effective technologies, free enterprise's scheme of planned obsolescence—in short, the ongoing downfall of the civilized world.)

But my mother—what did she do in Delphi? I can barely recall her presence at the farm, as we called it (though we never farmed anything except the red pine). She drove us to the swimming hole. Chatted with Diana Magoon or Violet Sleeper, keeping the social traces oiled. Once, with George and Mary's and my help, repapered the kitchen as a surprise for our father, who'd had to stay later in Annapolis that year.

I see her, slim and elegant, in the pretty green-and-white polka-dotted straight skirt and matching buttoned short-sleeved jacket she wore to travel in, doling out the sliced chicken-and-ketchup sandwiches on Pepperidge Farm bread she'd packed for the trip. One dressed to travel, she taught me—even, evidently, while riding in a sweaty station wagon the length of the New Jersey Turnpike—and I still experience a certain compunction if I wear jeans on a train or an airplane. She gave meaning to the designation *lady*; until the early sixties she wore white elbow-length gloves to go out in. She cared about manners, and often bemoaned the fact that we seemed unable to behave in our family with the same courtesy we'd accord to perfect strangers.

But what did she *do* in Delphi? I once asked her if she'd liked spending time there—with some trepidation, since by then, after a protracted, bitter divorce, mention of anything east of the Mississippi was by association within my father's purview, and risked being responded to by icy silence—but she remarked mildly enough that it had seemed to her that she'd had to spend all her time trying to keep the house clean, a comment I thought skewed and self-deluding, a product of her resentment, until I had my own house in the country to keep up.

But she couldn't have cooked and cleaned *all* the time, could she? What did she *do* while my father was reading or gardening or working in the woods? I can't remember her in the kitchen, or at the dining room table, or in the yard. So little of her is left.

An olla—a jug that Luz, the woman in Mexico who'd cleaned our house for the six months of my father's sabbatical that we'd lived in San Miguel de Allende in the early sixties, had given her. A packet of letters she wrote at the time of the divorce to my father's mother, who had sent them to him, and which I, inveterate family PI, read. Pleading with my grandmother to make him see sense; there was even a letter from my other grandmother, my mother's mother, to my father's mother, assuring her that "Rose Ann is a good girl. . ." My father's mother had sent them all to him. In perplexity? As evidence? It seemed a betrayal, although I could imagine that my grandmother would have found keeping them from him a betrayal too. I didn't wonder then why *he* kept them, though now I do. As legal evidence? But of what? He couldn't have wanted to read them over. She'd often written him letters when they were still living together, long exhortatory epistles, which she left lying on his desk. Easily available for anyone who might be interested to read. Anyone who, captive in the next room, happened to overhear their muffled and not-so-muffled fights and wanted to understand what they were about, as if they could ever be about anything except the fact that he didn't love her and she was trying to convince him to.

More than a decade after his death, it's still his house to me, but my mother came and went without a trace. Not only does the farm not recall her, no house anywhere stands as a memorial to her—she who moved her entire childhood, an army brat. Attending a new school every year or two, setting up house all over again. Wasn't that difficult? I asked her once. "I didn't know anything else," she said. "We were all used to it." Once, when I was ten or eleven, I told her that I was homesick for the farm. "People don't miss places," she said disparagingly. "They miss people." It was offered as a statement of fact.

She did love a place in the end—New Mexico, which her mother had warned her when she was young that she'd never want to leave once she'd seen it. "She was right," she told us, as she gazed up at the fluffy clouds she could still just barely make out, though she couldn't recognize her children's faces unless we moved to within a few inches of her.

My father's ashes are buried in a secluded corner of the lawn under the former granite threshold of the house. A meaningful stone, and he lies beneath, his ashes wrapped in his old gray zippered sweater, his Cubs hat laid on top, joined to the place he loved best on this earth. There are flowers planted around his grave, a loving inscription affixed to the stone. BELOVED FATHER, GRANDFATHER, BROTHER, MENTOR, FRIEND . . . and a line from a poem of his: MAY THERE BE A GREEN AND QUIET PEACE.

My feeling for my father is inextricably bound up with my feeling for this place, and vice versa. Even though he's no longer here it holds his memory. I look at my twenty-foot-tall lilac bush or the daylilies he hybridized and remember when he first brought them up as small shoots for me to transplant around my house.

My mother's ashes are buried on land in New Mexico that doesn't belong to us, in a peaceful meadow in which purple flowers grow, her favorite color. My sister and I smuggled them there. She died in Los Alamos, in a nursing home, even her familiar furniture given away. Only the photographs on her dresser of her grandchildren, which she couldn't make out, told anyone that she'd had a life before this last, reduced existence.

To think of where one wants to lie—what is this but a prayer to the future that a place you love will stay the same? It will shelter you, but you hope also to protect it. You'll have thrown your lot in with its, in the most final way you can.

My mother's life and her anonymous grave are the shadow cast by the Republic: people without homes, without company, who have nowhere to belong, no place to finally come to rest.

When I wonder how things might have been different had my parents been happily married, cared for this place together, lived out their old age in it together, I can't imagine it, can't imagine them. Or when I do—picture a couple in this house on the hill, happy, still in love—it's the Republic that fades away to a shadow. I can't conceive of the Republic having come into existence if my family had been intact, and I wonder what to make of that.

It's so quiet in November. It's a different quiet from that of deep midwinter, when nothing can speak. Now, it's as if it's chosen not to. There comes a day when, all unexpectedly, it warms up, and the sunshine brings out the rich, peaty smell of the fallen leaves. You can lie out on the grass, knowing it may well be the last time of the year. A single wrinkled brown leaf, drifting desultorily to the ground, sounds so loud.

Soon it will snow, and when the whiteness blankets everything it is so silent that, lying in bed in the dark, all you can hear is the tide of your own blood in your ears, as if everything in the universe has condensed to the single point that is you, darkest implosion of your most solipsistic dream.

It's in winter that you're lost without other people. In summer you can forget that you need them, so gentle does the world seem on sunny days, the trees listing in the wind, scripting their eloquent speech against the sky. If you see people it's because you're celebrating all of this with them, your good fortune in finding yourselves here together, not because you can't do without them.

In winter everything changes. After the delirium of the first falling snow, when the universe seems intending to cover all in softness, to circumscribe the world as you wish it were once and for all, the village embarks upon the long months of unremitting whiteness, the relentless cold. The world does not bid us welcome after all, we are forced to recognize; to go out of our houses we must swaddle ourselves in protection against the elements, which now seem not simply indifferent to us, but actively malevolent. Branches, sodden with wet snow and then abruptly frozen, snap off and make the road impassable. They fall on the power lines and then there are no lights or running water and you feel clever if you've thought ahead to outwit the weather: You have a gas stove and water saved in old milk containers, or you have gravity-feed. Nowadays, when there are more and longer power outages, a generator. If you don't, you go to your better-prepared neighbors. Woe betide the person in winter who has no neighbors, no one to call upon if your battery is dead or you get stuck in a snowdrift.

But it can take a while for a newcomer to be properly respectful of the weather. It took me knowing I really lived here, that it wasn't all a lark, that I couldn't just leave and go somewhere else when I was tired of it. The fall I first stayed on, waiting for the manuscript that Bucky Lefevre was threatening to drive down in his son-in-law's lavender bus to Manhattan to fetch, I was there long past the time anyone in our family had ever stayed in the house. The water had been shut off because without central heating the pipes would freeze. There was no bathroom so at night I used a makeshift chamber pot and in the daytime hiked out back where I'd dug a shallow trench behind the woodshed. I took baths in the brook through November, and when I couldn't stand it anymore I took showers at Swift and Chantal's. Every day I carried water up from the village for cooking and washing. Usually in the evening I'd walk the half mile down the winding road deep in snow, lit only by the moon or, if there were no moon, by the ambient light reflected off the snow. I had no car, so the town didn't plow the road. No one, as of yet, had built anything up the road past us. When I needed groceries, I hitched a ride into town with someone. I got milk from the Jewells and eggs from Lenny Hodge, who said, "Aren't you scared, to walk up that hill, all alone, by yourself, in the dark?" sounding like the foreshadowing caretaker of a haunted house in a movie I could still scare myself by thinking about. "No," I said, knowing he probably thought me unnatural more than he admired my independence.

But I wasn't afraid. I was alone, but not lonely. I worked on a book during the day, oblivious of my actual surroundings to the degree that once, rereading the line "A knock came on the door," I got up out of my chair and went to open it. And in the evenings, the other citizens gone for the winter, I had Ben and Swift and Chantal, the four of us holding the Republic together. In solidarity we ate dinner together nearly every night at one of our houses. Our cuisine didn't suffer despite the thinning of the ranks of our compatriots, and I well recall one wintry morning after a dinner the four of us had eaten at a card table in front of the woodstove in the Institute's living room (in February a five-foot radius from the stove the only place warm enough to sit comfortably), when Swift and Ben hiked up the road a second time to polish off the half of the Sacher torte they knew was left over from the night before.

Never before, and never since, have the boundaries between me and my neighbors felt so fluid. Swift and Ben came up to eat the rest of the cake and I didn't mind. Why would I mind? Anytime I wanted company I could go down the hill to their houses, and they would set aside whatever they were doing and make coffee. I visited Violet Sleeper, who fed me doughnuts while we played Yahtzee. I stopped by the Jewells' barn, so warm and welcoming in the early winter dark, and walked back and forth with Stanley from barn to milk house as he emptied the milking machines that looked like giant tea kettles into the bulk tank. I had seen that sight since I was a little girl, but it was something I never tired of: the big silver box, maybe six by twelve feet, four feet deep, whose lid lifted to reveal a swimming pool of milk. If I got there before they turned on the mixing blade I'd look in greedily at the inches of cream on top. As a child (well, long after, whenever I got the chance), if I was up in the morning before anyone else I'd open the milk jug and spoon cream off the top. Or—heavenly serendipity—if there was fresh homemade bread and homemade strawberry jam, spread the bread with the jam and then dip *that* in the cream, careful to leave no crumbs.

The differentiation between me as a summer person, someone with no stick-to-itiveness, and as a real resident dissolved. I had a home, and it was better than the home I'd had as a child because I'd chosen this one. Everything I did felt like a sacrament that confirmed belonging and seemed to promise that that feeling would never abandon me if I did not abandon the place. Belief had been engendered by place, but affirmed by people, who believed in it too.

When I came into the village in the snow at night, I'd stop and look across the wide expanse of snow-smoothed fields and the lighted squares of windows were like beacons across a body of water. Reassurance of welcome and comfort, food and drink, conversation. Help, unquestionably, if I needed it. Then I'd continue on down the road through the village, the snow squeaking as I trod on it, and look through the uncurtained windows and see my friends and neighbors or know who was inside if I couldn't see them. In some houses the blue light of a television glowed and I knew who was sitting before it and that they were home and snug, work over for the day. I could knock on any door at all and it would be opened and I would be greeted warmly and asked to come inside.

PART THREE

XVI

The Great Chanterelle Murder Mysteries: Part One

In which things get more complicated and detectives arrive to get to the heart of the matter.

The one thing they had in common from the first was that they didn't believe it was really about mushrooms. To be so distressed, possessed, so *ob*sessed, by a mere mushroom, a *Cantharellus cibarius*, la girolle, il gallinaccio, eine Echter Pfifferling, la chanterelle . . . the *chanterelle*. The purported crime, of whose precise nature they had yet to be informed, clearly concealed something else. Something, they were beginning to suspect, of profound, far-reaching significance, perhaps of national, even international import. (Reluctant though the detectives were to share their suspicions with the others, arising, as they did, they knew not whence.)

"If it were a truf-fluh," said Hercule Poirot, in his nearly incomprehensible accent. "Zat I could comprendre, but a champignon! Hélas, your customs are not ours."

"Zat is zee point, Herk," said Philip Marlowe, who could not help baiting the dandified French detective. He made a move to tighten the belt of his trench coat, as he habitually did when he felt he had scored a point off someone, but they were at breakfast, and he was not wearing it. Instead he reached for the platter of pancakes (or they may have been griddle cakes, or flapjacks; the time period is uncertain)—which were quite good—and for the pitcher of maple syrup—which was delectable in any era.

Now *that's* worth fighting over, he nearly said to Poirot. But he despaired of the Frenchman's appreciating American irony. It was hard to know *what* he understood, other than the oiling of his extravagant mustache—whiskers for a mouse, not a man. Now, Holmes—*he* would have appreciated the remark, but whether he would have revealed that he did was another story. He was a deep one, that Holmes, peering out from his half-lidded eyes and puffing on his relentless pipe. His sidekick, Watson, would have barked out a laugh; his laugh came out in short bursts, like audible smoke rings, yet it was hard to know what it meant either. Holmes, however, hadn't come down to breakfast. Marlowe had thought that Watson might, but apparently he kept his friend's hours.

Marlowe noticed Poirot making a small moue of distaste (he supposed you could call it) at the sight of Marlowe's syrup-soaked stack; then he sipped his chocolate and reached for a roll, which he broke in two and began to nibble on. A mouse, yes, or a rat—a conceited, dressed-to-the-nines rat.

This analogy cheered Marlowe, and he said companionably to Poirot, "How long has this been going on?"

"Ah!" said Poirot, raising his hands and making an expression that Marlowe recognized as typically French, although he had never set foot in France. He had a vision of an entire nation, palms turned upward, shoulders lifted, mouths downturned, eyes widened: a silent chorus of disbelieving disavowal.

"I s'pose you're going to tell me that it's our job to find out."

"Ah," said Poirot again—a different "ah," this time seeming to mean either "You've hit it now, chum" or "That's for me to know and you to find out."

"Lucy!"

A pretty girl in a maid's uniform came in from wherever she'd been standing. Eavesdropping, probably. How often did the Birchwood Hotel get foreign visitors?

"Lucy," Marlowe said. "More coffee, please."

When she came back with it, he said, "Sit down for a sec. Herk here and I would like to ask you a few questions."

"Oh, sir, I don't know as I ought to, sir."

"Sure you can. This here's the US of A. Don't stand on ceremony." Then he added, "In fact, sit on it."

Poirot raised his French eyebrows and Lucy blushed and Marlowe himself wondered why he sometimes found himself talking like Groucho Marx. (As he thought this, he experienced the prickly flush that comes over people when they suspect that what they're feeling may in fact belong to someone else.)

"What did you wish to ask me, sir?" asked Lucy, who remained standing.

"Are we the only guests in this hotel?"

"It's not the season, sir," she said.

"Do you live in the village, mademoiselle?"

"I couldn't say, sir."

Marlowe and Poirot exchanged a look. Their first as complicit detectives, sharing their recognition that they were dealing either with a flibbertigibbet or a very cagey witness.

"Can you tell us how long ago the murders began?" asked Marlowe, cutting to the chase in his hard-hitting way. He saw Poirot shaking his head slightly at this absence of subtlety. *I am not a subtle fellow, Leek*, thought Marlowe, feeling bolstered as he did whenever he recalled what Poirot's name meant in English. Though how he came by this knowledge he could not recall.

"Oi couldn't sigh, I'm sure, sir," said Lucy.

It took a moment for Marlowe to realize that she'd said she couldn't *say*, not that she couldn't *sigh*, as at first he'd thought, because Lucy had inexplicably begun to speak with a Cockney accent.

"Where are you *from*?" demanded Marlowe, whereupon, with a muttered "I'm sure I wished I could tell you, sir," Lucy burst into tears and ran from the room.

"Excellent work, Mr. Marlowe," said Poirot acidly. "If this is an example of your forenseek powahs . . ."

"It's not an example of anything, Lee—Herk. Either the girl's a brainless twit or the cleverest anti-sleuth since Moriarty."

"I beg your pardon?" came a voice.

Both Poirot and Marlowe spun around to behold Sherlock Holmes, in dressing gown, sitting in an armchair in the corner of the dining room. He was lowering a newspaper, behind which he had apparently been concealed.

"I could have sworn—" Marlowe muttered.

"I, also, could have sworn," said Poirot.

"Did you overhear our conversation with the girl Lucy?" demanded Marlowe.

"Alas, I had not the pleasure. I appear to have been absorbed by—" Holmes broke off, regarding the newspaper with some puzzlement.

"Anything of interest, Holmes?" asked Watson, who now entered the room from the hallway, looking wide-awake and ready for business. "You're up early, my friend."

"Indeed. As always, my dear Watson, your powers of observation do not pall."

Knock it off, Sherlock, thought Marlowe, but he found himself uncharacteristically intimidated. *Too many goddam Europeans*, he thought. And there'd been a rumor that there was another one coming—an English lord and his butler. Marlowe wondered how Sherlock would take to that.

Lucy came back in now, her eyes dry, seemingly with no memory—or certainly no self-consciousness—about what had transpired earlier.

"What would you gentlemen like for breakfast?" she asked.

Watson wanted the works but Holmes wanted only coffee and a roll, which made the Leek look smug. The two latecomers joined the other detectives at the table.

"So what's on the agenda today, gents?" asked Marlowe.

He thought he noticed wincing—one French wince, two English ones. He'd about had it with these bull-in-a-china-shop looks. Pansies, he thought. A bunch of fops and pansies.

"What do you suggest, Mr. Marlowe?" Watson asked agreeably enough.

"Phil," Marlowe said. "Call me Phil. We're all friends here, I trust." ("Phil"? Had he ever really been called "Phil"?)

"Kind of you," said Watson, but once again Marlowe felt he'd put his foot in it. It was like a sore tooth he couldn't resist prodding. But he trusted his instinct, and something was telling him that to keep pressing on this spot was going to get him somewhere, even though at the moment he had no idea where that could be. But he knew that he hadn't gotten to be Philip Marlowe, top-notch private eye, by being a pussyfoot.

Holmes took out his pipe (regarding it with some astonishment, since he'd not been smoking it a moment ago) and cleared his throat.

"I believe I should confess at the outset, gentlemen, that I find this to be an exceedingly peculiar case. Leaving aside for the moment the fact that none of us seems to have been informed under whose auspices or at whose request we are operating, there is the indubitably unusual circumstance of there being a crime to uncover, a murder or murders to solve, and yet we have been given such a paucity of detail that one might . . ."

Marlowe wondered with interest how Holmes was going to get himself out of this sentence. In his view (or at least that of his creator), detectives should express themselves with pithy brevity.

". . . one might suspect those who engaged us of themselves being implicated in crimes they purport to wish to solve."

"They're up to their necks in it," Marlowe said.

Holmes gave the twitch of the eye that was apparently as close as he got to a smile.

"You have put your finger on it, Mr. Marlowe," he said.

"Yes," said Poirot. "If only vee could discovaire vut ett is."

"Ah," said Holmes.

"I'll second that," said Watson.

"See you and raise you five," said Marlowe.

"I must also confess," continued Holmes, "that I am unaccustomed to being engaged in my undertakings *with* anyone. Watson has been my sole aide and accomplice and I find myself in something of a quandary as to how to proceed."

"I share your con-stair-na-tion, Mr. Holmes."

"Ditto," said Marlowe.

"I am at a further disadvantage in that you two gentlemen appear to know me by reputation while I must confess to having never had the pleasure of hearing of either of you."

"Nor I of you, Monsieur Marlowe."

"Likewise, Herk," said Marlowe.

"Whoever assembled us here is operating at a considerable advantage over the four of us in this respect," said Watson jovially.

"Too true, Docteur," said Poirot.

"Who did?" asked Marlowe. "I'll tell you who invited me if you'll tell me who invited you."

"Ah," said Poirot, although for the first time he looked ill at ease.

"Ah, indeed," said Holmes. "I find that I have mislaid my letter of invitation and uncharacteristically cannot recall the name of its writer.

Nor, I am afraid, did I mention it to my friend Dr. Watson."

"How very strange," said Poirot, in his surprise losing some of his French accent, though he quickly recovered it. "Zee same zing 'as 'appened to me! I was loathze to admeet it, I admeet, since I feared zat my powers were sleeping."

"Slipping," said Marlowe. "Me three. I never even got a letter. Here I just was. I took it for granted I knew why and how but whenever I try to think about it, like Herk says, it fades away like a dream you can't keep hold of."

"Perhaps we have been given an amnesia-inducing substance," suggested Holmes. "What have you gentlemen drunk since your arrival?"

"Wine, last night at dinner," said Marlowe. "Whiskey after. Water in my room. Coffee this morning."

"I had zee same, except for zee water."

"And I," said Holmes, "except that, as I now note, the girl has not yet brought my breakfast."

"Nor mine," said Watson.

"I believe I speak for all of us if I say we may therefore safely conclude that it is not the coffee. Wine and whiskey are all that we appear to have drunk in common."

"Whoever slipped us a mickey might not have used the same for all of us," said Marlowe.

"You have a point, Mr. Marlowe, if I comprehend your odd phrasing. But that would certainly have occasioned more work, and it is my experience that, with the exception of certain fiendish minds, and I need not mention any names for I heard the name I would otherwise mention earlier on in the conversation, criminals prefer the most expeditious route to accomplish their aims. Otherwise we would never find them out so readily."

"Ça c'est vrai, mon ami," said Poirot.

"Let us see if there be any wine left in the sideboard and retrieve the bottle of whiskey from the library. Did we remember to bring my chemical laboratory, Watson?"

"Yes, we did."

"Capital, my dear fellow. I suggest that, after we have breakfasted—where the blazes is that girl?—that we leave the analysis in the capable hands of my compatriot here and we three repair to the village and see what we shall see."

"Excellent idea, Mr. Holmes," said Poirot.

Repair, thought Marlowe.

"Lucy!" they all shouted.

XVII

The Great Chanterelle Murder Mysteries: Part Two

Deposition

Okay. So—yeah. What happened. Who did what to whom when. That's what you're after, right? (Not to mention why.)

Here's this bucolic paradise, this carnival of conversationalists, this—this Athens without the togas, this Rome without the centurions, this Vienna without—

The witness is requested not to embark upon flights of fancy—

Um, "flights of fancy"—now there's a phrase—to be held aloft by—the tendency to . . . That's really the crux of the matter, isn't it?

Impatient-throat clearing by the detectives.

Okay, okay. What happened. "Happened." Not really how this chronicler's mind works, but okay, she'll take a stab. Hmm. Maybe not the best metaphor to employ in a murder inquiry, but—

More impatient throat-clearing.

The witness is requested—

Please! Patience! Getting there! You insist it be spelled out, when spelling out, in a close-knit community, is generally to be avoided. It's not like there *is* a murder, an actual body, a perpetrator—

Yes, sure, it was predictable that the philosopher and Sasha's relationship wouldn't last. He could be difficult to live with, unpredictably moody and unreachable, even though with Sasha around he was more cheerful and more even-tempered than he'd ever been. But he was thirty years older, had already had a family and wouldn't have been eager, or willing, to start another, and she likely would have wanted one—

Witness is requested to stick to facts.

Oh, *facts*—

The point is, why shouldn't it have prevailed? More incongruous couples have existed in the world, after all. And what was West Delphi if not a place where idiosyncratic arrangements could be accepted and flourish? Wasn't that a hallmark of the Republic—celebration of oddity?

The witness is requested not to reply to questions with further questions.

Oh, she is, is she? The witness was *going* to say that certainly c. of o. was an article of our declaration of independence. The strictures and inevitabilities that prevailed in the outside world would not apply to us. Signs gauged elsewhere as warning, in West Delphi were simply marks of originality. The whole point of the Republic was that we had escaped the hidebound, the unimaginative, the ordinary. We had become permanent residents of a fantastical dominion in taking whose tacit oath of allegiance we had promised to believe each other's stories—

The witness is reminded—

Yeah, yeah, all right already. The witness was *going* to say that one of the stories we'd implicitly believed was that we'd persist in the same arrangements with which we'd arrived. However, though Sasha's departure was a blow, it was not a lethal one. We were very sad, of course, but once it was a fait accompli, the rest of us ruefully accepted it. The philosopher would still return in the summers, as always. Republics lost citizens from time to time and carried on, n'est-ce pas? The Threshold Institute might be one of the four cornerstones of the Republic, but the Republic could still be supported on three. Moreover the philosopher's daughter, even if not strictly a philosopher, possessed certain philosophical tendencies as well as the requisite culinary skills and could at least prop up her end. She was not unhappy, either, truth be told, to be, at least for an interval, the sole Institute representative.

The witness is further reminded—

Stop reminding the witness! I—I mean, she—

—that the purpose of this hearing is to determine if there be enough evidence to bring someone to trial.

That's not what—

What's not what?

Why I invited you here, I'd started to say, but this seemed inadvisable.

How about some*thing*? I said. Instead of some*one*—

What does Witness mean to imply?

Does she refer, peut être, to zee, how you say, mush-rooms?

But then—Otto and Gilda? And, eventually, Swift and Chantal?

Conceive of Adams and Jefferson together deciding to rescind their signatures on the Declaration—that gives an approximation of the cataclysmic effect of the departure of these founders.

And then not only the aforementioned but auxiliary supports: Gene and Diana Webb, Ivy and Dan Caulfield, Michael Suskind and Stella Swan. The astounding fact is that, of the couples who settled in the Republic during its formative years, all except the Meyers and the Silloways came apart and they were already of or near retirement age when they arrived. This was essentially double the national rate of fifty percent failure—what could explain this? Some zeitgeist riptide that had swept in unstable pairs? The stress of isolated living? Was West Delphi a proving ground—like a chemical test—to see what people were made of and most of us didn't pass? Did a pre-existing tendency to bathe the quotidian in the theatrical, which the citizens of the Republic shared, wreak havoc in private life? Or was it the opposite—did something about the very founding of republics, with their inherent beliefs in their uniqueness and superiority, sow seeds of dissatisfaction in couples?

What, in other words, was what?

Was it that, in a small village such as ours, it's inevitable that everyone eventually will have something against everyone else, but what isn't done—what *wasn't* done, before we newcomers gave in to gossip, was to spell it out to others. We ought to have learned this lesson from Violet Sleeper.

Need we remind the witness . . .

Oh, stuff it. Though I didn't say that aloud. But I'd had enough of these interruptions for the moment, so sent the pesky interrogators back to Birchwood. (Sorry, Lucinda.)

This time they got it out of her. Three seasoned detectives and one assistant detective were no match for one confused girl. They had the full weight of their fame behind them and she felt it. And yet what they did get out of her was nothing to set up shop with. Not even a flea market booth. It was a confused and confusing tale. She said she'd owned the hotel once, after her father died. She'd given water cures to the cosmopolitan dyspeptic, but after a love affair gone wrong she had drowned, and "I'm sure I don't know why I've been brought back to life for *this*," she concluded. Here the tight-lipped triumvirate could not suppress surprise but they covered it.

"*This?*" asked Marlowe.

"You," the girl said. "Whatever it is you're up to. Or after."

Holmes put his pipe in his mouth and took it out again. Poirot raised his eyebrows.

"Why don't you just show us the hotel, sweetheart," Marlowe said.

"It's not as it was in my day."

"Nothing is. When was that?"

"1915 was the year I died," she said.

"Is that a fact?"

"I don't know what year it is now."

"1930."

"1894."

"1962."

The three detectives stared at each other. It was a priceless look. Lucy's look at them was worth maybe $19.99, less if it went on sale. If they thought she was nuts, she returned the favor.

"You have been cruelly used," said Holmes.

"I cannot but think," said Watson, "that some of us must be suffering under a misapprehension."

"You don't say, Doc."

The main staircase was still grand but it looked like lipstick on a washerwoman. A window at each end of the upstairs hall had laid a wan rectangle of light on the bare floor, like a playbill someone had forgotten to put the words on. The dead girl opened doors and the detectives looked through them. Some furniture played ghost with sheets, waiting for someone to cut holes for eyes. In other rooms the beds and wardrobes and chairs were shoved into a corner, like a crowd around a body.

"I don't—I never—This was my father's room," Lucy exclaimed. "Look at it!"

Watson knew what to do. "There, my dear. Pray don't distress yourself. Gentlemen, I must request that we cut short our tour. It is too painful for the poor child."

"Is that so," said Marlowe, but he followed the others downstairs.

Poirot asked if the hotel kept a car.

"A hansom cab would do," Holmes said.

"The horses is all gone, sir," said Lucy, reverting to her amalgamated servant-speak.

"Any old crate," said Marlowe. "Or call a taxi."

Everyone except Poirot gave him looks empty of intelligence.

"Taxicab. Hired car. Any jalopy to get us from point A to point B."

"Where do you wish to go, sir?"

Marlowe looked at Poirot and Holmes. "The name 'West Delphi' comes to mind."

"Mine as well."

"Precisely."

"That you can walk, sir. It's only a couple of miles."

"A couple of—sacrebleu!"

Marlowe and Holmes exchanged an Anglo-Saxon look. It had survived since the time of William the Conqueror. He had not conquered it. A lot that had not been conquered was in it.

"I say we give the place the once-over," Marlowe said.

"There is but one thing to do, and it must be done at once," Holmes agreed.

"Sacrebleu," said Poirot again. "It is I, Poirot, who have said it," he added unnecessarily.

The road sloped up from the hotel as if it had its doubts about going that way. The detectives had doubts too but had to live with them. They had doubts because they were detectives, or they were detectives because they had doubts.

Marlowe was wearing his trench coat, Holmes his houndstooth deerstalker cap, and Poirot dapper outerwear of no clear description. They couldn't tell what season it was. One minute it felt like a day for the beach and they took off their cold weather wear and carried it. The next a nasty wind sliced through the trees, like a knife looking for something to cut, and they put it back on.

"Gentlemen," said Holmes. "The first consideration must be to share what facts we each may have gleaned."

"Precisely my zoughts," said Poirot.

"Thoughts," corrected Marlowe. "Mushrooms have gone missing, but no one will spill the beans. But damned if I know how I know this."

"Zat is vut I veeshed to zay. I know vut I know but not how I know it."

"A most perplexing case, gentlemen," said Holmes. "On this I believe we are all agreed."

"Zee knowledge appears to arise from nowhere—like zose voices zat bubbled forth from zee rock, and we are zee interpreters of zee oracle."

"You don't say," said Marlowe. Lord love a duck to death, a detective with a literary bent. But the Hat-and-Pipe went for it.

"It is without doubt a dark and sinister business. But if you will permit a digression—it has occurred to me that we may be the victims of an elaborate prank."

"Yes, zis has occurred to me as well. And yet—"

"What would be the racket?"

"Ah," said Poirot.

"Indeed," said Holmes.

"Let's stick to what we know, fellas. Did some lug do in some other lug or did he just think about it?"

"Murder, in such a place—wiz an appreciation of zee finer things—gastronomie, le vin bien sûr, conversation. . ."

"To your cosmopolitan pleasures I would add the lure of the countryside—"

"Ah, oui, you Eengleesh and your countryside—you are *fou* for zee gar-den . . ."

"I was going to say," said Holmes with a look—the kind you might get if you tried to dance the tango with the statue of a general—"that they desired to preserve a way of life that sadly may be vanishing, in the fashion in which monks in medieval monasteries kept knowledge safe through the Dark Ages—"

"Ah, but what you Eengleesh never want to recognize, zeese dreams—zeese, how you say? rêve pastorale?—it is a playzing—you will recall what 'appened to la reine Marie Antoinette . . . no more 'ed! Bye-bye shoulderz. . ."

"Appreciate the history lesson, Herk."

"Furzermore, it—la rêve communale—it will alwayz, but alwayz, be trumped by love! Amour! Amore! Lieb! La jalousie! Vengeance!

Vendetta! Rache—"

"We will take it as a working hypothesis—"

"En plus, alwayz, zare are zee ones around about whom zee rest orbeet, and zen ven zay depart—poof! No more gravitee! Bye-bye solar seestem!"

"You're a poet, Poirot," said Marlowe dryly. (If he got any drier, he thought, he'd die of thirst.)

"But non, mon ami, I merely use a figure of speech. Zat, if I may be so bold, is zee heart of zee problem here. Zare is a literal and a not-so-literal sinking at war—"

"Thinking, Herk. Th-, th-, th- . . ."

"Zee French, zee European mind—it ees so different from zee Eengleesh, zee American one . . . You sink I do not comprendre your ironee, Monsieur Marlowe," said Poirot, raising a finger, "but I understand it very well. Your difficulty ees, you do not know how to get out of it."

"Alas, it is doubtful whether two national temperaments can ever come to a true understanding of one another," said Holmes. "Irene Adler—"

Poirot bowed.

"Could we cut the philosophy and talk mushrooms?" said Marlowe. "That is why we were hired. Find out who took them and what they did with them."

"Brass tacks, Mr. Marlowe," said Holmes. "You would like us to come down to them."

"And what are zeese brass tacks zat we should descend to zare level?"

"Take the rap," Marlowe said to Holmes.

Marlowe, Poirot, and Holmes stopped walking. Coincidentally they had attained the crest of the hill. A long descent into, they presumed, the village of West Delphi and perhaps a less hard-boiled prose lay before them.

"Where the blazes is Watson?" exclaimed Holmes suddenly.

"Zat is a question I have been asking myself for a long time now."

"Didn't you ask your sidekick—" Marlowe began, but was interrupted.

"I am not my brother's keeper," said Holmes, then looked stricken—as stricken as the great detective could permit himself to be, even in someone else's prose. "I do not speak like this," he said softly.

"Nor I," said Poirot. "I have said many zings zat normally I do not say."

They looked at Marlowe; he caught the look and hit it back.

"Perhaps Monsieur Watson has stayed behind to tend to zee young lady at zee hotel—she wiz zee unfortunate belief zat she is already dead."

"These are deep waters," said Holmes. "But this is no time for despair."

"Don't get tough," said Marlowe.

The next thing they knew, the three detectives found that they had resumed walking, and the gentle downward motion lulled them into a kind of trance, out of which they spoke, indeed like oracles.

"From whom were the chanterelles taken?"

"From the woods."

"Whose woods?"

"I think I know."

"Do tell."

"I am unable."

"How many were taken?"

"A colander full at least."

(What was a colander? wondered the detectives.)

"What was done with them afterward?"

"Some were eaten immediately. The rest were dried and stored for winter use."

"How was the theft discovered?"

"The thief displayed his bounty to provoke those less fortunate in their seeking."

"Provoke to what end?"

"To drive them to conclude that they lacked what it took to fulfill their quest."

"Do those who do not find believe that they have not been deemed worthy?"

"They seek to confess their sins."

"Does a certain Grail quality attach itself to this mushroom?"

"Chanterelle seekers guard their spots with infinite guile and confide their locations only to persons of unimpeachable rectitude."

"Do such persons exist?"

"…"

"In certain countries people leave these locations to others in their wills."

"Is there any truth to the rumor that the chanterelle was the ambrosia of the gods?"

"To eat is to know."

"We have our web to weave," said Holmes, "while theirs is already woven."

But when the others looked at him expectantly, he found that he did not know what else he had intended to say.

"Irene Adler. . . ?" prompted Marlowe.

Whereupon they awoke from their trance and made their way on into the village in search of—it had just come to them—a Mrs. Violet Sleeper.

XVIII

The Great Chanterelle Murder Mysteries: Part Three

In which the detectives attempt to interrogate Violet Sleeper

As they descended the hill that led into the village of West Delphi, the three detectives had to pass by the house of the philosopher's daughter, and it dawned on her that they might stop off there on the way. A happenstance she contemplated with a mixture of eagerness and apprehension. The latter because, for one, in thinking about them, she was beginning to talk like them, and if she did this in their presence it would be embarrassing, to say the least. It would be exciting, of course—these three renowned detectives in her living room (or on her porch; on the whole, she thought, things would be more relaxed if they all sat on the screened porch—if there were uncomfortable silences they could all admire the hummingbirds, who fluttered around the feeder—birds with which at least two of the detectives were unfamiliar since these extravagant evolutionary inventions existed only in the New World) but—what would she *say* to them? Or they to her?

She imagined such scenarios as Marlow remarking, in his dry, cut-to-the-chase way, "Spill the beans, toots," and herself responding with an arsenal of clever responses such as "What beans?" "What do you mean by 'beans'?" "*Are* there beans?" or "We are living in a post-bean age, Marlowe," since, after all, she had invited them into this Delphic history in the first place (if "inviting" applies when the visitors in question had simply materialized). It's possible that she had gone off the deep end, narratively speaking—lost her marbles, jarred a screw loose, or lapsed into some other euphemistic lunacy. But since there was no way to answer this question definitively, she passed over it. If the trio of private eyes had been summoned to West Delphi by her imagination, she could congratulate herself on having done a thorough job. Like Frankenstein's monster, they were now acting autonomously. And, after all, she had not invented them, so they could not upbraid her for her presumption. She supposed they could have been appearing as a sign of something, the way the Virgin Mary is reputed to do to some people, though no one in West Delphi, to her knowledge, had yet seen Sherlock Holmes, Hercule Poirot, or Philip Marlowe in a tortilla.

But if they were apparitions, in response to what prayer, to alleviate what dire circumstance, had they appeared?

Though this was disingenuous. She knew very well why they were there. For one, she had reached the limit of her ability to analyze why the Republic had disintegrated, and, for another, there were things one couldn't very well reveal about other people if one wanted to go on living in their midst.

However, while all of this was passing through the mind of the philosopher's daughter, who had begun to worry about whether and what to offer them to eat, the three detectives had already made it to the village of West Delphi and the house of Violet Sleeper, who could be depended upon to deal with them.

Here is what happened next.

Violet invited them in and without ceremony set cups down on the table and brought the coffeepot from the stove. She poured, then passed around the cream and sugar.

"Do you gentlemen care for doughnuts?" she inquired.

Only Marlowe knew what she was talking about.

"Yes, ma'am," he said. "Rolls with holes," he added economically to the other two when Violet went off to the pantry.

Poirot raised a Gallic eyebrow and Holmes took his pipe out of his mouth and put it back in again. It was unlit, in deference to Marlowe's astonishing and weirdly folksy warning that "Some don't hold with baccy."

"Fresh yesterday," announced Violet Sleeper as she set down the plate.

"Extraordinaire," said Poirot, lifting the item in question and peering through the hole at Holmes. Holmes took his lorgnon out of his pocket and studied his.

Marlowe, perhaps to establish a patriotic solidarity with Mrs. Sleeper, took a bite.

"Excellent," he pronounced. "Top-notch."

However, Mrs. Sleeper didn't beam with pleasure, as he'd anticipated, or even thank him. She nodded, as if praise were nothing less than what she expected (Violet Sleeper was a good advertisement for the admonition that in order to get, one must expect), then said, "Now, what can I do for you gentlemen?"

The three sleuths exchanged a look of unsleuthlike surprise. They'd come to visit Mrs. Sleeper upon . . . that is to say . . . that is . . . someone's . . . recommendation, but now, it appeared, they could not remember whose. Nor, in fact, what they were investigating.

"It seems—"

"We aren't—"

"Perhaps you—"

"One at a time, please," said Mrs. Sleeper, who, the three now recalled having been told (though not by whom), had once been a schoolteacher.

The detectives held a silent parley. They had discovered that they could do this. Who was to be spokesman? Marlowe had the advantage of being the dame's countryman. Holmes, they conceded, was the deftest questioner. But Poirot could pour on the social oil—that is, if Mrs. Sleeper could understand him.

They looked at each other.

"Something appears to have occurred—"

"Are you fond of mushrooms, Mrs. Sleeper?"

"That is to say . . ."

Mrs. Sleeper gave a slight frown. She went to the stove and came back with the coffeepot and refilled their cups, as if additional caffeine might raise the IQ level of her guests. After this she took off her apron, hung it on a hook behind the stove, then sat back down and folded her hands together on the table.

The well-worn square table, pushed against the two windows that looked out upon the road and, across it, at the graveyard, was pulled out only when Violet was expecting company for supper. Impromptu visitors had to crowd around it as best they could. Violet was sitting now on her usual side, beside the easternmost window, whence she could keep an eye on Elton's and Alton's gravestones and at the same time reach behind her to answer the phone should it ring. (This scene occurred pre–answering machine, although it's debatable whether or not Violet would have scrupled to let a machine answer so long as she herself were actually present.) Marlowe sat across from Violet beside the other window; Holmes was to Violet's right; Poirot beside Holmes, around the corner from Marlowe.

"If you're asking about the McGranahan place, I've said all I have to say on that subject. It was a long time ago and it's over and done with. Why anyone would want to dig this up again is beyond me."

"The McGranahan place?"

"I assure you, we—"

"Irish. Or perhaps Scottish. How long is long ago?"

"Who did you say you're staying with?"

"We didn't," said Marlowe flatly, before his companions had a chance to equivocate. They hadn't discussed it but he knew that they favored the indirect method, whereas experience had taught him that striking first with the truth caught people unprepared. It left them off-balance in a helpful way.

But not, as it happened, Mrs. Sleeper.

"I am not the village idiot," she said. "Mr. . . ."

"Marlowe," said Marlowe, before he considered not saying. "Philip Marlowe."

"Mr. Marlowe. And . . ." She looked at Holmes and Poirot.

"Poirot," said Poirot. "Hercule." (He pronounced it "Air-Cool.")

"Holmes, Sherlock, at your service."

"And I'm the monkey's uncle," said Violet Sleeper.

She did not, however, seem out of countenance. She had these three pegged now: troublemakers. The ones she'd used to send into the corners with dunce's caps on their heads (although these had been invisible). "North! South! East! West!" she'd call out, pointing at each culprit in turn. (She didn't employ this method of punishment if there were more than four perpetrators.) For these three, however, there were other means. Besides, she was curious. If Violet Sleeper had an Achilles' heel, curiosity was it. People did not necessarily know, since she had cultivated the impartiality and receptivity of the father confessor, but in her heart of hearts Violet regarded information as currency, which, properly invested, resulted in more currency. This pecuniary philosophy she now employed.

"It was 1947," she said. "The whole family disappeared. Never heard from again. Roddy Slocomb went by to help with the haying and there was their breakfast still on the table, half eaten. Porridge in the bowls and bread on the plates. Bites out of it."

She said this last as if this clinched the matter, and fixed the three detectives with what could only be described as a gimlet eye. It was not clear to anyone present what a gimlet eye precisely was, but no one (including this writer, despite her having heard many times that it was what the fisher who came after Henry the cat in the middle of the night fixed her father with) had any doubt that Violet possessed one. Looking closely now, the detectives observed—how had they missed it?—that one of Violet Sleeper's eyelids was held open by a most curious device, something like a dressmaker's pin, affixed horizontally to the top rim of her eyeglasses. How had they not noticed this before? they each, separately, wondered. Were their powers of observation slipping? (Or "sleeping," in Poirot's case.)

They ventured to exchange a look: who *was* this woman? There was something of Irene Adler about her, thought Holmes, allowing for the differences in nationality, age, physique, and a host of other attributes about which there was no time to speculate. But she had the same ability that La Adler had of somehow finding her way *around* one's thought—or of anticipating it—or shunting it aside—he could never adequately explain to himself exactly how the Adler effect was achieved.

Marlowe also had met his match in a woman—several matches, in fact, though all had failed to combust. Violet Sleeper, past her prime as she theoretically was, yet possessed something of the indomitable spirit of the women with whom he'd hoped he might not be able to get the better of.

"Bites . . ." repeated Holmes. It was all he could think of to say, but instead of disparaging him for this, the others looked sympathetic.

"Bites," said Violet Sleeper, more firmly. "From humans."

"These are deep waters," Holmes said, rousing himself. "There's more to this than meets the eye, Watson."

Lord love a duck to death, thought Marlowe to himself. The Pipe appeared to use "Watson" as a term of emphasis, even when his sidekick wasn't present. It's me and the clowns, he thought, feeling sorry for himself in the self-ironically flamboyant American way that gives its users the impression that they're on the big screen, observed by an audience sympathetically chuckling.

Violet was studying the master detective, who drew on his unlit pipe. Nothing human was alien to her, or if it was, it was not her policy to reveal this. In their discomfort at not knowing what mystery they had been summoned to solve, the three detectives were not aided by the fact that Violet Sleeper, compact in her flowered dress, took it entirely in stride that three strangers, two plainly from across the ocean, one apparently believing himself to be a character in a book, were seated at her oilcloth-covered kitchen table. (As has been pointed out, Violet was the Republic's customs house, its border crossing, and could, invisibly and inaudibly, request passports. Also, issue them.)

"Either of you boys have a clue?" she asked, regarding Marlowe and Holmes with satisfaction. Mesmerized, they shook their heads.

"Fire in the cookstove still smoldering. Power didn't come in till—"

"Power?" repeated Holmes.

"Electricity," Marlowe explained.

"Ah. How many in the family, Mrs. Sleeper?"

"Five. Mother, father, three children. Had them in school. Benjamin, Frances, Roy. That Roy." She shook her head, as if to describe Roy's misdemeanors exceeded even her powers of articulation.

"It was down the hill then," she said.

"I beg your pardon, madam?" asked Holmes.

"The school."

"Vare has it gone?"

"It's Otto's now."

"Otto?" prompted Marlowe.

Holmes waved away this apparently tangential line of questioning.

"Any signs of a struggle?"

"Had zey le transport?"

"1942 Ford coupe," Violet recited. "Red. Still there. No signs of a struggle. Nothing packed, so far as anyone could tell. Dog left behind. Tied in the yard."

"Their usual practice?" inquired Holmes.

Violet Sleeper rewarded this question with a sphinxlike smile. "Sometimes."

"It is indeed a dark and sinister business."

At this moment, just when they said to themselves, individually and collectively, that they had no idea what to do next, Violet abruptly turned and rapped fiercely on the window with her knuckles, provoking a triplicate detective jump. Springing to their feet, the three peered outside, but all they saw was a black-and-white cat lying in the road. Violet had meanwhile already stomped out onto the porch. "Now, Wil*bur*!" she said, in her guilt-inducing schoolmarmish way. Whereupon Wilbur, the cat, sheepishly stood and strolled over to Violet to rub ingratiatingly against her legs. Meanwhile a chipmunk, on top of whom Wilbur had been lying, looked around in surprise, got up, shook itself a little, and scampered back toward the stone wall that marked the lower border of the graveyard. It did this rather half-heartedly, however, as if it didn't much have a mind to do this but since scampering was apparently what was expected of it, it would oblige.

"That Wilbur," Violet said when she came back in. "Him and that chipmunk."

The chipmunk's apparent alacrity to be caught and Wilbur's apparent lack of alacrity in killing and eating it had led her to the inescapable conclusion that they—cat and chipmunk—had developed a mutually satisfying game whose ultimate goal was to make Violet emerge onto the wraparound porch in her house shoes and apron and say, "Now, Wil*bur* . . ." and, if that didn't work, "Shoo! Now stop that, you bad cat!"

It's almost impossible to imagine what the three detectives were thinking during Violet's disquisition. Had they *seen* the chipmunk? Did any of them even know what a chipmunk *was*? The chances are slim. It does not live in Europe. And even dwellers in the contiguous United States have not always seen them—or known what they were if they did. When Thomas Jefferson visited the state of Vermont in the 1700s, he noted in his naturalist's journal the many "small red squirrels with black stripes." And Marlowe was an urban PI.

They were, in any event, thoroughly astonished by now—off-balance, at a loss, at sea, and kerflummoxed, just to begin with—as Violet, providing further evidence of Wilbur's devious pastimes, continued to trip merrily along, but her talk, contrary to appearances, was not truly self-referential; she did not look upon conversation as an opportunity to draw its focus toward herself, but instead talked on to give other people a chance to steer it in their own direction. She talked something like a conductor of an orchestra tuning up, but as if she hoped that, instead of her having to raise her baton, initiative would strike one or other of the players and they'd embark upon a melody on their own.

The detectives were also befuddled because Violet was a person whom it was completely impossible to patronize. If there be a single quality that typifies native Delphians—Vermonters in general—this would be it. People who attempt this do so at their peril.

The detectives had assumed, when they first laid eyes on Mrs. Sleeper, that she would be a soft touch. A beldam, a sweet little old lady, a country bumpkin, une vieille—and Violet was fairly short, it's true, and not young, but "sweet"—with its implication of docility—was not a word that sprang to mind when one thought of Violet. Generous, yes. Neighborly. But with a quality of alertness and appraisal that did not conform to the innocuousness that "sweet" contains.

Habitually ready with the mot juste, the pithy remark—part of the point of their existence, after all—here were three celebrated detectives, in a village they had never heard of, in a country none of them had visited (Marlowe, a native Californian, considered New England another country), sitting at the kitchen table of a village matron whom they should have got around within ten minutes and they were next to tongue-tied. In fact, they were tongue-tied.

Moreover, they were falling prey to thoughts of a kind they had never encountered before. To begin with, they were getting the uncomfortable feeling—and it was not a feeling with which they were familiar—that they were not earning their keep. Were letting their employers down. "Time is money, money is time" was a phrase that revoltingly occurred to them, though they had never heard it before. And "Something always has to be happening. You can't just have detectives sitting around a table—this will not advance the plot." They—none of them religious men—found themselves thinking of their "creators," though no sooner had they thought this than they found themselves thinking that their original creators had absconded, or lost interest in them, and they were now in the hands of a new and decidedly less sympathetic creator who meant to do they did not know what with them. Violet Sleeper, they could tell, was not in the employ of *anyone*. So it was no wonder they found themselves at a loss, at sixes and sevens, in the dark, topsy-turvy, and possibly at loggerheads.

The three detectives now mentioned that they'd walked over from Birchwood and Violet naturally concluded that they'd been sent—she still hadn't figured out who'd sent them, but it could have been anyone; visitors with a few screws loose were no surprise in this village as of late—to ask her about its history, since she'd worked there in the kitchen in the 1930s. But she had lunch to get on the table so she told them only that the hotel had closed down for good not long after her time there and had burned to the ground in 1958.

The detectives exchanged their—by now—trademark look while attempting to hide the fact that they were in fact exchanging it.

"I believe you have been cruelly used," said Holmes thoughtfully. "You have done wisely to confide in us. Yet you have not told us all. Pray go on with your narrative. This is no time for despair."

"Who's despairing?" Violet said, astonished. "You're a talking book."

"Let us consider the situation and see what may be deduced from it," he said.

"And what situation might that be?"

"Zis one," said Poirot.

"The beans, toots," said Marlowe. "Spill them."

And now something did happen, though whether it will advance the plot or not remains to be seen. A loud crackling noise, emanating from the little room off the kitchen, made them all jump for the second time. When it was followed by a voice calling "Mother? You there? Come in, Mother!" the triumvirate once again sprang to their feet and spun around, courageously prepared to meet this new threat. Once again, Violet had anticipated them. She disappeared into the little room and they heard her say, "Roger, Leroy. I read you."

"Hawk Hollow, home under fifteen."

"Under fifteen," repeated Violet. "Roger. I'll get things going."

"Sings?" echoed Poirot.

"What things?" wondered Marlowe.

"Over and out," said Leroy—or Roger, as at least one of the detectives believed him to be.

"My son," Violet explained. "On his way for lunch."

"Ah," said Poirot and Marlowe, who had grasped that Violet had been employing some sort of radio communication, although they had never encountered its usage between a mother and son and for such a purpose. But, apparently, this Leroy liked his food to be on the table when he arrived.

Holmes, however, thought that they had witnessed nothing less than an apparition, of an auditory kind—that is, the semblance of an apparition, meant to hoodwink them all—and he concurred with Poirot's and Marlowe's "Ahs" with one of his own.

Whereupon the three judged it prudent to take their leave.

XIX

The Great Chanterelle Murder Mysteries: Part Four

Deposition (with speculation—calm down, detectives)

It's not only that it's difficult to convey the atmosphere of contagious excitement of the era. How significant daily life felt and at the same time how homey. It had been a shipboard romance, the discovery of Troy, the Yalta summit all rolled into one—and taking place, metaphorically if not always literally, in Violet Sleeper's kitchen. So what was the catalyst of the dissolution? It is apparent in the comparisons used above that they are all experiences with an end point, yet nevertheless imbued with the belief that henceforth everything would change. But this still doesn't explain what had gone wrong in the Republic of West Delphi. That was what the three press-ganged detectives were supposed to ferret out. But now, it seemed, I couldn't even lay out the case for them.

We'd been in a near-constant state of elation, we were never bored, we were learning new things all the time. Doors were flung wide; there was always someone to talk to. Around the dinner table we made the world intelligible. Surely our endless interest in each other, our new capacious worldview, should have found room for any variations in human nature that might appear. But apparently for a too-long interval we'd remained in that stage of infatuation in which warnings sound irrelevantly, like foghorns heard romantically offshore when one is solidly on land.

In the village, there came a day when Otto was gone and Gilda, aspect subdued, stoically visited neighbors on her own. Having never conceived of her as an entity apart from Otto, we were as taken aback as children who'd always thought that their parents got along perfectly only to be informed one day that Mama and Papa can no longer reside under the same roof.

Particularly those of us who were not ourselves half of a pair, like Ben Metcalf and me, were shocked. What had *happened*? Incompatible desires, different ways of seeing a relationship, varying levels of commitment?

But that these hackneyed explanations should apply to our Otto and Gilda! To Swift and Chantal! Weren't they—weren't we—*above* such things? Or beyond them, or out of the way of them—whatever preposition would best describe our immunity? Besides being shocking it was also aggravating, in the manner of a two-year-old's tantrum that holds up an expedition. How could they have let their private problems interfere with the collective well-being? Hadn't our charter made it clear that the ensemble was the important thing? Though branches of the military stood ready to defend the Republic against invaders, no one had thought to guard against threats from within.

Throughout West Delphi, many an impromptu summit conference took place to assess these threats to the body politic. We had talked about each other before this, of course; often we talked of nothing but. The fabric from which our patriotism had been cut had been woven out of marveling at our fellow citizens and at our good fortune in ending up together in the same place. If we had flaws (of *course* we did; naturally we did) these were lovable eccentricities—merely further material from which stories could be constructed. They weren't *serious*. They weren't *consequential*. It was not that everyone was always on their best behavior: Swift and Chantal, for example, frequently engaged in tremendous arguments—flamboyant, screaming, bilingual shouting matches, which they did not scruple to break off for visitors. "A couple is not a *nice* thing," Chantal proclaimed in her Gallically certain way. "There is always a violence in love."

Disparagingly I had envisioned Mr. and Mrs. Settled, reading and knitting by the fire. How hackneyed, how trite, how *cowardly* this image seemed beside such stormy passion. Who, after all, would not prefer Heathcliff to Linton? Nick and Nora Charles to Rob and Laura Petrie? Swift and Chantal's fighting was simply another attribute of their uniqueness. Human relationships were fraught with difficulty and why should they censor themselves for the benefit of others? We did not think less of them for their stormy scenes. After all, we were so witty, accomplished, generous, likable, so *interested* in each other—each of us a major constellation in the new cosmology we had collaborated to create.

After a time Gilda brought new boyfriends to West Delphi, to test them out against the exigencies of Republic life. We were polite and welcoming, but when they left we tore them to shreds. Who could hold a candle to Otto? "That one was wearing a *leisure suit*!" we marveled. How could such an item have even made it into the Republic without being held up at customs? Otto himself meanwhile brought up various candidates for our inspection. Had we noticed, Ben pointed out, that this latest was a dead ringer for Gilda? Whom Gilda and Otto were involved with, when they would be coming up next, and where Otto would stay, since it was Gilda who owned the Schoolhouse, dominated our conversation. We clung to the hope that they would get back together again. Who knew that what happened between two people could shiver the timbers upon which society was built? Could only people happy in love form stable governments? Or was it that private relationships took their template from the larger relationship of the state to its citizens, the way children learn by unconscious imitation of their parents how to conduct intimate relationships, and if this governmental progenitor isn't functioning then woe betide the hapless twosome?

There was *something* there, but I couldn't identify it. I could feel its outlines, recognize some of its features, but not catch hold of the whole.

For one, to which state, then, had we referred for guidance? The behemoth putatively authorizing our social arrangements, or the rebellious pure-of-heart youthful newly charted one that rebelled against it—our own arrangement that we felt we'd recognized as much as invented? Did I have to impress the likes of Gibbon and de Tocqueville into service to answer these questions? But even my fancy hadn't the temerity to invoke their perspicacity and gravity.

Or was it simply more pedestrian than that? Such as that, being new to village life, the founders of the Republic had not been adept, unlike either their fictional counterparts or villagers longer in residence, at the habit of maintaining in equilibrium their social and private selves. So that when, for instance, the citizens began to realize that the eccentricities of fellow citizens that they had found so novel and endearing in the beginning were inextricable from deep-seated character traits—not to say weaknesses, not to say *flaws*—they reacted with astonishment and distress?

These are questions, however, that only hindsight can suggest, not ones we thought to pose at the time. Even the most cursory investigation into any utopia or commune throughout history could have told us that no such ordering endures very long when individual needs come into conflict with group demands. Engendered in heat, by a feverish desire for union with like-minded others, such arcadias seem inevitably to contain the seeds of their demise in their inception. All over our own state such wishful arrangements had foundered, if a decade or so before ours.

But nevertheless, even so, okay, but . . . *why*? Is it as mundane as the fact that they're too small, so that a rupture in private arrangements cannot be absorbed by the public one? Were we simply too inveterately individualistic to cooperate for very long? Too idealistic? But what does that even mean? Is it that, without actual *laws*, the tension between individual ambition and care for the common good can simply not be balanced?

I myself had not felt personally implicated in all this, however. Like everyone else, I mourned Otto's departure, but I was not a principal, except as observer. I remember then the surprise I felt, the sick feeling, when I discovered that I, too, could be a subject of gossip. A boyfriend had visited, eccentric enough for the Republic, surely: an accomplished storyteller, he believed in ghosts, one of which he'd encountered one night in the west of Ireland (she had reeked of the grave, which is how the villagers to whom he'd mentioned the strange woman he'd seen had been able to identify her and how he'd learned she was dead); he foraged for all kinds of unusual things: cattails, wild leeks, daylily tubers. My father enjoyed remarking that he expected to come back to find all his flower beds devoured. This boyfriend took a liking to Bucky Lefevre and we drank vodka with him in his trailer. In fact, my visiting friend liked Bucky more than he liked Otto and Swift and Chantal. Swift he especially didn't cotton to. "He grows on you," I tried to persuade him. "Yeah, like fungus," he retorted. After he left I discovered that they didn't like him either. They had been discussing my taste in men. I felt myself enveloped in the queasy quagmire all too familiar to me as the child of divorced parents who abominated each other: who was right? How had Delphi, a place free from such miasmas, become infected by this unsettling question?

Eventually Gilda fell in love with a man from a neighboring town who, though not a founder of the Republic, was yet deemed worthy of citizenship. Chantal pronounced them well suited. Upon the eve of their departure for the Northwest, we conferred passports upon them. From beyond the borders Gilda reported back that they were very happy and eventually she sold the Schoolhouse to Otto; we began to adjust to the new arrangements. It was a little ungainly, a little asymmetrical: Otto refused to come to Chantal's house if Gilda and her new companion, back during the summers, were also invited and this was inconvenient, but, well, this was Otto. Chantal would not refuse to invite them, as Otto would have preferred, but neither did she find Otto's demand presumptuous. She came from a country that, after all, deems thwarted passion a mitigating motive in murder.

To the rest of us, doubtless inhibited by our Anglo-Saxon sensibilities, such outward displays were as liberating as they were startling. In my upbringing, it was risky to say what you thought. For one, it could be used against you later. Now here was all this drama, not, as in the household I'd grown up in, hidden behind closed doors, raised voices whose import had to be decoded, but out in the open, like avant-garde theater requiring participation. To discuss people's private lives—not simply as gossip but to analyze and adjudicate—this was not Chantal's temperament alone; having spent a year in boarding school in France, I was familiar with this national habit. It was not that I and my friends back home had not talked about other people, but these discussions were driven by the attempt to understand motives and foretell the future, in which efforts we felt ultimately tentative and inept; opinions were never delivered with such certainty, as if they were facts. My French roommate regularly ran down the intrinsic values of all the girls on our floor. "Christine is a child; Anne-Marie is not honest; Sabine is a whore." In West Delphi, "the Church" was apparently still a place where one went to understand the ultimate worthiness of things, to distinguish good from evil, to experience a life more thoroughly adjudicated than one did outside its walls.

Gilda and Baxter—her new partner and later her husband—were away; Sasha and the philosopher had separated. But we now entered upon a Second Republic, in which Otto, Ben, Chantal and Swift, and I strove to keep the dream alive. The philosopher appeared on occasional weekends. We retrenched; we endured the winter; we held the fort. We could see that it would never again be quite the way it had been but we were determined not to be overcome by postlapsarian rue. Even if all republics contain in their DNA the gene for their dissolution as well as their growth, the Republic could not really die as long as we were there to recount tales of it, could it?

It was during this era that the uneasy tone crept into the chronicles, concealing sotto voce questions for the oracle. How could this happen? What had we done wrong? Hadn't we reached a point where we *couldn't* do anything wrong? Where nothing very bad would ever happen to us?

Perhaps we were, if not flatlanders anymore, still, at base, summer people, without the endurance and mud-season staunchness of real residents. (You have only to listen to the way people talk about mud season to figure out who's a "real Vermonter." The astonishment and complaint about the impassability of the roads also contains, unmistakably, bragging.)

Had any of the previously cited commentators on the Republic applied their analytic acumen to this question, they would certainly have hit here upon the critical mother lode, to wit: the question of the healthy relationship between public and private realms and what maintaining the one has to do with the health of the other and vice versa.

Since these commentators, however, seemed to have absconded, as pundits are wont to do when the answers to questions become urgent, we are left to struggle on alone with this one. Did the demands of citizenship in the Republic interfere too fundamentally with the demands of our own, idiosyncratic lives? Can conviviality sap too much energy from intimacy? What about the reverse? Did the group love affair carry the individual ones along in its flood, and when that began to dissipate the private connections dried up? Or were the individual relationships tributaries that ran into the river of state and when they slowed and narrowed the Republic ran dry?

All of which questions lead, horribly but inexorably, into other miserably intricate questions, such as what private life even is, and whether its nature changes as the size of the surrounding community changes. Intimate friendships depend on privacy, just to begin with—on confidentiality—and this is difficult, if not impossible, in a tiny community.

Cranford and the *Lucia* books convey the sense that private life is the anomaly, an alcove off the common room, not a separate dwelling. One great appeal of reading these books is that you feel you are never alone, people are always thinking about you, and the less admirable parts of your character (which you've always been at great pains to hide) are in fact already known to everyone and not considered the evidence of damnation you have always feared. Yet these, we must perforce recall, are novels—comedies. Nothing truly dire occurs. Maybe only in fiction can the boundary between public and private life be held in perfect balance.

In West Delphi none of us had yet confronted the problematic truth that, in friendships as in republics, subscribing to the same interpretation of events is a large part of what they are founded on. In a larger place, a certain percentage of people may default on this agreement and the entity will still stand. But in one the size of ours, even one person's apostasy had the power to undermine everyone else's faith.

We lapsed into an unpleasant evaluating mode. Up on the hill I was thinking about these neighbors' lives more than felt healthy, feeling alternately oppressed by whatever new information I gleaned when I descended into the village, yet even now somewhat envious that I wasn't more in the thick of things. Qualities that previously had seemed refreshingly eccentric now appeared to conceal a darker side. Ben let it be known what he had previously kept to himself: that, to maintain his cats' family succession, Swift drowned successive litters of kittens. Then, returned from a trip out West, he told of having laid his father's spirit to rest, having taken his ashes on a symbolic journey across the country. I was touched by Swift's coming up to the Institute on purpose to confide this affecting story to me. It seemed in keeping with his flamboyant, idiosyncratic temperament that he would drive his father's remains across the country.

Except, it turned out, he had not been alone. He had been accompanied by a young woman, a fact that emerged when the woman's husband sued Swift for "alienation of affection." (Who knew that such a legal category existed?)

The ensuing court case drove yet another nail into the Republic's coffin. It was tawdry and humiliating, especially for Chantal, who rallied to defend him. After a sensationalistic trial in which it was revealed, among other things, that Swift and his paramour had carried out their affair in all the village graveyards and taken on the identities, respectively, of "Violetta" and "Boris the Pirate," the case was dismissed, but people's feelings about Swift had been permanently tarnished. Chantal had visited each of us in turn and confided additional details about Swift's domestic shortcomings. Like the offspring of divorce reluctant to give up our role as uninvolved children, we had now to consider them as individuals with needs and personalities of their own.

When a relationship comes apart, a door opens into a house one has seen only from outside and one is given a tour of the interior. So—the ironic, self-contained violence that had formed a part of Swift's charm concealed a real violence, of not so amusing a character. When Chantal reunited with Swift and wanted us to welcome him back into the fold, this was difficult to do. The door of the couple's house is shut in your face; flowers are back in the window boxes, and you must pretend that you don't know what goes on behind it.

Chantal had a more inclusive view of human nature than the inexperienced rest of us, perhaps, but we were stuck in our shifted allegiance. This was for most of us also our first encounter with the triangulation that can occur when a relationship comes apart and how thankless, if it reestablishes itself, the role of supporter can prove to be, particularly if one has become invested in the outcome.

It was all too much for Ben, who sold his house and moved to Lancaster. Chantal went back to France and eventually Swift followed. Otto, after living for a few years in the Schoolhouse, bought land in another part of Delphi and built a house there. I went into exile for a teaching job in the Midwest. The philosopher returned to his solitary pursuits. The Republic, just like that, was no more.

XX

The Great Chanterelle Murder Mysteries: Part Five

In which the detectives make a last attempt

I had thought I was done with the detectives but I suppose it was inevitable that they should show up at my house with tired questions about the nature of truth.

"Mademoiselle, let us speak franchement. Zare are sings you are not telling us."

"*Things*," Marlowe said wearily.

"Things, yes," I repeated.

Having thought them still safely gathered around Violet Sleeper's table, I had been lost in recollection of Leroy Sleeper, of various stories involving him over the years—the time he and my brother and another friend borrowed our family car and drove to Canada (having intended to go mountain-climbing in New Hampshire, but, deciding it was too foggy, had set off for the border instead—no passports then required to cross it), or how, at his own wedding, when his suit coat opened slightly, in Leroy's shirt pocket could just be discerned the vinyl pocket protector he always wore—with pencils in it. (*In sickness and in health? Let me just write that down . . .*) And of another story involving the Sleepers—the time a visiting violist friend of our family played a concert for them in their house, his head (he's tall) nearly brushing the low ceiling, when in the midst of a soft passage of Mozart could be heard a clip-clip-clip sound; it turned out to be Alton, in the armchair, taking advantage of the enforced idleness to cut his fingernails. The violist, to maintain his composure, had to turn his back to his small audience and play the rest of the piece gazing out the little window above the sink, as if overcome by musical emotion.

Ignoring the detectives for the moment, I'm thinking about the fact that every attempt to develop some line of inquiry skids into anecdote. Like Violet Sleeper's story about the McGranahan place, which I've never heard from anyone else but which, like Dexter Tapper's stories, has become part of my history of Delphi.

I further am worrying that, while what I find appealing in these stories about Leroy and Alton is the principals' flouting of convention—their remaining who they are, regardless of circumstance—to retell the stories may seem patronizing, or worse, class-driven. Class, that thing we supposedly don't have in America; social division an aspect of Delphic and Vermont life it's painful to think about. Which, for good or ill, was not something on anyone's minds during the heyday of the Republic.

Meanwhile the quasi-invited guests are still in my living room: Marlowe and Holmes sitting on the slip-covered couch; Poirot on the love seat, whose springs, pre-reupholstery, protruded from its worn cover. Whenever he moved I watched anxiously to see if they were going to bayonet him. Like most of the furniture in the room, the love seat had been given to me; whoever previously owned it, some friend of a friend, had tired of lugging it from place to place and never having the money to repair it. Now I had been doing the same. However—"Zare are sings you 'ave not told us, mademoiselle," Poirot reminded me.

"That's true," I said. "I can't."

I saw the detectives exchange detective looks. But they did not know whether they were getting somewhere or if I was merely being cagey.

"The mushroom murders are a sham, aren't they, toots?"

I smiled. I liked Marlowe. In some ways I liked him the best of all of them. I liked his candor and his hard-boiled prose. I wondered who had first used the term "hard-boiled" to describe language. I admired the way he cut through the strings of subordinate clauses that increasingly tied Holmes up in knots. Yet at the same time I envisioned a tea table on which the estimable Mrs. Hudson had just set a laden tray and this was the world in which I'd been brought up, by a series of nineteenth-century narrators, not the world of gumshoes in slouch hats, and I was confused again. Certain things one simply did not speak of, particularly to strangers. I didn't owe them anything, did I? These characters only provisionally mine? I'd borrowed them[54] [(55)] [(56)] [(57)] in anticipation of their being able to detect the crux of the question, which so far I had failed to identify. What was at stake here? What was I really trying to understand?

Yet as I sat gazing at them, I could take little pleasure in their appearance in my living room—Sherlock Holmes! Philip Marlowe! Hercule Poirot!

I was experiencing such a bewildering mixture of feelings that the phrase "tongue-tied" seems mild for the muteness that now silenced me.

Distress about the collapse of the Republic. Shock at our loss of innocence. Nostalgia for what had been. Frustration at not being able fully to grasp why it had all fallen apart.

And, not least, the desire to call someone up and exclaim, "You'll never guess who just showed up in my house!"—when there was no one any longer to exclaim to.

The Chanterelle Murders, we'd called them in the village. We knew what we meant. A way of referring to what had happened without having to spell it out. But then newspapers were calling up, wanting to know what our relationship was to "the deceased." What had been funny, wasn't. *Flatlanders*, we muttered, *literal-minded lug nuts*, but we were uneasy. As happens with the IRS, absence of imagination could impose itself on us. It could, it seemed, bring in the Law. Spiritually speaking, it could audit us.

I didn't say this aloud but something of it communicated itself. I should have known that this was what the detectives were here for—to ascertain what deeper strife the mushroom rivalries concealed—not to clear up interpersonal quandaries.

"Friendship . . ." I said. "Privacy . . . We didn't realize . . . Maintaining a sense of identity . . . Requiring enemies . . . In a small community . . . I don't . . . I'm sorry. I can't *think*."

---

54 A mechanism as unpremeditated as that which brought them to my pages can be termed "borrowing" only in the sense that the visitation of the Magi could be termed "borrowing" by the authors of the New Testament—

55 and here, of course, I have invariably lapsed into the self-aggrandizement without which the Republic would never have come into existence in the first place, yet which habit was,

56 if not the source of the present difficulty, then certainly an impediment in the way of extracting ourselves from—

57 well, this sentence, to begin with.

Holmes and Poirot leaned forward in their seats. Marlowe didn't budge.

I paused—stopped, actually—since I didn't know how to go on.

Three penetrating, narrowed, lidded gazes were now directed my way. I tried to ignore them.

"Spit it out, toots," Marlowe said.

"Would anyone care for something to drink?" I asked.

Deflection by ingratiation—it had worked for me in the past, but they weren't falling for it.

"There are things that can't be said," I said, taking an oracular tone. (One naturally acquired it, in Delphi.) There was always the hope that vagueness would turn into profundity. That *they* would turn it into profundity. That's what they were here for, wasn't it? They with their mystery-solving doctrine: first you identify the crime, then you discover the guilty party.

"Relying on someone—what people are like—even the people closest to us—it's so difficult to know—to find out what people are capable of—our views shift . . ."

They frowned. One American, two transatlantic frowns.

"Everyone has illusions, I suppose, but when everyone shares them . . ."

Six eyebrows elevated themselves.

I wasn't prevaricating. I really wasn't. But what would you do if you'd lived through fin de siècle Vienna, Paris in the twenties, or Greenwich Village in the fifties, and three impatient detectives showed up and asked you to explain just what had "gone wrong"? *Had* anything gone wrong? Had there been a cataclysmic event or was it a slow deterioration? Had the Republic been doomed from the start or was there something we could have done? And what would that have been?

"It's just so hard to explain . . . You had to be there . . ." I began. "If you weren't then I can't—"

But as I said these words I was struck by a terrible vertigo. *Had* we ever been there? That is, had what we thought happened, happened? Or had we been besotted by an idea of ourselves, residing in the future perfect of the stories we'd spun out of what was happening in the present? Had the denizens of fin de siècle Vienna, Paris in the twenties, and Greenwich Village in the fifties ever really been there either? Hadn't we who read their redolent memoirs made the mistake of thinking that they'd known what they were living at the time they lived it?

But—I objected (to the invisible interrogator who always stood ready to cross-examine me)—how could an experience be imaginary if you were living it?

No doubt we had been naïve, to think that we could all simply get along, march on into our dotage singing the battle hymn of our Republic, but how could we have foretold that friendships would founder upon the shoals of wrecked love affairs? Was it, as Poirot had said, that the pastoral dream was always deposed by "l'amour"? Or did the latter risk splintering against the bulwark of communal esprit de corps?

How could I explain to scrutinizing detectives the particular seasickness you feel when you go from trusting and extolling people to suspecting their motives? That nauseating volatility in one's view of a person. How it took me back to the era of my parents' long-drawn-out divorce and the pressure I'd felt to choose between them. It was bad enough to feel distressed when one citizen announced that another was an unprintable word; yet however queasy I felt at having to decide whether or not this judgment was justified, I had still been outside of the controversy, or so I'd believed. I could still retreat to the safety of my perch as observer.

But then, apparently, I couldn't.

How could I tell the detectives how much time I had spent obsessing over why X had said the cruel thing to me he had, why Y had told Z what I had told her about Z in confidence, why W had become great friends with X despite the cruel thing X had said when W had been my friend first, why V could possibly have asked what he did, why U communicated secretly with T, why S never invited me to dinner when I had invited her so many times? About how *embarrassed* I was to have these feelings.

To catalog such resentments seemed petty and small-minded. What did I *expect* from people? Yet these reproofs did nothing to dispel the anger and hurt or the even more disturbing question: did I deserve this treatment? What had I done to incur it? What were my own insensitivities and obliviousness?

If I could bear to hear the answers to these questions from anyone, I supposed it would be from the detectives, they with their impartiality and keen sense of justice. These clever private eyes who could discern the guilty parties through the perusal of cigar ash or the timbre of a whistle.

But when I opened my mouth to speak, a strange thing happened. Instead of the words I'd meant to say I said this instead:

"Here's the thing. West Delphi was a Republic. It wasn't a large republic, but it was still a republic. We had an army and a navy. We were all generals and there was one admiral.[58] There was no rank and file. We were all the supreme command. We were ready to defend our way of life at all times but because the rest of the world didn't know we existed we didn't worry about being attacked. Now I realize that we were under attack all the time, by the forces that perpetually seek to undermine republics such as ours, we just didn't know it."

"And what forces are zeeze, mademoiselle?"

Don't interrupt, Frenchy, I wanted to say, but I was too polite. I couldn't talk like a character no matter how much I wanted to. But I was annoyed. He'd thrown me off my stride. Just as I seemed about to get to the central point, he sent me veering into reminiscence and a smart comeback.

"The forces to whom we constitute a threat, I meant."

"And what forces are zoze?"

"Don't interrupt, Frenchy," said Marlowe. "Listen and you might learn something."

"I don't know how to explain," I said. "Something that prevents—that doesn't want—that wants everyone to be themselves but only at the expense of others, so if we subordinate ourselves we think . . ." I sighed. "I don't know. It's hopeless. I know we have to make a leap—a different way to understand ourselves with others but . . . I don't know. When I try I just . . . I can't think . . . all the buzzing! It's like being in a beehive. I feel as if I'm going to disappear."

But try saying this to three persons trained by profession to mistrust all such hazy talk, to consider it, in fact, a sign of insufficient clues.

And all three certainly antedated the apprehension, now commonplace, that there is no such thing, entity, concept, as the essential self—

The lucky ducks.

Once upon a time (I'd heard it proclaimed) there were good people and bad people. Honest-to-god villains! But various clever thinkers like

58 Not the one of Generalissimo's appointment, but Swift, reaching for an additional title.

Freud and Darwin and others had done away with them. Reputedly one may find them nowadays only in certain mass-market paperbacks. So to search anachronistically for a *culprit* . . .

"Some coffee? Tea? Something stronger?" Though I offered the latter before remembering that all I had on hand were a couple of beers and some crème de cassis, which I used in cooking.

They, however, had no trouble recognizing this for the dodge it was and declined.

Which rekindled the hope (I was going to say the "wild hope," but this was just the kind of exaggerating and embellishing of experience I was trying to wean myself from)—aroused the hope, that is to say, that if I *could* put everything before them, they, with no stake in the outcome except to solve the case, would prove to be the sympathetic but impartial listeners one always longs for but never finds. Even one's dearest friends respond out of their own biases, which become clearer the longer you know them. But these were *detectives*. All they wanted was the truth—to know who had done what to whom and why. Like secular father confessors, if I told them they would then give me the absolution of making sense of what had happened.

But they preempted me.

"What, pray, can you tell us about chanterelles, Miss . . . ?"

"Um . . . I like to eat them?"

"You got any around the joint?" asked Marlowe.

"They're not in season."

"Which is when?"

"July."

"When in July?"

I shrugged. "Depends on the weather. A good rain, then sun—they come right out."

"Ah, who doesn't, Mademoiselle?" said Poirot.

I relented and smiled at him. Unlike my father, I am partial to the French. In particular I admire their certainty about absolutely everything, from food to love. Even existentialism and deconstruction, those philosophies of uncertainty, sneakily define the indefinable.

There didn't seem to be anything to say to this, however, so I didn't.

"I believe you have been cruelly used," said Holmes thoughtfully. "You have done wisely to confide in us. Yet you have not told us all. Pray go on with your narrative. This is no time for despair."

"I wasn't despairing," I said, experiencing a sense of solidarity with Violet Sleeper. "Are you sure you're not quoting yourself?"

"Let us consider the situation and see what may be deduced from it," he said.

"Okay," I said. "Be my guest."

"I zought zat is vut we already are."

"Tell us all that you can about this deep business, that we may proceed accordingly."

"We are in zee dark."

"Spill the beans, toots. Throw them down in a big heap."

They said a number of other things, exhortatory and sententious, but these did not promote the bean-spilling. I was getting increasingly fed up with "beans." To spill them would a) mean that they were already in my possession and b) to oversimplify, to take to a tawdry level what had been magical and rare.

I wanted to make sense of things but at the same time I didn't want people to think that we had been an experiment: a petri dish in which to observe what happened when you combined competing storytellers into a too-small space: a litmus test; a miniature metonym; a metaphor; a synecdoche—whichever of these it was—for what was occurring to the greater republic of which we were an inevitable, if recalcitrant, part.

"We do not comprehend how a mere mushroom—"

"Join the club," I said.

"Zere is a club?" asked Poirot hopefully.

"You bet. We're hitting ourselves over the head with it," said Marlowe.

"Tut-tut, gentlemen! We must act, or we are lost. Nothing but energy can save us. These are very deep waters."

"Dive into them," said Marlowe.

I gave Marlowe a patriotic look. We could have used him, in the Republic. The way he resuscitated dead metaphors and made fun of them. A republic needs someone like that in residence, like a king a court jester. But I wasn't going to give the detectives names and dates, to diagram the whole sad dissolution. Aside from the fact that I wanted to go on living in this town, I wasn't convinced that lurid details—who did what and who said what to whom—would help to understand the central question. Which I was evading, I sensed, but since it wasn't certain what the central question was, evasion seemed like a sensible way to proceed.

Or so I slipperily reasoned.

I did, however, tell them about the time when, as a young philosopher's daughter, I'd sat at the dining room table while the philosopher stood at its head and ingested several bites of the eponymous fungus. How my sister and I had watched, riveted, to see if our father would collapse, mortally stricken, into his chair.

The detectives continued to observe me: Holmes still leaning forward, his fingers steepled together in front of his chin; Poirot sitting up very straight on the edge of the love seat, having evidently discovered the protruding springs; Marlowe slouching back, peering at me from under the pulled-down brim of an invisible hat.

At the time we did not know (as did our father) that no mushroom poison acts so quickly. One of the deadliest, an *Amanita*, the destroying angel, does not even produce symptoms until it is often too late for a remedy to be employed. Attractive and pristine-looking, easy when young to mistake for puffballs, these mushrooms reputedly taste bland but do not announce themselves as inedible. Besides, cooked in butter and garlic, even cardboard would taste appetizing.

"Is the sobriquet 'destroying angel' not rich with implication?" an oracular voice inquired, but no one else seemed to hear it.

I imagined that the detectives asked me why a father would let his children think he might actually die before their very eyes and I replied, "He was sometimes bored by the everyday."

"The everyday?"

". . . " I thought it best not to attempt to elucidate.

Considering that for many years the philosopher and his family were the only chanterelle hunters in West Delphi, did they resent the sudden influx of competition? Did they not ascribe to the belief that all the chanterelles in Delphi were theirs, and theirs alone?

Can the incipient disintegration of republics be located in such a belief?

To avoid dwelling on this question, I took a detour into considering the chronological progression in the three detectives' worldviews. Holmes had no doubt that the guilty could be found and brought to justice;

Marlowe would find them, but justice, to him, was certainly peeking over her blindfold and he had a sympathy for the underdog. He had been called a "shop-soiled Galahad," and that fit. For Poirot, as far as I could tell, detecting seemed to be more of a hobby, an antidote to boredom, than the desire to redress the world's wrongs.

So there they were, with their English, French, and American detective mentalities, in my living room. It was all very well when they'd showed up at the old hotel, which I had never seen standing, and conversed with its nineteenth-century proprietress, Lucinda Dearborn, whom I had invented. I was perfectly comfortable when they sat in Violet Sleeper's kitchen as she gave them doughnuts and admonitory schoolmarmish looks. (Naturally I did not invent Violet Sleeper; Violet is fantasy-proof, and moreover perfectly able to invent herself, should the need arise.)

But it's one thing to talk about Violet, whom I loved and still miss, and another to talk about myself, about whom my feelings are more divided. So I reverted, instead, to the by now tedious reflection that in Delphi the border between the real and the imaginary is more permeable than elsewhere. It is not policed. I recalled how citizens of the Republic, instead of bringing others' flights of fancy to earth with a thud, hitched rides on them, kept them aloft. There were no air traffic controllers.

Yet if the solitude and serenity of Delphi had served as a spur to the imagination, perhaps it had done so in the way of an agreeable asylum keeper who makes it a point not to contradict the inmates. "Good morning, Your Majesty," says he cheerfully, bringing them watery porridge. "And you—how did Your Holiness sleep last night?"

Having Sherlock Holmes, Hercule Poirot, and Philip Marlowe materialize in my living room was not unlike a delegation of cardinals appearing outside the asylum gates and requesting to be shown into the presence of the pope.

"Zee mushrooms, mademoiselle?" said Poirot gently.

"You're still here?" I exclaimed.

XXI

The Great Chanterelle Murder Mysteries: Part Six

In which a summation is offered to the jury

As I'd told the detectives, sometime every July, depending on weather, the chanterelle returns to the north woods. A wet few days, not too cold, then sun and a little drying are the conditions she favors. These mushrooms like best to grow beneath the spreading branches of hemlock and spruce, not deep in the woods but at the border—at the edge of a clearing, along a tree-shaded road, in a sparse stand—as if plying the limits of the need for shelter, waiting to see what goes on in the wider world.[59]

One may be simply strolling dreamily along and then—a flash of brightness arrests the eye, and there on the ground is a loose gathering, like concertgoers waiting for a performance to begin in order to coalesce into a tighter formation: tawny orange, the color of caramelized sugar, of butterscotch, of well-oiled boot leather; fluted stem, lacy edges on the larger ones, the little ones round; bright buttons inexplicably sprung from the ground.

Here. The essential mystery of the universe, enacted before our eyes.

Why *here*, one wonders, and not *there*? Why in this grove and not that? Why two-thirds of the way up the hill and not lower? Why on their land and not ours? One may know the terrain a particular mushroom frequents, the conditions it prefers, the season in which it flourishes, and yet—never find it.

Having espied a likely stand of hemlock, hospitably spaced, and

---

59 "Mushrooms of the border"—in short, threshold mushrooms, the reader will recognize, with all that this implies.

clambered down, or up, to it, only to find—no chanterelles, not one!—one feels betrayed. Chastened. To think you thought you knew something! Such presumption. Such hubris. By contrast, when you *do* find them, you feel commended, blessed by the dryads and hamadryads and other sylvan deities that concern themselves with mushrooms. Virtue has been rewarded, the land has tested you and found you deserving, the only affirmation, you feel in that moment, that anyone has ever really needed. Why, after all, should creation have conspired to make something so utterly delicious, yet so hard to find, and mistakable by those not in the know for something poisonous, if these temptresses were not loitering with intent? Could the serpent have offered a mushroom instead of an apple? There are certainly no atheists among mushroom hunters, if that's an answer.

The chanterelle is the disguised royalty among mushrooms. The morel, the *tout* of gastronomes, may stand resplendent and wear the crown, but the chanterelle smiles to herself in the shadows, recognizing her royal cousin for the impostor she is. The chanterelle, like Cinderella (whose etymological similarity we may well note),[60] knows her claim to the throne will one day be validated, but, like Zeus in camouflage, is content for now to be recognized only by select mortals.

Moreover, the morel is often unpredictable, showing up once or twice and rarely reappearing, fancying the earth around decaying elms, or ancient apple trees, though only at a particular moment, like overbred nobility too fastidious in their tastes to survive into future generations. The morel is the fickle Calvinist deity among mushrooms: you can do all the right things, but there is no guarantee your ardor will be rewarded. Though this may initially be true with the chanterelle, once you have found a growing spot, you can usually rely upon finding the mushroom year after year. If you do—if you do not!

Let us not mince words.

It is not only that you realize with a titanically sinking feeling that someone—someone else! —has come upon the spot before you, come

60 I know people who have named a daughter "Chanterelle," but who has ever run across a human "Boletus" or "Ink-Spot" or "Chicken-of-the-Woods"? D. H. Lawrence called his main character in *Sons and Lovers* Paul Morel—perhaps to suggest his earthiness if not his phallic preoccupations—but he is fictional, after all, and Morel is merely a last name.

upon . . . yes . . . *your* spot! It is not only that one *likes* to eat them, one *needs* to eat them! Chanterelles are the communion wafer of the woods, the fountain of youth, the philosopher's stone—emblem of benediction from the land. You are among the elect. (It is possible to buy this mushroom in certain sacrilegious grocery stores, but this would be like paying a friend to take communion for you because you're too busy to go to Mass.)

If we're looking for obvious motives, I explained in my world-weariest voice to Sherlock Holmes, Philip Marlowe, and Hercule Poirot, there's the uncontestable fact that mushroom hunters practice the highest levels of security to keep secret the location of their hunting grounds. Only on the rarest of occasions do they share these, and then only with someone they judge of unimpeachable probity. These persons must have shown themselves to be worthy, like postulants. The assumption is that this person will never seek to profit by this knowledge. Like knowing the location of the Holy Grail, the knowledge itself will suffice. So that when you suspect—when you *find*—that someone has trespassed upon *your* spot, *violated* it, *desecrated* it, your dismay knows no bounds. The words *horror* and *rage* are not too strong. To people who do not hunt mushrooms, the idea that anyone could commit a crime, a *murder*, on their behalf, defies credulity. Surely, they think, there has to be *something else*, some deep-seated antagonism, built up over the years, a competition underlying all other competitions, which mushroom poaching merely catalyzes.[61]

I stopped talking and looked at them hopefully.

"And vut is zis ressentiment?"

"Spit it out, toots."

"This is no time for—"

"Yes, I know. Despair. It's just . . . I can't . . . I just can't."

---

61 Honesty compels me to confess that on one occasion Ben Metcalf and I did visit the property of some friends of his, occasional residents of a township adjacent to Delphi, who yearly amassed vast quantities of chanterelles and lorded this fact over Ben the verb is chosen judiciously. They displayed for his benefit jars full of chanterelles they'd already dried, only very rarely doling out a small sample to him. Thus, when they happened to be away at a time when the chanterelles were fruiting, we considered it only just and reasonable that we look for them. We had no luck, however. Retribution, perhaps, for our temerity in seeking by nefarious means what is properly some earthly spirit's prerogative to mete out. In the final irony, Ben later discovered that his friends harvested the mushrooms on someone else's land and said they found them on theirs to throw him off the scent.

In our house (I did not say), we'd always liked chanterelles, but we had taken them more or less lightly. No one else in the village even hunted them, so far as we knew. But now . . . now! There were *other* mushroom hunters in residence. Who *worked* at it. *Methodically.* One, in particular, who, like the third little pig outwitting the wolf, always got up earlier, traveled faster, covered more territory, and found more chanterelles than we. Took to horseback to cover more ground, conscripted his girlfriends in the foraging, even trained his toddler daughter to crawl beneath low-spreading spruce branches to reach where he couldn't. Not to mention practiced the sport of baiting hapless mushroom excommunicants. Baiting . . . ! Bragged, boasted, chortled, gloated, teased—and generally and sadistically rubbed it in in the most heartless and depraved way. There are few spectator sports where we live, and observing one village inhabitant attempting to feign indifference in the face of this mushroom-taunting by another could figure as one of them.

Holding out a colander full, the way a new fiancée might flash an engagement ring as proof of having been desired, he'd say, "This is such an incredible year! We were just driving to town the other day and found several pounds along the road—we couldn't even *pick* them all . . ." "We've found so many we're sick of eating them." Or, alternatively, "Have you tried the Inky Cap?" "Or the Boletus? The King Boletus is excellent . . ." The implication being that one is too obsessed by one species, too monotheistic for one's own good. Thus adding to the injury of his superior collecting the insult of his superior knowledge.

The philosopher, it must be confessed (if not to the detectives, no one was out to implicate anyone in particular), took this hard. Clearly this was about more than chanterelles, although Mushroom was the language in which parleys were held, strategy discussed. This—but the time has come to not mince words. This was about nothing less than one's favor with the universe. Who did they think they were, these upstarts? These nouveau riche mycologists? The philosopher's familiarity with the place had never been challenged, just as he'd never had to wonder if the relationships he had with the "villagers" could have been other than they were. It was one thing to invent institutes, to speak fancifully of "the Republic," even to march in a parade celebrating its independence, but mushrooms were *material.* (And *matériel.*) Not to be able to take for granted one's primacy—to have to recognize that others might want what one had always simply had—this took one rapidly right out of the teatime-genteel into the slouch hat hard-boiled. This was *war*.

"Well, shiver my timbers, it's a village!" "What else would one expect, it's a village." "Eet's un village!" the trio of detectives from LA, London, and Paris responded in unison. "Every little thing—every leetle zing—seems so important."

But every little thing *is* important, I retorted. Though not aloud. It was not that things were "more than themselves"—or that we had, that dread accusation, an inflated sense of our own importance. To the contrary, it felt as if things had assumed their proper importance, that life had richly expanded—into the space it was all along intended to occupy.

This is as it should be, I wanted to say, as if I had been put on the witness stand and it were my job to defend the village way of life. There's a reason people elect representatives to deal with the larger things. Our minds did not evolve to think in global terms. Only megalomaniacs and generals instinctively do that. Yet now it seems we are constrained to know what's happening on the other side of the world. If we want to preserve not only the way we live, but the very earth. Otherwise, besides being foolish, we're solipsistic. Greedy and stingy. Hiding our heads in the sand. We're—

"Zee mushrooms, mademoiselle?" said Poirot gently.

All right, all right, yes, the mushrooms.

How much of what I'd been thinking had I said? It didn't matter. I despaired of their understanding. City slickers all. (Yes, at last despaired, Mr. Holmes.)

Just to say *something*, I explained to them then that, like the secretive truffle, wild mushrooms have heretofore been impossible to cultivate; to identify the multifarious conditions they depend upon to thrive, and then to duplicate these, has appeared to be an insurmountable task. They grow where they do according to some inner directive in the earth that has until recently escaped human discovery. Methods for growing truffles have found their way into murder mysteries but that has been where they stayed. Until recently. Now there are cultivated truffles (reputedly truffles are, after saffron, the single most expensive raw food in the world), morels, and, not very long ago, chanterelles. Someone filed a patent on the "isolated mycelium of a chanterelle"—that is, the underground part of the fungi that produces the "fruiting body"—that is, the mushroom.

Furthermore, it's not as if spread underground is a root system of which the mushroom is a shoot. The mushrooms are parasites—but parasites useful to their hosts. They take up starches and sugars from the vascular systems of plants, but at the same time, by injecting some substance into the roots, give minerals and other nutrients to them, help them absorb water and resist pathogens. These are not parasites in the traditional sense of freeloaders; they take, but they give.

This individual who patented one strain of the mycelium also patented a "method for propagating the chanterelle." How is this even possible? (Or allowed? It's as if someone were to take out a patent on a tree.) To have been able to identify the interdependence of these fungi with the trees around them is mind-boggling enough but then to *replicate* the products of these mysterious forces with the intent to *sell* them is, in the religion of mushroom hunters, akin to the creation of a golem, desire for advantage and control displacing reverence and awe. This arrogance and heresy cry out for a new Reformer to nail some theses to some church door.

Appalled as I was to read about this (I'd researched it as a lark, expecting to find mycologists scoffing at the very idea, and instead turned up a patent number), I was subsequently gratified to discover that the cost of producing the chanterelle is too great to make this commercially viable. (The morel, I might mention, has succumbed, and it is possible to buy morel-growing kits on the sacrilegious internet.)

"You see," I tried, "it's just that . . . If you . . . You see . . ."

Then, all at once, as I gazed in frustration at the three detectives, studying me—so skeptically, so hopefully and improbably—in my own living room, it hit me that the crime in question, though it involved mushrooms, might be, after all, not a theft, or retribution enacted upon a thief, or the putting out of commission of a competitor, but a crime for which there was no legal terminology, a crime certainly unlike any in the experience of Messrs. Holmes, Marlowe, and Poirot: in short, a crime *against* mushrooms.

Against the mushrooms *themselves*—these immobile, graceful, defenseless manifestations of the divine. In our internecine mushroom rivalry, they were the real victims.

"I know who did it!" I shouted, springing to my feet, being as dramatic as possible, intending for all their combined detective brilliance to beam in upon me and give me their triplicate forensic blessing—and it did, for one profound, unforgettable moment—before they vanished.

XXII

Interlude Three: *Defending the Old Stone Wall*

One autumn afternoon a number of years ago, I headed up our back road for a walk. (We were still calling it "our" road then—the hunting camps[62] since built at the far end of the road weren't there yet and a passing car was rare enough that if we heard an engine we'd hurry to the door to catch a glint of metal as it climbed the hill.) It was late August or early September: leaves still on the trees, but the air becoming still as it does when fall is coming on, as if winter's hidden somewhere in the loosening breath of summer. These days are shot through with an elegiac sweetness like no other and I was in the abstracted mood this time of year can inspire. The hard-packed dirt striped by the grassy median, every rise and hollow of the road that I know as well as I do my own body, the slopes on either side (up on my left, down on my right: to the east and, when the leaves are gone, the view), the border of ferns and reddening jacks-in-the-pulpit and three-leaved trillium—all seemed to be as much in my mind as out of it.

As I strolled along in this solitudinous state, a sound worked its way into my consciousness—a dissonance in the atmosphere, gradually translating itself into canned music, some sort of pop rock, getting louder as I climbed the hill. Cresting the rise, I came abruptly upon a gray pickup, smack in the middle of the road, a large black radio atop the cab, parked there as if in the driver's own asphalted driveway while he went about his chores.

Here the road has sunk and, up the steep embankment to the right, at the edge of the red pine plantation my father and Merle Magoon had

62 The term "hunting camps" persists even if they're not exactly camps and the occupants don't necessarily hunt.

put in as seedlings more than thirty years earlier, a man I recognized as new to the area was heaving rocks down into the road, dismantling an old stone wall. It took me a moment to register what he was doing, but then I bristled. Literally. The feeling intensely physical, a mixture of repugnance and fear, a recognition of something not right as instinctual as a guard dog's.

"What are you doing?" I called.

The man—a neighbor (he was renting a house in the village, I remembered now)—glanced down at me but went on with his work.

"What are you doing?" I called again, moving closer.

This time he paused.

"Just looking for some rocks," he said.

"Well, this is my father's land," I said, "and I don't think he particularly wants his stone walls taken apart."

"Oh, is this Corky's land?" he repeated. "I didn't realize . . ."

He was a sculptor, he then explained, in search of a particular size and shape of rock; he was taking only a few, but he'd talk to my dad. The twenty or thirty boulders in the bed of the truck belied his story, even if they hadn't all come from our wall. To my discomfort at having been provoked to speak like a tough six-year-old was now added the embarrassment of having caught him in a lie.

But maybe he doesn't know, I thought, exoneratingly. Maybe he really believes old stone walls aren't wanted. He *ought* to know, he *ought* to ask, but what are a few rocks after all? I asked myself. Did I really care about rocks?

Neither of us moved. Was he actually going to keep on loading them? What was I going to do next?

Another truck drove up and I was momentarily alarmed—accomplices? Now what? Could I actually be in *danger*? *Here*?

It turned out to be two men neither of us knew and they needed to get by. Since the neighbor was blocking the road he packed up and left; I cut off to the right through the pine plantation, along an overgrown track. Only if you know to look for it can you still find the two indentations and the ridge in the center, heavy with russet needles. An old field road, crossing what, when we first came up here, was a field. Yet as I slipped through the ranks of the reddish trunks, picking my way over branches left to rot when the pines had been thinned a few years back, I didn't feel the serenity I ordinarily do once I step into the shadowy quiet of the pinewoods. I was still bathed in an adrenaline high, taken aback by the welter of proprietary outrage, self-satisfaction, and shame that the encounter had aroused in me. At the time I neither owned the property nor subscribed (so I held) to the idea of private ownership of land in general, and yet I had leapt right into the role of entitled noble, ousting a poaching peasant. I was embarrassed but also simultaneously still afloat in the wake of the powerful, unmediated impulse that had compelled me to accost a stranger who could, for all I knew, have become belligerent if the other truck hadn't come along. I regarded my response with surprise and some admiration. I didn't know that *that* was in me, I thought.

I'd always told myself that my feeling for this piece of earth was distinct from the need to possess it—I didn't care if I owned it, I'd maintained, so long as I could *be* there—but apparently this was not the case. Something stronger than reason translates caring into a sense of proprietorship. This was *my* land. Or—more to the point—it was *not his*. I might think whatever I liked about the fairness or lack thereof (why shouldn't a man who had no stones be entitled to some of ours?), but what I felt was clearly something else entirely.

Before I built my own house, I often recalled the morning when, as part of my parents' divorce proceeding, a local realtor arrived to show prospective buyers over our family house. I was there alone and, hunched beside the woodstove, was as recalcitrant and unwelcoming as I thought I decently could be, silently putting a hex on them so they wouldn't like the place.

How dare they consider my *home* something they could *buy*? Give *money* to someone and afterward think it was *theirs*? It was obscene—and terrifying—that the acquisitiveness of strangers and the cold, hard world of money, something that, after all, isn't strictly real, had the power to deprive me of *place*. This was my home. It was the place I could always go; it, at least, was intact when my family no longer was, endowed now with all the sense of safety and comfort that "family" promises, even if many, including mine, never fulfill the ideal. And it was the more stable for *not* being a person, given to moods, unpredictable, untrustworthy. It would never walk out of a room or shut itself up in another and refuse to come out. People came and went, but it didn't. It couldn't. It was a *place*; that's what a place *was*.

When a reasonable offer was made, my father had the option to match it—that is, to pay my mother half. This he did, taking out a mortgage for half of $75,000. This was in the 1970s. In 1958 the original price—for the house and 125 acres—had been $6,000. Even so, he had taught a night class at a local community college (in addition to his regular full-time college teaching job) in order to make those first mortgage payments. During the divorce, my mother had offered to let him have the property if he'd make an irrevocable will leaving it to my brother and sister and me but he refused. He wanted the expedient of being able to sell it if he had to; he wanted to control it. There was a practical sense to this, but there was more to it than that. It was *his*; he'd invested himself in it and he both wanted, and didn't want, his children to, literally, take his place.

That day of the encounter with the "rock sculptor," I understood all at once why families break apart over land, why people stop speaking to each other, why people fight to the death over it. I understood, on a visceral level, why whole populations continue to hate other whole populations who have conquered their land, even when centuries have passed. Fighting to the death over land is an abstraction to most contemporary Americans, and to discover that I contained the primordial emotions such a deed springs from frankly pleased me. There is something gratifying in discovering that you have the roots of time-honored tragedy in you. Given the scenario of someone's threatening someone I loved and my property at the same time, I would, without hesitation, defend the person. I know that. But if the land were threatened and I had no other recourse, how far would I go to defend it? I really don't know. Because we *want* it, we want to feel not only that it belongs to us but that it wants us too. Possession may be nine-tenths of the law, but the one-tenth is desiring, and as anyone who has truly desired anything or anyone knows, desire renders fractions irrelevant. There's only the frenzy of not wanting to lose—though mine, I had to recognize that day, was the frenzy of a lover without a legal claim.

I believed then, and do now, *philosophically*, that ownership of land is a myth, albeit a legalized and time-honored one, that any genuine claim to land can only take the form of stewardship—it's our job to safeguard it while we're here, to preserve it for all those, human and animal, who come after us—but something else in me evidently disagrees. Beauty does that, desire does, or we think, as John Locke famously claimed we should, that we've *earned* our land by the work we've done on it; we've made it our own. *We* may not live forever (though this we can scarcely credit either) but at least the *place* will be here, a testament to our passing.

Like the constitution of a republic, a title or deed is a fiction: words on paper that—only because enough people have agreed to recognize them as referring to some entity beyond themselves—have weight. *Real* estate. Real property—as distinguished from *goods and chattels*; you can't possess land in the way you can a shovel or a chair. You can't take it anywhere. It's real—yet not exactly. It's a paradoxical idea, yet society will sustain this paradox by force, if need be. If you default on your mortgage, the bank will repossess your property; the town will sell it for back taxes. The government can seize your land by exercising its right of eminent domain if it's decided yours is the best location for a highway or a missile defense system. Not to mention a new settlement for coastal populations if the rising sea level drives them inland. The property-minded Puritans wrote out deeds for the land they "bought" from the people who were living on it first, to whom the concept of landownership had no meaning. Just as in the old country titles went hand in hand with landownership, at first here too only those who owned land could vote. Folded into all this hypocrisy and judgment is all that is most instinctual about living in a place.

That afternoon, as I continued on my ritual circuit—down through the pines to what used to be a tawny knoll with a large stone all alone in the center like a druidic marker, now overtaken by maple and poplar and cherry—I continued my justifying reasoning. I see the land both ways, as people who have been friends a long time can still see each other's youth in their aged faces, and what new person, I inquired of whatever arbiter I was appealing to, could know that about the land who came here now? How could anyone else care for it as I did?

After grappling my way through a thicket of saplings I climbed over another stone wall and came out in what we've always called the "far field"—a long meadow with a narrow glimpse at one end of blue mountains; it's here where, in a grove of old maples, I began to build the tree house the summer Sasha lived with my father. To the northeast rises a diminutive wooded ridge—a mysterious area, in part, perhaps, because nothing ever takes us there. But there's something suggestive about its configuration: the way it invites you up to an invisible, magical place that you can never quite reach as you ascend. There might be a gateway to a *completely different* place up there, one of those *otherworldes* that the branching roads and hills behind hills of the country around here so often seem to promise—that is, if you knew the password or were purer of heart.[63]

In the time since that day, my then-teenage son built a log cabin in the far field; it serves as the "three-season dwelling" that the conservation easement we've placed on the land permits; he used the pines that Merle Magoon and his grandfather planted, cutting them himself and hiring a neighbor with a horse to pull them to the building site. He chose it independently of knowing that it was where I'd originally wanted to build before I realized I couldn't afford to be so far from the power line and the road. Someone who's hunted on our land for many years recently told me he'd told his father, who'd hunted there before him, "You know where you always said would be a good place for a cabin? Well, there is one."

What is it about that place that we've all recognized? When my son and I were out in the field looking over the various sites he was considering, we looked at several before he said, "There's just something about this one." It was only then that I told him that I'd wanted to build right on that very spot. It was late afternoon and as we headed home, just before we left the field we turned and the entire meadow was in shadow—except for that one little knoll, flagrantly lit by a last, lingering beam. How had we known whatever it was we'd known?

Leaving the field that day of the encounter with the neighbor I took the lower road—used last when the far field was hayed, twenty years ago at least. Small spruce have sprung up along the median and farther into the woods the road is dark with dead leaves. It's muddy in places and in spring takes a long time to dry out. I had a cat who used to follow me around this circuit, complaining bitterly, and here he always looped down into the woods below the road so that he wouldn't have to get his paws wet.

In the last segment of this walk, I come out into the steep, mostly

63 My father named this ridge Monica Vitti Hill in honor of his favorite Italian actress.

unhayed field below my house (growing up to blackberry too, although we now pay to have the sections of the fields not cut for hay brush-hogged every other year) and routinely pause, gazing eastward at the hills—the green patched here and there with the darker green of spruce stands, and beyond, the soft mountains, only a little darker than the sky. I look at them and feel whatever it is I feel after I've studied them for a while, which seems articulate only because it's so familiar, a message heard so many times it seems as if I could translate it. Though translation is maybe not the point.

By the time I got back to my house that day, I'd already decided not to say anything to anyone about what happened. No harm was done, I told myself, no irreparable damage had occurred; I wasn't afraid that the "sculptor" would return under cover of darkness and divest the property of stones. I knew that if I told my father, he'd be furious—*Goddam son of a bitch! What the hell!*—and I didn't want to hear it. There was nothing more to do; I'd dealt with the "problem," so what would be the point except to provoke his predictable outrage and garner myself brownie points for having been a good watchdog? And if I told anyone else—even one person—the news would move through the community faster than sound along a telephone wire and before he knew what had hit him this new neighbor would be branded a thief. I wanted to give him the benefit of the doubt. Despite his falsely innocent manner he really might be just a dim-witted newcomer and I didn't want to ruin his reputation on such puny provocation. Too bad he'd never recognize my magnanimity.

But what was I really up to? I kept asking myself. I suspected that there was more than one buried metropolis of feelings beneath the one I'd already unearthed. The ambivalence I felt about my reaction—it arose from more than simply a discomfort with confrontation. So much history lay concealed within this one encounter.

It was no news to me that I cleave to this place, to these pastures and woods I've known since I was five, and that I belong to it if not it to me. And yet I'd always maintained that I didn't care if I owned it, so long as I could come there when I wanted—but there was the rub. What could assure that except ownership? What was going to happen to the farm when our father died? No one knew. It wasn't something we discussed.

He was deeply bound to the farm but was regularly overwhelmed by the amount of upkeep it required. Once he'd retired and was living there full-time, he had to migrate somewhere every November since the house wasn't winterized; he was fed up with high taxes and the dearth of "real conversation" to be had in the vicinity ("I once had high hopes for this village"). I had only to hear the words "I'll just sell the damn place" to feel a kind of internal withering, and I knew my father knew I did. ("He's never going to sell it," my friend Sally scoffed. "He just likes to jerk your chain.") It was a way of assuring himself of the power he still wielded. Lear-like, he wanted his children to prove their affection. He wanted us to evince an obligation and loyalty to the place without its being entailed to us. And I was irritatingly both Cordelia and Goneril, the loving and solicitous but also self-serving daughter: I proved my attachment by settling here, but I settled in my own house, contriving an end run around the ownership blockade. It wasn't he, apparently, whom I was most attached to; it was the land.

I'd had a little money from selling a book: twenty thousand dollars minus agent's commission and taxes. I was tired of the nomadic life. Even if I couldn't stay in one spot all the time—if, as I assumed, I'd have to keep moving for teaching jobs—at least I'd have a place to leave my books and the few pieces of furniture I owned. Including a couch now, the only object I'd ever owned that I couldn't move by myself. No nomad ever owned a couch.

At the time I was living in New Mexico, in Santa Fe, where in part I grew up; land went for up to a hundred thousand dollars an acre anywhere near town. There were 125 acres in Delphi that I didn't have to pay for. There was no math to do.

"I'm ready to build," I announced to my father. "This spring," I added.

He suggested I build in the pasture. Easy access to the road. I wanted to be farther away, out of sight of his house. I wanted to build where my tree house was, but the far field was too far away and I couldn't afford solar energy.

What about the field in back of the house? he suggested.

No, that was still too close. I wanted to build up by what we called the "first foundation," the closer to the house of two cellar holes on our parcel, left from the time when all the land back of us to the copper mines, now abandoned, had been settled. He argued that the road would be impassable in winter. "You'll never be able to handle that road, Kate." And it was true that the slope, contained between high banks like a luge run, regularly washed out. But he had often told me what I *couldn't* do, and I saw his life in part as emblematic of never-enacted plans and had already discovered that most of what had mattered the most to me in life someone had advised me against doing.

He didn't tell me I could go ahead but he didn't tell me I couldn't either. And I feared, accurately or not, that his threats to "sell the damn place" might be made good if none of us put down a stake there. Like settlers out West, I might make the place mine by working it. Not to put too fine a point on it, I squatted.

Throughout the building process we fought often, about everything from my not taking his suggestions about where to situate the house to my spending a Sunday on the newly finished deck by myself, cutting two-by-fours into wall studs with a radial arm saw. "She won't listen to anyone," he complained to anyone who would listen to him.

I learned only later that he didn't want me to build where I did because the "first foundation" was the best, or at least most accessible, building site on the place, and my taking it precluded his being able to sell it, should the need arise. He reasonably worried, among other things, about having access to money if he entered a long illness in his old age. But he never said any of this to me. I heard it from my sister. He never talked directly with any of us about what he specifically wanted or what we might want in order to find a practical and equitable solution, not only because as a family we didn't talk openly about precarious subjects but also because his desire to be fair to us was in conflict with his desire to see the land preserved intact. "Land is not a *commodity*," he often emphatically stated. "I don't see who the hell's going to be around to take care of the place when I'm gone," he'd throw out, aggrieved (this even after I, the squatter, had already built my house and was living in it). My brother and sister were too busy with their own lives; the grandchildren "showed no interest" in the place (meaning that they didn't set out on their own to plant Christmas trees or go down in the field and cut brush). He was sure we would squabble among ourselves and the property would end up being sold to a developer.

Yet after the house was built he dug up lilacs and irises and daylilies for me to transplant and when he came up always walked around the yard to see how they were doing. "She did a good job," people told me he had said. When I was in the hospital giving birth to my son he sheetrocked and taped the living room. Every time I notice the buckling tape up near the ceiling, which he, an impatient worker always, hadn't been able to get to lie flat, I feel affection for him; I remember how, when it was dark, he'd go into rooms he'd taped and spackled to shine a flashlight at the ceiling and then swear at the wrinkles that were now revealed. The forces of the inanimate, as usual, conspiring to outwit him.

He often gave the impression that he was about to go under financially and needed immediate practical and monetary help if we weren't to lose the property. Child of the Depression that he was, he could be frugal to the point of parsimony and liked to talk as if he were one step away from the poorhouse. I'd walk into the house in the afternoon and find him sitting disconsolately in his usual chair—the squashed-looking upholstered rocker beside the woodstove, where he sat whether there was a fire or not. "Well," he'd remark gloomily, "I lost ten thousand today." "What!" I'd exclaim, fears of bankruptcy and house foreclosure besetting me. It turned out he meant there'd been an option he hadn't exercised in time or a stock he'd been thinking of selling that he hadn't—a virtual loss that he counted among the actual ones. (The latter, strangely enough, he'd speak about more sagely, telling me often that if you were going to play the stock market you had better have a stomach for financial ups and downs. As, he enjoyed pointing out, I clearly didn't.)

I spent a lot of time coming up with plans to save the place. Maybe we could turn it into a land co-op or donate it to some sort of charity that would allow us to continue to live there. I drew up a draft of a co-op agreement and wrote to my brother and sister and some friends about it. To my brother, I said that I'd shown the outline to our father and he was "somewhat disposed towards it, but then his usual foretelling negativity came into play and he began to recite all the communes throughout history that had failed and to explain to me the flaws of the human spirit . . ." Or we could transform the Threshold Institute into a real think tank, I suggested—a place where leaders in various fields who otherwise wouldn't encounter each other could come together and simply talk. We could get grant money for this, I asserted glibly. My father, with his belief in the power of conversation, liked this idea. He liked to listen to all my plans for saving the farm. He always enjoyed speculating about what *might* be done.

After he retired and was living on a fixed income I was so worried about his financial situation that I used to buy groceries for him unasked or undercharge him for things he did ask me to buy. So when he died and my brother and sister and I first looked at his E*Trade statements and found that he had accumulated an estate of several hundred thousand dollars, we were flabbergasted. We'd expected to find debts, and either to lose the farm or ourselves have to go deeply into debt to hang onto it. It was true, we knew, as he had known, that if he'd needed certain kinds of long-term health care at the end of his life he could have run through his savings quickly. As it happened, had he died even a few months later his stocks would have plummeted in value, and yet we grieved in the midst of all the other grieving we were doing to think that by using only a small percentage of the money he'd so painstakingly accrued he could have made his last years easier—put a furnace in the house, for instance, which would have let him stay in Delphi past Thanksgiving if he'd wanted, so that he wouldn't have had to migrate to temporary housing as he did every year, finding places at the last minute. "The gods will provide," he'd say—as his children and a former student who was a close friend scrambled (divinely) to find somewhere for him to go—and he'd wind up in Provincetown, or Kittery, Maine, or San Miguel de Allende, in Mexico, in someone else's vacation house that was cheap because it was off-season and as often as not uncomfortably cold and "without a single goddam reading lamp."

Over the years he often spoke of an image in Ford Madox Ford's tetralogy *Parade's End*, "Groby Great Tree," a symbol of the continuity of landowners to the dying Tory Mark Tietjens; my father conflated Groby Great Tree with the giant elm in our own backyard, which was slowly dying, from the top down, of Dutch elm disease. Toward the end of his life, when he knew he might not have long to live, he chose to sit in the backyard with its tall stump of elm instead of in the front, with its demanding mountains, because the more circumscribed view—his last, reduced vegetable garden, the hillock of field beyond—gave him, he said, a feeling of closure.

Just as Groby Great Tree's merging with the elm in our yard gave a kind of literary and historical imprimatur to his personal situation for my father, "the farm," for me, has always been more than just a place; it's been the single most enduring stability in my life. The equation between the failure of my original family to survive and the potential loss of the place I loved was formulated early. But because there was no law of primogeniture to ensure a Groby Great Tree–like continuation, he had to decide how to leave the property but filibustered himself with objections. In the will he finally did write, he left the place to the three of us, with the stipulation that the last one living would then decide which grandchildren should inherit, based on their interest and investment in the place. I, having no child as of yet, saw no problem with this; my brother, drafting the will, did. I mentioned this to my father, and my brother felt attacked. "There's a worm here somewhere," intoned our father, unable, as he often seemed to be, of trusting more than one of us at a time.

I lived in my house for five years before I owned the land it stood on, and then only because I needed to take out a mortgage and put in a septic system. (Banks, in their uncongenial way, insist that owning property and doing what you want on it are inextricable.) This occasioned some strained feeling between me and my brother and sister, who were hurt by our father's not subsequently deeding them acreage of their own. I didn't see it that way—he hadn't favored me; it was simply expedient. I still wouldn't have owned the land had not the bank required it. Ownership succeeded investment (in my conveniently Lockean view); if they wanted to build, fine, but why did they need to carve acreage out of the whole just to have it? And *you're* not carving out acreage? they objected. You just want to have the whole place to yourself. We eventually revised the terms of the will so that our children would inherit our shares and most recently agreed to sell the property to my son, who'd been living in the family house with roommates, for the tax-assessed value. I gave him my third and he paid each of his four cousins a quarter of the two hundred thousand dollars remaining. (Once again, a mortgage. As my dad said, "Don't worry, Kate, most people are in debt most of their lives.") I was relieved by this, though it did not happen without some bruised feelings on the part of one of the cousins. And yet. It's not the same. Once again it's not mine. I look at the familiar fields and they look somehow different. Less welcoming. No longer a part of me. I pass the house, often empty of late, and it looks (and I feel) forlorn. The feeling is physical, and I still don't understand the connection between words on paper asserting ownership and the disturbed feeling in my blood.

I could well be a hypocrite, I thought that day I defended the stone wall. It wouldn't be surprising. Most people who want to keep something to themselves that others lack generally wind themselves up in some self-serving line of reasoning. With land one says that it's better for everyone if one hangs on to it; if it's broken into little pieces, everyone loses. The law of primogeniture is based on this assumption. The firstborn son gets everything; the others have to be clerics or go to the colonies. In Vermont if we don't keep the countryside attractive—not broken into suburban lots like the rest of the East Coast—we will lose tourists and (the theory goes) everyone's income will decrease. Wildlife habitat depends on uninterrupted tracts of land. A group of landowners in Delphi and adjacent towns have already conserved a bloc of over seven thousand acres, giving up their development rights, and we are among them. Our land happens to sit close to the center of this conserved bloc. Dartmouth College owns the land on two sides of us; the land across the road was bought by a venture capitalist who bought many hundreds of acres in Delphi and conserved them, and has since been sold to people who live in another part of Delphi. The narrow southern end is bordered by unconserved land owned by people from Rhode Island, but they're hardly ever here and the land right across the property divide is steep and rocky and they're not likely to build on it. So here I sit, deep in this kingdom, protected from interference of many kinds, able to contemplate the possibility that grandchildren of mine might have the same experience of the place that I do. How nice for us, but—why should *I* have had the luck to end up here, in the heart of this peaceful realm? And then essentially say, We're here but you can't come. As people have always said, once they've laid claim to somewhere: *Private Property: Keep Out.*

Moreover, the fact that land is conserved also means that it can be sold only to people who can afford to buy large parcels of land and never divide it up. It says "Keep Out" to young Vermonters starting out. "Groby Great Tree" is a compelling image but it's also a staunchly class-specific one. You can't have a "great" tree if it hasn't been in your family for generations, and land can rarely stay in families for generations if it's worth much unless you have a lot of money.

We know that there wasn't always private property, in the sense in which we now mean it; that the aboriginal peoples on this continent didn't think of the land as theirs, even when they fought over territory. They took what they needed from a place and moved on. Sometimes they planted crops and stayed for a season, or longer, but it took European settlers with their ideas of "improving" places, of staying put, with their charters and deeds, acreage and parcels, domains and territories (not to mention states and nations), to impose ownership. And by now the globe is so thoroughly owned that people can't wander even if they want to. Nomads are forced into trailer parks; Native Americans, long ago onto reservations. The only intentional wanderers left may be retirees in RVs and expatriates in boats.

Yet it's clear that if this sense of owning—of land as ours to do with as we please, a place where no one, but no one, can tell us what we can or can't do—doesn't give way to another kind of feeling about the earth that it—let alone we—will not survive. If we don't recognize that we own it only in a temporary sense, that proprietorship is about the land, not about us.

Land is horrifyingly fragile. You have only to watch a bulldozer clear a small piece of ground to realize how rapidly what has seemed impervious to change can be altered beyond repair. The land can recover from ice storms and forest fires but some kinds of man-made destruction kill its spirit. Invasive plants and insects, the vanguard of climate change, are making this ever more palpable. Birds who used to be common here no longer appear. A recent summer was the first in which I did not see a single monarch butterfly, because their habitats in Mexico and on the way up here are being destroyed. They used to be all over the milkweed.

The land won't know when I'm gone, however much I might like to think so. It won't feel anything when I'm buried in it, or scattered on top of it, even if contemplating that end softens my sadness a little. I tell myself that the health of the land is what I feel enjoined to guard and this is true, yet it seems I can't separate this protective impulse from self-protection. Why is it comforting to think that I will cease to exist here, rather than somewhere else? It's all a projection, a hopeless one-way love affair, except in this: though land may not be aware of us, if we neglect and mistreat it, then everything that lives on it, including us, will die.

My encounter with the "rock sculptor" had an unexpected sequel. I kept the event to myself until the day Stella Swan happened to tell me the story of some fellow in West Delphi working as a stonemason somewhere who was stealing all the stones he brought to his job site. He claimed he found them out in fields, but they were too clean for that. The other men on the job figured he was taking down old stone walls.

So I told. As I had anticipated, the retellings multiplied exponentially and before long I got a call from Ben Metcalf, who'd heard I'd "driven" the thief off my land. He, Ben, knew the foreman of the job on which the guy was working and this foreman had been terribly upset to learn where the stones came from, not only on behalf of the landowners but because he knew how distressed the owner of the new building would be. The stones were being used in building some kind of chapel for a—evidently spiritually minded—survivalists' group and if the stones of the chapel had been secured by impure means . . . Well, the peril was self-evident.

Would I mind if he gave the foreman my phone number? Ben asked. No, I said, I guess not, though there's really no need, it's over and done with . . .

Within the hour the foreman was on the line, full of outrage and apology. I, feeling more fraudulent by the moment, told my story yet another time, assuring him that no great harm had been done—wishing all the while that I'd kept my mouth shut, since the brave and virtuous defender of property I'd become in the tale did not jibe with the shame-riddled umbrage with which I'd reacted in the moment. The revulsion against being a tattletale is strong, regardless of the justice of the tale one's telling. And I still wasn't sure, in the scheme of things, if the guy didn't after all have a perfect right to take these stones that were effecting no purpose anymore other than decorative—yes, I knew he would have had to pay money if he'd bought them at a stoneyard and so yes, technically it was stealing, but nevertheless—

"It's all right," I said. "Tell the owner that I absolve him of all wrongdoing."

I was surprised that the irony in my tone didn't clog the phone lines, but the contractor said, "He'll be relieved to hear that."

He might be relieved, I thought, but whatever spirit it is that oversees his chapel-building would surely discover my own fraudulent priesthood, and how unauthorized my absolution.

PART FOUR

XXIII

After the Fall

It would be convenient if the end of the Republic were the end, but the end is never really the end, and so it is with republics. Civilizations do die, but usually less succinctly than people. Even Rome, it's been said, didn't fall when Gibbon liked to claim it did, but lingered on, with invaders in charge but looking something like the original for long after the date he fixed for its demise.

One by one, the founders departed. Chantal and Swift went overseas. After harboring a number of tenants (including the marriage counselors), the Church was sold to a couple with children, who have, slowly but surely, been turning it back into a farm. They've installed a giant hoop house and operate a CSA and a weekly farm stand where they sell bread they bake in their outdoor bread oven. Their bread oven is, by last count, one of at least half a dozen in existence in Delphi, the first having been built by Baxter Fledge quite a few years ago. He has two now, both on wheels, and once every summer he pulls one across the road from his house to bake bread at the outdoor Saturday café, held near the post office. A few years ago the Church's latest inhabitants added pizza to their list of baked goods and once a week in summer turn the field across the road into a pizzeria. Sometimes there's live music. People gather at little tablecloth-covered tables and feel a kind of prayerful amazement at having access to this experience in a location as out of the way as West Delphi.[64] Perhaps the place is making use of them, as places may do, to work its way back into its first incarnation, as the Free Will Baptist Church.

64 The reader of these pages will know that, to citizens of the Republic, "out of the way" is always preceded by a tacit "seemingly."

Ben Metcalf, as has already been mentioned, moved to Lancaster; after this went west and made a fortune, lost it, came back. He is still in the technological vanguard (installing giant solar panels on his lawn, installing a device to whom he says, "Marigold"—or whatever its name is (I am only pretending not to know)—"please play me 'In-A-Gadda-Da-Vida'"—cognizant of the likelihood of its (her) transmitting any seditious comments he may make directly to National Liberty-Suppressing Headquarters. (Naturally I've cited a song title I never heard Ben play in order to throw "Marigold" and her henchpersons—henchdevices?—off the scent.) Ben is still busy amending the dull quotidian; not long ago he gave me a photograph of an Icelandic steppe into which he'd inserted a troll. "Everyone talks about them all the time," he said in explanation.

Gilda married Baxter and they came back from the West Coast and bought a big house in Center Delphi that was once an inn. Gilda continues in her lively and generous way to be a force for social cohesion, organizing dancing lessons at the town hall, walks in the town forest. Baxter, having practiced as a doctor in his spare time (an expert diagnostician, whom people call long-distance to have their symptoms diagnosed, but less enthusiastic about the day-to-day demands of doctoring, especially as insurance companies and their regulations increasingly inserted themselves into everybody's business), restores old cars and builds things full-time: wagons, bread ovens, sheds, porches. When one has questions about most anything, it's often Baxter one thinks first of asking. When he and Gilda visited Chantal and Swift in the French village to which they repaired (and where Chantal had recently been elected mayor) he was made a Grand Talmelier of the Talmeliers de Saint Honoré d'Aunis et Saintonge. According to Baxter, "talmelier" is an "archaic term of art for a sifter or bolter of flour." (Uh, Bax, what's a "bolter"?)

Other friends from the town next to Delphi happened to be passing through at the same time;[65] one of these, a photographer, snapped so many photos of Baxter receiving his award that the citizens of that village suspected Baxter of being a visiting dignitary. (Which, as we know, he was.)

Otto sold the Schoolhouse to some people from Boston who sold it

65 "happened to be"? Since when does anything connected to West Delphi simply "happen"?

to the venture capitalist who recently sold it to the people who own the Church because they wanted the land attached to it, which abuts theirs. Then their niece and her husband bought it from them. With Hans Furness's daughter Magda and Stella Swan, Otto bought thirty acres on Perrin Hill, not far from Center Delphi. Over the years Magda's sister Cecilia and a friend of Magda's, with their husbands, bought houses on other sides of this hill. Recently Magda's other sister, Lara, bought land abutting Otto's on the other side. (This enclave, West Delphi notes, not without a certain wariness, has the potential to form its own breakaway republic.) Hans Furness, after years of resisting the pull of Delphi, bought an old barn down the road from his daughters, which he transformed into living quarters, complete with workshop, a collection of garden sheds under the barn roof he used as guesthouses, and a greenhouse. (After the bread oven explosion, Delphi has seen an explosion of greenhouses.) During his earlier days, Hans regularly disappeared to far-flung parts of the world in pursuit of adventure, scolding his daughter and other mothers for coddling their children, who instead should be sent into risky sectors of the globe to learn how to fend for themselves. Hans's recent death has left a great gap in our world and not incidentally made us aware of the narrowing windows of time we have left to reside in it. Magda has continued to make a living in various ways that involve being on or writing about boats. Another resident, who writes sailing guides to the Caribbean, spends six months in Delphi. Magda's former husband captains boats for other people or sails their boats back to their home ports when they don't want to. Another couple, retired from working as carpenters, used to take off in their boat for warmer climes when winter came. One could find oneself at a gathering on a hilltop in this landlocked settlement in a landlocked state and overhear lively (if incomprehensible) discussions about ocean winds.

Otto, too, has continued to be a major force for social cohesion. The self-styled mayor of Delphi, he likes to welcome new settlers and facilitate their indoctrination. In a few instances, these have begun as renters either in my house or down the hill in our family house. Some have bought places of their own; others have taken an intermediate step and moved into Otto's guesthouse. The philosopher-mathematician-carpenter was one of these, though after a few years he decamped to Hawaii, from which he posts occasional gnostic communiqués. Sally, my close friend from college, followed this route, although after a summer she moved to a rental and eventually bought a house on the next hill over from West Delphi. Another, who rented first my house and then our family house, moved "temporarily" to an apartment Otto built beneath his studio and has never left.

The most recent tenants down the hill, good friends now also, were here for several years, though recently decamped to a town a ways away because of the exigencies of employment and school. They originally responded to an ad in Craigslist for a nine-month rental—at the time they were living in London—and in the course of a phone conversation Derek said to me, "Is West Delphi anywhere near East Appleton, by any chance?"

"Yes," I said, "it's the next town over." As it is—but only by way of the Birchwood Road, over a rough hill and a Class 4 road, not maintained in winter.

"I lived on a commune there when I was sixteen," Derek said.

Of course you did, I thought.

Derek and Aruna were the first people ever to spend a winter in the house (my brother and sister and I insulated it and put in a heating system after our father died) and in recognition of this watershed event were given an appropriate award by the Threshold Institute, whose tenets they enthusiastically embraced. One evening a few years ago as I was driving up the icy road to my house, my car lost traction and when I tried to back down the steep hill, the anti-lock brakes, disdaining their instructions, locked, and the car sped down backward, out of control. Suddenly it spun, turned sideways, and headed over the bank toward the other house. I had entered the strange, suspended state of mind I remembered from a similar situation many years back when I'd also thought that I was going to be killed. But the car came to rest against a tiny tree, half off the bank, its front wheels hung up in the air. When it seemed as if it weren't going to move any further, I very, very delicately opened the door and jumped the five feet to the ground, deeply grateful to have had neither my son nor my dog in the car with me. Shakily I went to knock on the door of the Institute. Derek opened it, looked at me, then at the car, perched against the tree, its headlights illuminating the second story of the house.

"I had an accident," I explained.

Derek regarded the car suspended in air and shook his head. "I knew I shouldn't have been working on evil in the Kabbalah today," he said.

Did all these people arrive here by chance? The reader is free to judge.

It's true that there was a time after everyone dispersed when people didn't speak to each other. Grudges were held. There were things it was painful to recall, things people had said and done that it was not easy to get over. Some wrote other citizens off. We had, after all, been a citizenry fond of the grand gesture. Yet time passed. Society broadened. We grew older and more tolerant. We forgave, if we didn't divinely forget. We'd seen the worst of each other by then, as well as the best. There was a comfort in that. We could say matter-of-factly, Oh, that's X. That's how they are. The effort one makes with people one doesn't know well—is *this* the real X? Is *this*?—we didn't have to make anymore. We had developed a kind of double vision—seeing people as myths of themselves at the same time we saw them as changeable, imperfect, but by and large well-intentioned individuals.

Had we lived in a bigger place, or scattered more widely, we might never have reconciled our differences. Umbrage would have reigned. But confronted with someone week after week, year after year—either you ossify into resentment or your friendship evolves. It gets hard to remember who isn't speaking to whom and why. Circumstances had taught us that we were all fallible and irritating people—people *are*—and we'd learned this about each other and gone on.

As for the Republic, those of us who founded it are united by an experience we increasingly understand to be a rare and irreplaceable one. When any two of us are together, the conversation not infrequently reverts to those times, and it doesn't take long before we're in the thick of remembering. The occasional visits by Chantal from her current embassy in Morocco or by Ben Metcalf from his in Lancaster engender particularly fervent debriefings.

"No, that was when . . ." "Oh, yeah, that's right . . ." "I can't believe I forgot that!"—as we fill in the gaps in each other's memories. The story about the balloonist arriving is a particular favorite. Or Cochon's eternal trip to Istanbul. The philosopher's nabbing the chicken-of-the-woods after Otto had mentioned having seen it. The Great Zucchini Contest. The abduction of Gilda and Chantal by the Aliens of the Blender. The postmortem theft of Violet Sleeper's chocolate zucchini cake. And we like to tell other people these stories; having an audience reaffirms our citizenry. Some people generously marvel and encourage us, while others find such patriotic hymns cloyingly insular and exclusive. Who wants to feel on the periphery? And who doesn't like being inside the circle? But, as we know, there can't be a circle without a periphery—the whole, seemingly insuperable, problem.

One recent fall, when Chantal came back to stay for a month, dividing her time between Otto's and Gilda's houses, festivities naturally ensued. She'd come before, and seen people individually, but this was the first time that all of the founders, with the exception of the philosopher and Swift, had been together like this since the fall of the Republic. First Otto made pizza in his bread oven, located out by his pond. Then we went indoors, where we ate a complicated sort of pot roast Chantal had prepared (to honor my father's memory I am only pretending not to know the French name). For dessert I'd made an elaborate French cake from an intricate and confusing fifteen-page recipe in Julia Child that a friend once sent me as a dare. (It tastes amazing, but I've never had any idea if it has turned out correctly or not.)

Except for Swift and my father, there we all were: Otto and his partner, Deirdre; Baxter and Gilda; Ben and his partner, Lewis; me. And what a convivial, nostalgic, and intoxicating occasion it was. We covered a lot of ground, narratively speaking. Filled in gaps in our memories and mythologies. Yet the gathering was also something it hadn't been in the past: gentle, sweet, and comforting. In our sixties and seventies now, we were solicitous of each other. Deeply valued each other. Not everyone had kept in touch with everyone, but if there'd been any apprehension about enduring resentment, that was dispelled in the first minute. How much we had grown up.

I had found a cache of chanterelles that day and as I left I gave some to Chantal and Otto—"l'omelette pour le matin," she said—and Otto looked on appreciatively. "We are all friends now," he said. "We are over all that."

Otto, Magda, and I have all raised our children here. There is a second generation of citizens now, brought up on the legends we have imparted to them. They have not had a conventional American upbringing. Just to begin with, for a long time none of us had, and in many cases still don't have, televisions. Cell phones don't always reliably work here; GPSs direct one to uninhabited regions. Our children all grew up in houses in a continual state of becoming, since none of us could afford, or wanted to borrow enough money, to finish construction before we moved into them. Inspecting the progress of one another's building projects has long been a pastime in Delphi. Unlike to the founders, the community seems ordinary to our children—until they go out in the larger world and try to explain it to people. The only successful method, they've found, is to bring people to visit. Even then it's not easy to convey the quality of life here, the freedom people have to be their eccentric selves, combined with the anchoring relationship to the natural world. Full-fledged citizens since birth, they have never known what it is to be left with babysitters so that their parents can attend grown-up dinner parties. While this may be because there were no babysitters, it never occurred to any of us to exclude them. Since birth, they simply came along, a growing posse that found its own identity. *BEWARE!* they wrote backward on the window in the ice forming outside one New Year's Eve.

There's a fluidity to life in Delphi—a permeability of boundaries. It is, in fact, literally not always certain where one's own property stops and the next landowner's begins. The town records aren't clear, and what use are GPS measurements if markers are maples that no longer stand? Compare this to suburban demarcations, neatly trimmed bushes, and hostilely decorative white picket fences. In Delphi the absence of strict ownership passes on to possessions: at any given time you might have X's sander, Y your jigsaw, Z Y's ladder, and so on. Or you take something to A's potluck, forget to take the dish home; A takes it to B's, who one day inadvertently returns it to you. "That's my plate!" one hears. "Oh, look, my breadboard!"—not in possessive outrage but in excitement at seeing whatever it is appear in this new place.

Coming back from the outside world to Delphi feels more like changing eras than changing location; the closer you come the more the evidence of the modern world—gas stations, souvenir outlets, pizza joints (our village pizzeria has yet to display a neon sign)—disappears. Except for the power lines and the paved roads, someone waking after a century's sleep might not at first think that anything had changed. When I was commuting across the state to work, as soon as, coming home, I began to descend the eastern slopes of the mountains that bisect the state, Delphi's gravitational field began to exert its pull. I'd begin to revive. What preoccupied me elsewhere—a class that wouldn't gel, the self-protective irony of academia, an overdrawn bank account—here hardly seemed real. It was just pages, just numbers. They didn't touch me at all.

Back in Delphi I was sometimes baffled by the strength of my antipathy for this other place. How could a place affect me so much? It was just a *place* . . . I had friends I felt close to, with whom in certain respects I had more in common than I did with my friends in Delphi: sympathies of profession and sensibility, a long-shared place of employment. But over *there*, I felt insecure; my voice seemed to me to lack conviction. I was a stranger. Like Heidi, when she has to live in Clara's city house and can't see the mountains, when I had to stay for long in that western enclave I pined away.

By the time I turned off the blacktop onto the back road from Delphi Four Corners to West Delphi, I had come back into focus. I felt visible again. My voice (had there been anyone to hear it) had reacquired authority; I meant what I said. It was the same point at which, during the years I rented a house in that foreign enclave, our cat and dog woke up after a two-hour ride; human and animal, some sense wakes us, it seems, or something wakes senses dormant elsewhere.

But this is absurd, I'd tell myself. How can this be? Do molecules receive some directive from the view to rearrange themselves? That barn against the green hillside? Those overlapping, sparsely forested slopes to the northeast that affirmed that I was entering the territory? The house on the green in Tewksbury that I always recall was once used in a movie—not a single Hollywood star in it was able accurately to reproduce a Vermont accent.

Perhaps weary of hearing me complain about my commute, my feeling of alienation, colleagues asked why I didn't sell my house and buy a place where I worked. I was as shocked by this suggestion as if someone had idly wondered why I didn't give up my young child for adoption. Quite aside from feeling an obligation not to extract my two acres, other than on paper, from the larger family property that surrounds it, I'd have felt about doing that as I would about abandoning any living creature for which I am responsible. That it's a reciprocal dependency I remind myself is an illusion—someone else could keep it up, likely more efficiently than I, enjoy as much solace from looking out the windows at the view; it's I who would be gone, not the place—yet I balk at believing this. I'm as convinced of my indispensability as any primogenitured duke. Caring for this place is my *job.* Since I feel that it guards me, so must I guard it. And vice versa: since I guard it, it will guard me. I imagine that somehow we agree about this.

Home. Into the village, past the turnoff to Lenny Hodge's, the Hodges all gone now, their land also bought by the venture capitalist, then sold to the brother of the people who bought the Church, the Hodges' sagging house pulled down, the ten children whose names I can still recite moved away; past where Violet Sleeper's house stood—it burned down some years after she died, she lying these many years in the graveyard beside Alton and Elton. Next the Schoolhouse; across from it the Jewells' farm, though farmed by someone else, trying to hang on—first cows, then goats, then hay, which he's getting certified as organic in the hope that he can milk cows again; around the corner and into the road now officially named Mill Street after the state decreed that all roads had to have names to comply with the 911 system, past the Church, past Ben Metcalf's place, long since owned by Bess and Gabriel, now concealed from the road by a tall lilac hedge; across the brook whose rusty iron bridge has been replaced by a modern cement one; past Bucky Lefevre's lopsided trailer that, uninhabited, has been pushed over the bank.

Then I'm starting down our road, past the pond put in by the people from Rhode Island who own the log cabin and are never here, so that we have a pond to swim in without having to maintain it; then up, around the blind curve whose HONK YOUR HORN signs are long gone. And always after that steep curve comes the feeling—more pronounced in winter but still there year-round—*Made it!*—as the road flattens out along the pasture, on the right the sugar bush of old maples, which, for a few years, the neighbors who live behind the lilac hedge tapped. One March morning I took our dog for a walk and then held him still so that I could listen to the plink, plank, plunk of sap dripping all up and down the road at different tones and intervals like a steel drum band in the woods.

In the last years of commuting, when I came home from over the mountains, I no longer stopped first at my father's house but drove on up the hill to my own, still experiencing a brutality in not stopping, though it had been more than a decade since he died. The final end, for me, of the Republic, though it had already deteriorated beyond repair before that. Coming home for the weekend from over the mountains we'd pull into the yard, and he, hearing the car, would come to the kitchen door and give me and my son his great strong hugs, and in the kitchen would be the smells of dinner cooking—his marinara sauce that from childhood I associated with the *Traviata* playing; Violetta's consumptive death I can never experience as truly tragic since it's inextricably bound to the hopeful smell of garlic simmering in olive oil. He'd have made bread, root beer popsicles for his grandson. He'd offer me some home brew.

Sometimes we'd eat in the dining room, at the ponderous carved medieval-feeling table, but usually, especially when it was cold enough to need a fire, we'd eat in the living room, plates on our laps, watching the news, if it was time (it was usually time)—"Peer Jennins," my young son called the anchorman. We'd look past the television out the eastern windows at the view: in a cleft formed by the nearer hills, the ones beyond overlapping as they change from dark green to blue to light blue until they are mountains—the kind of impossibly beautiful and serene landscape that painters like Maxfield Parrish used to illustrate children's books and that now, on the page, seem kitschy to the contemporary sensibility. Something from a bygone era, when peace and harmony were achievable on this earth. But there it still is, and I am never not amazed by it, nor do I look at it for long without reminding myself how rare, how next to impossible it is in this day and age to look out the window and see nothing that bruises the eye with ugliness. Every day the news brings some new horror, friends send links to some report about yet another destructive act out in the world or yet another demented move by some benighted politician—and I glance at and delete these and then go outside and am preoccupied by the population of potato bugs. Or all the weeds. Or how fast the grass is growing.

But my experience is no longer innocent. I rarely wake up in the morning and luxuriate in the quiet and peace without thinking of all the people who can't do this or without asking myself what relationship my having plays to others' not having.[66]

I have been deeply privileged, I am daily aware, to have known half a life here, to know what it is to walk where I see no one, where most of the time the only sounds are those of birds calling, squirrels scolding, grouse thundering up from cover, or the wind in the trees. Maybe the bucolic hum of a chain saw, distant and soothing. To know the experience of falling asleep with this quiet and uninhabited space around me, a template against which to measure peace. I've never not known this attachment, which, of all things in this world, should not be a privilege, but is. Not to have experienced this, to not live in a place one loves—I have heard myself deliver the opinion that character flaws, not to mention international conflicts, are occasioned by not caring for land, not having land to care *for*. At the same time, I remind my pompous and sententious self, possessing land is the root of conflict: because someone else *doesn't* have any, or wants more, or wants yours.

It feels like boasting even to write about it, shamefully self-congratulatory to describe my good fortune when so many have not only not a beautiful place to live but none at all. How dare I feel protective and proprietary about this land—as experience has taught me that, despite wishing to believe the contrary, I fundamentally, inadvertently, instinctually do.

I've been to places I regard as more stunningly beautiful, in terms of natural splendor, or places where human husbandry has given a gracious gentleness to the landscape that this one lacks; I've sometimes wished that, in the late fifties, when my parents were scouting for a summer place, they'd settled on a more populous and convivial (not to mention warmer) spot. The coast of Portugal, say, or Provence. Even somewhere where I could readily make a living.

Yet such speculation is finally irrelevant. It's like wishing that someone you love irrevocably were different. We may do it, yet we know where our loyalty lies, that it's not even a question of loyalty. If I abandoned this place it would destroy something in me more than it would harm the land.

66 There's not a word for this feeling of guilt or shame at one's good fortune, unless it be a multisyllabic German one, the opposite of schadenfreude, the enjoyment of the misfortune of others. Something that, in the optimistic postwar 1950s and the even more militantly hopeful 1960s in which I grew up, was not anything anyone would have given a thought to.

Home, I'd say to myself, when I left to drive away from it across the mountains—*I'll remember*. This time I won't let that *other* place affect me. I promised myself that I'd remain a Delphic citizen, as foreign legionnaires wear their identifying uniform, and everyone would recognize that I was from *somewhere else*, a visitor, whose peculiarities could be attributed to different cultural practices. But each time, as soon as I began the descent from the mountain range that separates our kingdom from all those other principalities and found myself in that western river valley, my sense of certainty evaporated. I might speak the language but I'd never be a native; if I weren't careful, I could be picked out as a spy.

For a long time it didn't occur to me to wonder why, in my discomfort, I felt compelled to compare the two, why cleaving to one place appears to mandate a repudiation of all others as if it were a vow of marriage. And once I did ask this question, I then had to ask why it is that we can't maintain a sense of identity without exclusion. Why, in order to *be* something, is it necessary to insist that one is not something else? That someone else cannot also be what one oneself is. This pernicious habit of valuing by comparison—is this why republics founder? Why ours did? Why the larger one of which West Delphi is a part is undergoing the same kinds of resentments, accusations of lack of patriotism, and confusion as to what patriotism even means that West Delphi did? As it becomes increasingly clear that our survival as a species, the survival of our planet, hangs by the precarious thread of our learning to think differently.

These essential questions ring round my private universe like a hostile advancing force as I quixotically guard the fortress of my certainty: wherever I may go, however long I may live, this hillside will remain my touchstone. It's where I know my place in the world, where I know what I feel and where I feel most certainly that I exist. I don't know if it's meaning I've discovered or meaning I've made, but it's where I can most consistently harbor the illusion, if it be an illusion, that something out there in the universe acknowledges my presence. I am more than myself, when I walk in this place, or less than myself, because I experience myself as a part of something more. I don't understand how this works, how years of looking at a particular line of hills can make something of the person who looks at it, yet I experience it. When you've spent a long time in a place you love, tending it, overseeing it—*knowing* it—after a while it gives you something back. And once this happens, you need to be there in order, in some fundamental way, to breathe.

XXIV

The Vortex Expands
or
The Goat Man Cometh

Some years after the fall of the Republic, a man on the blacktop, just past Center Delphi heading to Lancaster, began to keep goats. He hired a couple of people to build him a pretty gambrel-roofed barn. He bought state-of-the-art cheese-making equipment. He was setting up in style.

Everyone in the neighborhood, naturally, observed this enterprise with interest. There'd been no venture on this scale as long as anyone could remember. Former citizens of the Republic, even if they'd some of them moved to other sections of Delphi, took a particular interest in this visionary's improbable endeavor. We recognized the genre of ambition driving the project.[67] It helped that we knew the carpenters[68] who'd been

---

67 *Quixotic* is the adjective that most readily proposes itself.

68 Like many people in Delphi, to make a living these carpenters did not do only one thing. One was a sailor who'd arrived in Delphi because he'd married Hans Furness's daughter Magda (as has been mentioned, herself a sailor of renown). Another was a chef and restaurateur. A third, who'd been enticed to Delphi all the way from Florida by inspiring stories told him by the goat man's son, who lived down there—his father was breaking down the barriers between animal and human and, as his son would soon tell the newspapers, if people didn't like it, "that was their problem"—had joined the first two. In his spare time this third carpenter was writing a treatise that would explain the universe. (Why wouldn't he be? And where else should he have come to work on it?) One of the mathematical diagrams that would contribute to this explanation was tattooed on his shoulder, and on occasion he'd tap it meaningfully to suggest the interconnectedness of all things.

hired to build the barn and they became sought-after dinner guests, able as they were to regale the assemblage with stories about the goat man, as he'd come to be called.

The goat man was, it became clear, very fond of his goats. He began with three, but, as can happen, one goat led to another, and before he knew it he had...well, a crowd. He didn't hold with castrating the males because the surgery could be dangerous and in any case he believed that goats had as much right as humans to "maintain their own society." He refused to sell any of them because he couldn't be sure they wouldn't be killed and eaten or would be well cared for if not. By the time things got interesting, as we say up here, the goats numbered in the scores.

One winter when it got especially cold, he brought the less hearty ones to live in the house with him. In time his house grew to be a foot deep in hay and goat droppings, and the floorboards were so soaked with urine that it was doubtful the smell could ever be gotten rid of. But what mainly bothered the goat man was that the depth of the new floor coverings permitted his companions the more easily to reach the table when he was trying to eat dinner. Most distressing, he complained, was that they liked to eat his books. Milton, he told a reporter (the newspapers had begun to pay attention), was a particular favorite. Perhaps this was the goats' comment upon the author's attempt to "justify the ways of God to man." (If these required justification, one presumes the goats grumbled, how sound could they be?)

Among other things the goat man didn't believe in was fencing, since this would interfere with the goats' freedom to roam. One of the places the goats liked to roam was into the road. On the one hand it was kind of nice, in a nostalgic sort of way, to see animals repudiating human-made impediments such as pavement and automobiles, as if we lived in an earlier, more bucolic time, one of public greens and community barn raisings. It took me back to the days when cows had escaped from their pastures and wandered into the village of West Delphi, and Stanley and Billy and Ernie and Mary and I would drive them back to where they belonged, if we knew, or ask from house to house till we found out. Citizens of West Delphi were delighted to behold the boundary-relaxation ethos of the Republic springing up anew in Center Delphi.

On the other hand, cars went fast by there. People were in a hurry and didn't always feel like stopping to let a goat meander across the road. There were chickens too. We didn't want to hit the animals.

Some people took it upon themselves to stop and ask the goat man to please keep his goats out of the road. They explained that they were afraid of hitting them, but the goat man didn't take kindly to these requests. He swore at people. He shook his fist at them. He picked up a rock and smashed Baxter Fledge's car windshield when Baxter asked him to restrain his goats. When the school bus driver pulled over to ask him to remove the goats from the road the goat man so terrified the schoolchildren by pounding on the windows that the bus henceforth had to take an alternate, roundabout route.

Then, in addition, it became apparent that the goat man wasn't taking proper care of his charges. He couldn't. Even if he'd had the money, and he didn't (having, according to one article, sunk more than half a million of his mother's dollars into the place), one man alone could not care for so many goats. Quite a few of them were weak and sickly. In winter, since he couldn't bury the corpses of the ones who'd died, he piled them up in the nice new barn. The corpses attracted rats and they, in addition to the marauding goats, inflicted thousands of dollars of property damage upon the goat man's neighbors.

No one knew what to do about this. The state police were called. They put in a few appearances and told him to keep his goats out of the road. People informed the humane society and this group arrived and seized a few dozen goats but the others were healthy enough that they couldn't be taken. A certain percentage of animals in a herd has to be unwell before the whole can be impounded, Delphi learned. The goat man was clever and resourceful enough to know these things already. He knew, for example, that a man he enraged enough to take a swing at him would be in more trouble if the man assaulted him on his own property and thus, by stepping back out of the road, though it was the goat man who broke the other man's arm, it was the other man, not the goat man, who went to jail for assault and battery.

The goat man's story made first the local, then the national news. Said one article:

What is occurring in Delphi is occurring all over the world: all the passions, all the prejudice, all the petulance are to be found there. . .

This, of course, was no news to those of us who'd lived through the heyday of the Republic, and who were not surprised that once again Delphi, if not specifically West Delphi, had proven to be a vector for eccentricity. We were delighted that, after a long period of dormancy, newsworthy things were once again going on. Things that got to the heart of civilization's conflicts and revealed Delphi's far-reaching, even archetypal significance—if only civilization could interpret the message the oracle was transmitting.

Yet greater Delphi had no more idea how to handle a single person's waywardness than had the village of West Delphi. No one liked how erratically the goat man cared for his animals—a horse he left out in freezing rain and didn't feed, the goats left to wander, a llama disconsolately staring out at passersby from its pasture. But people were divided as to how much it was anyone's business to get involved. He was mentally ill, some said, diagnosed with "animal hoarding," a new category in the psychological lexicon.

The town had no regulations, it was clear, adequate to deal with the situation, and how would we have enforced them if we had? The secretary of agriculture and the governor's office had been called, but though these expressed their concern they also confessed themselves helpless to do anything. *Condolences* rather than counsel might be the more accurate term for what they expressed. Said an "animal health specialist" at the Ag. Dept., "I have no choice but to say he is not acting in an agriculturally accepted manner." You don't say.

A special meeting was convened at the town hall in Center Delphi to discuss the goat man and what to do about him. Suggestions ranged from getting everyone together to build a fence around the goat man's property to everyone in town adopting one goat. There was no law preventing people from building a fence around someone else's land, the person whose idea this was pointed out, so long as it wasn't on that person's land. What the goat-adoption advocate envisioned is not known. Tiny goat dwellings all over town, perhaps, transmogrifying Delphi into the most goat-friendly settlement in the nation.[69]

---

69 Now that, as of this writing, "goat yoga" (likely a precursor to goat-accompanied activities of all kinds) has burgeoned in popularity nationwide, it might be argued that once again Delphi anticipated the zeitgeist, even though at the time we had no idea why all these goats had descended upon us.

Maddening though the situation was, especially to the goat man's immediate neighbors, our feelings were not uncomplicated. There was something salutary as well as aggravating at being reminded how limited were not only our powers but those of outside *organizations* and *agencies*, tasked with *administering* and *enforcing rules and restrictions*. Those known, in other words, for getting up in other people's business.

Recognizing the symbolic import of this impasse, reporters took a deeper interest. The story was picked up by the AP and CBS. There was a charming picture of the goat man holding a newborn goat as his llama nuzzled it. A pastoral scene—a man trying to be both Noah and Adam and allow the animals to live a free and unlegislated life, heroically battling the unfeeling and unimaginative bureaucracy.

This, of course, had been the supreme quest of the Republic of West Delphi, and, just as had the Republic, greater Delphi—if in a somewhat unsubtler and less flashy fashion—was running up against the age-old conflict between the individual and the community. How tiresome to have to mention it! How tawdry! Had this not been resolved by now? Hadn't we—in West Delphi, and, by extension, in the ever-larger republic that surrounded us, cosmically rippling outward—hadn't we formed our bodies politic to celebrate a freedom greater than we'd ever previously had, one that would leave us freer to be ourselves, untaxed by foreign governments, unrestricted by irrelevant laws? What had gone wrong? Had we, despite all our most laudable intentions, forgotten that we were still, er, ourselves? Was it that simple? Really, we came down with *that* thud?

Apparently. The paean to group identity we'd deliriously sung in the Republic could subsume one only to an extent. Patriotism, it seems, can take one only so far. Once the battles have been lost and won, the bugles ceased blowing, there you are, fumbling around in peacetime, face-to-face not only with the essential irritatingness of other humans and their perpetual insistence on holding other points of view, but also, it turns out, limits as to how much you can let a person do their own thing. Particularly if their own thing involves goats, metaphorically or otherwise, marauding all over someone else's lawn.

At the time, we were preoccupied by resolving this dilemma and didn't spend much time wondering how the goat man had come to this point.

None of us knew, or paid it much mind if we did, that once he'd had a family, a lovely, friendly-looking wife and seven children, with whom he'd once lived in Costa Rica. I know this now only because research led me to a book he wrote about how to buy anything and everything at the "least cost to yourself and the environment." Written with his wife, it was published in the early 1970s, ahead of its time, advising with clearly extensive knowledge about issues now in mainstream consciousness: avoid using plastic, don't consider animals as being here for your benefit, suspect the drug industry, to name a very few. The writing is engaging, smart, and funny. Lazy architects, the writers assert, will build "tasteless 'Colonial' townhouses with cat food-colored brick . . ." The authors assure one that they "don't for a moment advocate ostrich-ism" but do recommend buying only the Sunday paper to cut down on paper waste because most of the week's news can be found therein (and will be better digested, too). While deploring the cosmetics industry they acknowledge that deodorants "just barely qualify as a useful class of goods. There are times when a human being two hours out of a shower can smell like a rhinoceros."

How did the goat man go from this wit and earnestness to disillusionment and anger? He himself smelled so powerfully of goat (if not of rhinoceros) that from quite a distance away one could tell he was coming. In the photo on the back of his book, the goat man and his wife are young and attractive, smiling at the camera; they look warmhearted, interested, thoughtful, hopeful. What happened?

Was it a nervous breakdown or a mental health crisis? Visions of a better world thwarted could certainly deform the psyche. Even if regarded solely symbolically, the goat man's story is in hypertrophied form the story of the rise and fall of the Republic: delight and hopefulness soured into disillusion and resentment. Is there no way to design republics so as to make lasting room for individual aspiration, while preventing their deforming themselves into xenophobic self-absorption?

Certainly mental health isn't assisted by knowing what needs to be done to save the world and not being able to do it. And maybe being too much in the company of other people who also feel this can end by alienating us from each other, in the way that standing by helplessly as a child dies can destroy a marriage. How can you keep looking at the other person without hating them for doing nothing?

When groups of politically like-minded people get together, they wax eloquent castigating those standing in the way of cure; they don't berate each other for not doing more. As we discovered during the heyday of the Republic, having an enemy—even if a vague and fanciful one—results in a bountiful esprit de corps. That's what esprit de corps is. But—esprit de corps is the spirit of the army. Is there no way to experience that without being at war? Can we not subordinate our need to be first to a desire to tend, shepherd, aid? Why are we not taught early on (aside from varsity sports—which, as has been much written about, is a kind of war simulation) how good it actually feels to be part of a group effort? Why is so much of our education designed to pit us against each other? Evidently you have to reach the point of really and truly believing that we are all in this world together to accept the necessity of limits to individual freedom. Yet what, in this land whose religion is self-reliance, needs to happen to bring about the apostasy of solidarity? I don't know the answer to that, though dread suggests it may be apocalypse.

A few summers ago my son and his then girlfriend, who were living with me for a time, were keeping chickens. Someone had given them a chicken tractor, which looks like a miniature Romani wagon and can be pulled around by a truck. They first positioned it on a flat area down below the house, but after coyotes made off with a chicken or two who were living in the stationary coop beside the family house down the hill, they (the humans) decided to move the tractor to another part of the yard, above my house, and closer to the road. Conventional wisdom has it that when you relocate chickens, you're supposed to leave them shut in their coop for at least twenty-four hours so that they'll know to go back to it, but Nicolas reasoned that since the chickens already knew the territory, they'd figure it out.

The chickens, unfortunately, had studied the same manual. Come roosting time they returned to the spot where the wagon had previously stood and, finding it not there, instead of scouring the grounds in search of it, as you'd think any reasonable chicken would do, they sought safe spaces in the near vicinity in which to spend the night. Some opted for hollows beneath bushes, others for tree branches. As dusk fell, Nicolas came in and announced, "We have to catch the chickens!" It was pronounced in the same way that, during my childhood, someone called, "The cows are out!" The same urgency, the same command to drop every inessential occupation and *do what needs to be done*! I, who had never caught a chicken in my life and hadn't the first notion of how to go about it, put on my shoes and hurried outside.

Meanwhile Nicolas had dragged the extension ladder out from under the porch, where it's stored, and positioned it against one of the trees. His girlfriend steadied it while he climbed. When he attained the higher rungs, my emotions ricocheted between maternal anxiety and the thrill of the chase. As he captured each chicken, he descended with it (well, *her*, except for Spoon, the rooster) and handed the escapee to one of us. I was taught how to hold them with both hands or under my arm, so they couldn't flap. The first time I was nervous, expecting the chicken to peck and struggle, but she didn't resist. It was a little like clutching a pillow, but this comforter was alive, and trusted me. Or didn't think not to trust me. Or knew it was pointless. I had no idea, but I felt privileged. Honored, really.

Besides that, there was the satisfaction of being helpful combined with the particular pleasure of working with someone else. Doing something necessary. And that it was out in the soft night air, striding up and down the damp lawn under the stars, wasn't only uplifting, it was intoxicating. How long had it been since I'd actually worked *with* someone like this? Possibly since I'd built my house, two decades before: carrying lumber, holding a wall stud steady while the other person used the nail gun, positioning a window.

This is what is wrong with the world, I asserted silently. Carrying on the family tradition of making extravagant leaps of thought, I opined that the problem is that we don't work often enough with people for a common goal, hand something off to someone else—whether it be a nail to someone with a hammer, a bucket of water to someone putting out a fire, or a chicken to be put to bed in its chicken tractor. Work physically, materially, training neural pathways to understand ourselves as plural. That's what we need to do.

It's hard to know how things would have turned out with the goat man had the state of Kentucky not got wind of the controversy and invited him and his goats to come down south and eat kudzu. Maybe this state, being the next after Vermont to join the Union, wanted to show that they could succeed in dealing with ornery individuals where we had failed. They sent a cushy air-conditioned bus and rescued them all in style. But they didn't know our goat man. In under a year the state had seized and euthanized his goats and he himself had left, never to be heard from again.

But—wait. No research corroborates this story. Its sources are obscure. Perhaps he went to join his mother in Maine, and then . . . Or he left in his car with three goats in the back seat. Perhaps he and his goats resettled on an island somewhere and are there to this day, continuing to perform their critical exegesis upon *Paradise Lost*.

According to actual newspaper reports, he went to West Virginia and then Ohio, in both of which states he was charged with animal cruelty and his animals confiscated. In Delphi what we knew for sure was that his house was repossessed by the bank and sold cheap. We marveled that anyone had the temerity to reclaim a house filled waist-high with goat droppings. We realized that we'd had the best of the goat man before Kentucky got him—if "best" can be measured in quantities of story production.

Sad though the story was, at least for the goat man and his goats, clearly the spirit of the Republic was not dead. Where else, we said, but in Delphi? The goat man's saga, if it didn't resurrect the Republic, certainly breathed new life into its diaspora. And we began to rebuild the Republic—dispersed, it was true, but not gone—and the goat man was enshrined in legend.

Let one astonishing victory against the bureaucracies of the world stand for what the goat man, however Pyrrhically, achieved.

One morning he called Ned Sable, his neighbor, because he feared that he might be having a heart attack. Ned rushed over and drove him down to the ER at Dartmouth's spiffy hospital—accompanied by a baby goat the goat man was bottle-feeding and couldn't leave behind. At the hospital the goat man refused to be admitted without the goat, so after much argument the nurses—inscrutable Delphic idealism mixed with goatish intransigence having evidently forced them to put patient welfare above regulations—adorned the baby goat with a diaper and admitted it too. Which story, when I am frustrated by that particular medical behemoth, I take comfort in recollecting.

XXV

The State We're In, Revisited

Chapter II lists some of the things in which the state where Delphi is located claims priority. We have other boasting rights. Or rites. Just one article in *Vermont Life,*[70] for example, gives us, per capita, more writers and artists, more colleges, more Peace Corps volunteers, more cows, more wildlife-watchers, more artisan cheesemakers, more patents, and—get ready for it—more people eating oatmeal than any other state. (One wonders how this last fact was arrived at. According to how much oatmeal sold, presumably, but how do the researchers know it's not going into cookies?) Recently I've read that we are notorious for being the least religious state in the nation (has whatever august body calculates such things ever observed a mushroom hunter in the woods?), though there are, should this last fact trouble anyone, pilgrims from south of our borders taking it upon themselves to remedy this situation. It should, however, be pointed out that when you're the second-least-populous state (hate to admit it, but Wyoming has us beat),[71] you can probably be the highest per capita if you have more than three of anything. On the other hand, while storytelling may be the fabric out of which nations are woven, as in the Republic of West Delphi the stories sometimes obscure inconvenient truths.

Well, yes, as boasted earlier, our soil *is* different from New Hampshire's, but that's because, when both states were covered with water, Vermont was closer to the shore. As a result it's richer in lime and other minerals.

---

70 Which magazine's subtitle, unsurprisingly, used to be "A Special Place." First appearing in 1946, ***Vermont Life*** ceased publication in 2018.

71 Our numbers have gone down since the last census, however, while theirs have gone up, so there's hope yet for our reclaiming this distinction.

Yes, we did come out against slavery before other states but at first only for people when they reached the age of majority (twenty-one for men, eighteen for women) and some people, including a judge, still kept slaves after they were legislatively freed. We did declare a "state of belligerency" against Germany to get a jump on WWII before the US Congress announced it but this was motivated by the fact that the only way for the legislature to vote a pay raise for the underpaid members of the military already drafted into service was if we were at war. (As it happened, this resolution didn't pass because there was no money in the state coffers to pay for it—the reason the opponents had argued against it in the first place.)

And if we've had the highest number of soldiers (per capita) to die in some wars it may not have been out of an excess of patriotism but because it's been one of the few available ways for young men, and now women, to make some money. You don't have to be Karl Marx to note the economic underpinnings to things. And yes, we have the only state capital without a McDonald's but this self-extolling bit of information is repudiated by a short drive east from the statehouse's golden dome along Route 302, where you'll shortly find the golden arches.

Bragging, as we know from fairy tales, can come back to haunt you. Trumpeting your good fortune can land you in big trouble. If nothing else, people may want to get some of what you have for themselves. In West Delphi, we thought irony was protection. Not so fast, citizens.

As has been said, two centuries had intervened between the Republic of Vermont and the founding of the Republic of West Delphi, but in the state, things hadn't changed all that much, zeitgeistically speaking. Sheep-herding had given way to dairy farming: since the 1920s the number of farms had steadily declined as had the portion of the population who lived on them; where 75 percent of the land had once been open was now the reverse. But even so we "leapfrogged urban industrialism" to remain the most rural state in the nation until 2010, when Maine beat us out for that title. *Drat.*

Yet around the same time that West Delphi's republic disintegrated, the state overall did begin to go through a fundamental change. Arguably more of a change than at any time in its history. Even if I'd never left my hillside as a wage-earning commuting parent I'd have noticed the goings-on. Thinking back to the Vermont I knew as a child and then as it is today, it's as if I went over to Violet Sleeper's one day and found she'd exchanged her flowered housedress and apron for a sleek pantsuit.

It's not just that there's a greater proportion of people "from away"; it's the nature of the species. Through most of the past century these were summer people who, whatever outlandish ways they brought, would at least, come cold weather, go back where they'd come from. Some ill-coiffed academics and artists and a few enclaves of well-to-do city folks, mainly clustered around lakes. In the sixties came the hippies, the back-to-the-landers, the Helen and Scott Nearing wannabes, practicing free love and living in communes, but though some longtime residents were suspicious and disapproving, these newcomers were relatively harmless and by and large they respected and often sought out advice from old-timers, who, like Violet Sleeper, would consider them exceptions to the general rule when they got to know them.[72] Except for their sexual mores and outlandish modes of dress (which mostly fell by the wayside) they didn't try to stir things up too much. By and large they came with a desire for cooperation, to live and let live, which has long been the watchword of the residents of the Green Mountain State.

But then things did go through another sea change. Instead of wanting to live up here because they'd recognized something sympathetic in the place—whether this be its much-heralded independence of spirit or its scenery—and desired to be part of it, newer-fangled immigrants imported their own way of living with them. They came not as members joining a congregation but as consumers—and proselytizers. They liked what they saw, and they bought it. Though not to leave it as is, but to improve it.

As if they wanted to reinstate Vermont's previous name, New Connecticut, they worked to make it resemble its namesake. Paved driveways, landscaping, no chickens running around in anyone's yard. No clothes hanging on the clothesline where someone else might have to look at them. (In at least one town, I've heard, they even made sure their neighbors couldn't do these things either.) They built new, energy-efficient houses with double-glazed windows or rehabbed old houses and

---

72 Alton Sleeper once remarked to my brother that hippies had moved in over to Lincolnshire. "What's a hippie?" George asked. Alton replied, "I dunno but they've got long hair." "I've got long hair," George said. "Ayup," said Alton, "but I ***know*** you."

put in kitchens with gleaming granite countertops, in which no one, to all appearances, ever actually cooks anything.

And like parasites following a host, new goods and services sprang up to accommodate them. Restaurants on whose menus things like "mesclun salad with goat cheese and candied pecans" or "crêpes with wild mushrooms, leeks, and artisan ricotta in an arugula cream sauce" or "pasture-raised lamb with strawberry chutney and baby leeks" have become clichés. These newcomers and previously installed sympathizers founded private schools, brought in Buddhist meditation centers, made a crusade of organic farming, opened food co-ops where, besides grains and flour in bulk, you can now buy cheese from all over the world, forty-two types of olive oil (as I recently counted in one such store), and—as new entrepreneurs have sought ways to stay afloat—such elaborate "value-added" products as Bourbon Goat's Milk Caramel or Jalapeño Goat Cheese Popcorn (note goats again) or Apricot Chai Paleo Granola that have made "local" a code word for "unaffordable." Not to mention the craft beers that have made us the state with, yep, the highest number of breweries per capita, among them one judged the "world's best" by whatever entity it is that judges such things.

These changes have not been peculiar to Vermont, of course; this growing disparity in wealth and the advent of wealth's support systems has been occurring in "desirable" venues all over the country. Effected, as with our landmass, by the aforementioned squeeze, "possibly from Washington." But it's especially noticeable in a place where heretofore people adhered to a modesty in display, so that there'd been a kind of general shabbiness, whether it came from the neglect by a college professor who was too busy thinking about *more important things* than scraping and painting his clapboards or that of a farm family who had more than enough to do to keep the place going without taking time to get rid of the various vehicles that no longer worked or were being kept for spare parts. Now when you drive around the state you can pretty much tell who has the money to subscribe to this neatness-will-save-you-from-death aesthetic. No peeling paint, no rusting automobiles on these folks' property. Certainly no houses whose sheathing stops with Typar or whose roof has yet to acquire a covering beyond tar paper.

Around the state, one often sees small signs advertising such things as maple syrup, eggs, honey, rabbits, and so on. Not long ago I drove by a yard displaying a vintage VW bug with a For Sale sign on its windshield. The letters were faded, the car's paint dull, and grass had grown high around the deflated tires. And this sight—indomitable hopefulness mixed with not giving a damn—filled me with such pleasure that I actually said "That's so great" aloud in my car. Before, that is, I registered the troubling mix of voyeurism, detachment, and sentimentality that lay snuggled like parasites in my reaction.

The vacation brochure vision of Vermont[73] has us a bucolic enclave blissfully munching locally raised organic food, driving hybrid cars, refitting our houses with solar power, standing in line to buy Heady Topper and the other newly invented beers that are springing up around the state like mushrooms. Not unlike the "latte-drinking, sushi-eating, Volvo-driving, *New York Times*–reading, body-piercing, Hollywood-loving, left-wing freak show" that the Club for Growth PAC ad, inveighing against our former governor Howard Dean when he was running for president in 2006, told him he should "take back to Vermont, where it belongs."

Unacknowledged in my reaction to the sign and in this vacation vision are issues of class and privilege—who's been poised to benefit from the resources of the state and who hasn't. The Take Back Vermont movement that arose in 2000 may have been catalyzed by opposition to civil unions (we are the first state to have established this right through our legislature) but had been simmering for a while over resentment of the latte-drinking Volvo drivers who had moved into the state in the eighties and nineties and made Vermont "work for them." Who'd prospered while people who'd lived here their whole lives were left behind. That this also happened to places all over the country and has multiple causes is beside the point. Vermont is a small state. When someone starts building millionaire mansions where before there were faded farmhouses and double-wides, it tends to advance a stark announcement.

I came here as a child, I thought as a child—and eventually put away childish things. Distinctions I never noticed, let alone articulated, became

73 The image, that is, that the state likes to convey to tourists on whom our livelihood in a substantial percentage depends. Supposedly one in ten Vermonters to some degree makes a living from tourism. (Hard to know if, were we to secede, tourists would be more or less likely to visit, considering they'd have to show a passport to get over the border.)

clear to me. I am glad I didn't notice them, that my parents never pointed them out, as they might have. Their own backgrounds—my mother's as the offspring of a career army officer, as a result having to adjust to a new place every year of her life until high school, and my father's, growing up in a working-class family during the Depression and witnessing people coming to the door hungry—perhaps contributed to their egalitarianism, if that's the word. Whatever the source, they both possessed an absolute hatred of pretentiousness and condescension, which I am grateful to have been brought up around. I played every summer with Stanley Jewell and Billy and Ernie Magoon, but if I was aware of any disparity in our backgrounds it was to feel envious of the fact that they got to stay up in West Delphi all year while I had to migrate southward.

Since I lived here full-time I haven't seen them as often as I used to—the Magoons moved to East Delphi and I stopped buying milk from the Jewells because Stanley wasn't able to keep their farm after his father died[74]—but whenever I've run into them I still feel the same sense of comfort and familiarity I do when I'm around my own family. We go so far back. If anything, I'm a snob in the other direction. If I hear that accent I feel a deep instinctual trust that maybe was born out of getting to sit in Hiram Jewell's lap as he drove the tractor around the hayfield, or of being the recipient of the particular kind of gentle, serious attention Merle Magoon gave to what a child said, but also identifies a quality in people that can't be simulated: of knowing a place, the land and its workings, its animals and plants and weather.

These qualities are not particular to here, but common to people deeply connected to place anywhere. They are grounded, literally, as if conscious of the elements we've all sprung from, when many of us have forgotten. Without such people, life here would feel very thin. Also, just to mention: impossible. I feel a reverential gratitude when I hear the snowplow coming up my steep hill or see the road crew clearing a stretch of Delphi's nearly hundred miles of roads. For the electrical co-op whose workers are out in all weather, day after day, when we've had a storm that's knocked out power. For all the people who know how to fix the things that break,

74 He wasn't alone in this. In 1970 Vermont had over four thousand dairy farms, many of them small. West Delphi had two large farms and three other households who kept cows. Now, in the state overall, there are only a little over a thousand.

without whom I couldn't live here. Instead of intoning "Hail Mary, full of grace," I instead murmur prayerfully, "I have a plumber, I have an electrician, I have a carpenter, I have a heating expert, I have someone to fix appliances . . ."

If I'm home when someone comes—to deliver propane or wood, or fix the power lines—I always go out. I can tell right away if someone is not from here—they don't want to chat. They don't know the routine: how like letting go on a long slide, you travel with great rapidity from weather to the problems with other humans to the state of the world. Somehow there's a big difference in talking to someone outside—out in the woods, or the fields—really *in* place, especially if work is going on, that makes what is said feel more substantial, more authentic than it does indoors. Maybe it's because both people know it's temporary—there's not much time, besides which they know they can take off at any moment—but it's undeniably the case. Maybe psychotherapy would be more effective if conducted standing up, out in the woods. A summer or two ago a logger cutting the ash on our land before the emerald ash borer could get to it said, "These new folks—they don't know what it is to have a feeling for the land." He'd say periodically, "You've got a nice piece of property here," and he didn't mean for the value of the timber. He meant the disposition of the woods and fields, the variation of trees, the views, the quiet—but more than that, something indefinable, something inarticulable that animals, and some people, instinctively recognize.

I feel a grief that hits me like a physical sickness when I see how that relationship with their home of the people who've lived here all their lives has been interfered with by the changes in demographics—that cold, empty word—that have occurred in the past quarter century. To retain the respect of the people I've known here all my life and the people from here whom I've come to know later matters deeply to me and nothing raises my hackles more than listening to certain kinds of recent transplants describe some long-term residents as if they're an interesting species of bird they're cataloging. Maybe their underlying values are well-intentioned—now that they drive hybrid cars and drink soy lattes and stump for our latest progressive presidential candidate or sell pasture-raised beef and organic arugula. But there can be a repugnant self-exalting tone of the kind that provokes the slighted fairy to swoop down and put a curse on the utterer that they'll have to strive for years to undo. And often on everyone associated with them. When Beauty slept, recall, everyone else in the castle got turned into statues. As if in equal and opposite reaction to this sequestering of prosperity there is a large percentage of the population suffering in this state right now. People without enough to eat or a place to live. Without meaningful work. Or work, period. People addicted to drugs,[75] angry, without hope. As there are all over the country. But to reiterate: we're a small state. We have made it a point of pride to look after ourselves. We should be able to do better here.

Not long ago an issue arose in Delphi that brought some of these social divisions into stark relief. A vote was being held to determine whether or not to build a new firehouse. The old one was unusable, falling apart. No one thought we didn't need a new one; the issue was cost. Why do we have to spend close to a million dollars? people complained. We aren't Connecticut! (From which scapegoat of a state our fire chief retired from. A volunteer, like all the firemen, investing untold time and energy in training the firefighters, using his connections to get fire trucks for Delphi for free, but rubbing some people the wrong way by his seeming to know better than people who'd been carrying on just fine before he showed up, thank you.)

Those in favor of the bond argued that the costs had been brought down as much as possible. We needed space for several engines, a place where the firefighters could wash contaminants off their clothes. New regulations are such that if certain procedures aren't followed we could lose our insurance. And so on.

Some people were in accord with this reasoning: spend this much now so that we'd be good to go. Others couldn't make it past the price tag. Some people can barely put food on the table, let alone absorb another tax hike. People opposed, those in favor said, were living thirty years ago; they just didn't realize what things cost these days. Besides, the tax liability was proportionate to property taxes; at most it would add about thirty dollars a year for each hundred thousand dollars of value. The payment to diminish each year and last only twenty years. This controversy pitted

75 In a recent survey, Vermont had a rate of deaths from opioid overdose of 20 per 100,000 people, compared to the national rate of 14.6 deaths per 100,000.

townsfolk against each other more sharply and vocally than even the disagreements over civil unions. This hit not only our philosophies, it hit our pocketbooks.

I'd always liked to think that I inhabited some area in between the born Vermonters and the "latte-drinking Volvo-driving" newcomers, so it was particularly painful when as a result of this controversy I found myself perceived as a traitor by a lifelong resident—someone I'd never met before but had waved to for years and thought highly of by hearsay. I'd been in favor of the bond, had heard a lot about the fire department's side of things. My son was a volunteer so I'd heard all the arguments in favor. Moreover, I'd experienced the need for firefighters firsthand when one New Year's Eve my house filled up with methane gas and ten minutes after my son called and said, "Chief, it's *my* house," not only a full-size fire engine but several pickup trucks arrived at the top of my snowbound road and several cheerful men[76] proceeded to hoist a ladder up onto the roof and sent my own dearly beloved fireman up to unblock the sewer vent. We all stood on the ground chatting, as the person at the top of the extension ladder steadying the roof ladder periodically called "Doing okay, Nick?" while he plunged the heavy iron rod repeatedly into the PVC vent pipe until suddenly a great plume of white smoke burst forth, as if sequestered cardinals had at long last decided upon a pope. I kept thanking them over and over, apologizing for having had to call them out on New Year's Eve. They not only were amazingly cheerful, but actually seemed to be having a good time. "Well," said the chief dryly, "now you know who aren't the drinkers in town."

Before the bond vote, I'd written up a list of pros and cons to pass out at the dump (Delphi's town square, agora, crossroads, social club), and went to talk to the neighbor, Melville King, whom one of the selectmen had told me would be a good person from whom to get the opposing point of view. I sat with him in his milk house and we had a cordial discussion. He showed me a paper with some figures his son-in-law had compiled that listed how much the town had spent on the fire department over the years. I thought it useful and asked if I could borrow it and make a copy. I showed it to my son, who asked if he could take it to the fire

---

76 It's not all men; there are women on the department as well. They just didn't happen to leap to a call at 9 p.m. that particular December 31st.

department meeting that night. Apparently some people laughed about it—or about Melville's resistance—I'm not sure what, exactly, but it got back to him and the next day he called me, furious, and said, "You *used* me!" Devastated by his anger, I wanted to protest my innocence, yet I had to admit the truth of some of what he said. I hadn't, it was true, gone to visit him with any real thought of changing my mind. I'd looked honestly for opposing points of view, with the intent of presenting them fairly, but I could see how the language in which I'd couched my presentation was slanted toward support for the proposal. I rewrote it to make it as neutral as possible and left him off a copy but I doubt it satisfied him, and every time I drive by his house I remember unhappily what Melville thought of me.

The lens looking at these disparities was adjusted even more sharply when, after renting our family house for twenty years, we had to evict tenants. Or I did, being the one who then oversaw the property. Since we'd mainly rented for a nine- or ten-month period, so that family could have access in the summer, the arrangement generally appealed to people in transitional moments in their lives. (One year, four recently divorced men answered the ad; another, three women who were leaving their husbands.) Derek and Aruna stayed for five years, but they were willing to leave for two to three weeks every summer.

This last time, only a half dozen people had any serious interest; I showed the house to two couples. The first seemed promising—until I discovered they had three beagles (which I'd had to ask to find out about). The second I knew were a credit risk—they were twenty-five and had three young children and worked an hour's drive away—but they were gentle with their kids, which seemed like the best recommendation, and I liked them. I asked for references and got not exactly enthusiastic ones but enough to let me believe what I wanted: that it was a risk worth taking. When they called up, excited, to say they'd come up with the deposit, and then scrounged in their pockets for quarters and dimes to make the last hundred dollars, I said don't worry about it. I wanted to give them a chance. Where else would they find the space for the money we were asking? Eleven hundred dollars for a four-bedroom house in a serene place. I doubted they'd had many breaks. Both were smart, curious, well-informed, but hadn't had access to enough education, had had children too young—she the first at fifteen, from an abusive relationship. And he was from a large family, had grown up at the end of a snowbound road, as ours could be, and wasn't fazed by it. He talked with great concern and thoughtfulness about his wife's difficulties. (Outside, when he'd come up to borrow something or I'd stopped as I drove by and saw him splitting wood.)

The rent came in pieces, but came at first. When the electric bill turned out to be higher than I'd anticipated, I lowered the rent to a thousand dollars. When they acquired a dog without asking permission, I said, "I would have liked to be asked," but I didn't make them get rid of it. Or the kitten who came next, whom they said they'd found by the side of the road. Their daughter, three years old and already an insomniac, had been able to sleep through the night for the first time with the kitten by her side.

I overlooked the chaos of the house: stuff everywhere, dirt building up. A broken window, which they said had shattered one day when they shut the door, even though he had bandages on his wrist, and my son impatiently said, "Mom, he *punched* it."

When the rent came later and later, I was sympathetic. They'd had a run of bad luck: hit a deer shortly after they moved here; had to buy a new car; she had a lot of medical expenses. There were more expenses involved in fighting to keep custody of her son. I believed him when he said he'd soon be getting some money and would settle up. I was aware he'd say what he needed to to placate me but I felt bad about his being in that position. And, as with the man taking stones from the stone wall, what would have been gained by saying I didn't believe him?

Then, when I was away for a month, they stopped paying rent altogether. They ran out of firewood and when I came back I saw that he'd cut nearly a dozen trees on our land without asking if he could. They stopped paying the utilities. Legally I couldn't not pay the electric bill even though, according to the lease, they were responsible for it.

And so it went. When I saw him in the yard I'd ask what was going on and he'd promise money before long. We had to start eviction proceedings. These are lengthy in Vermont. Eventually, on the advice of lawyers, we offered them a month's rent and a cessation of all legal proceedings against them if they'd leave. They did. They put much of their stuff in storage, left more. We stored it in the chicken coop; they never came back to get it. After four months we got rid of the bulk of it. I saved personal things, such as photos of their children, in case I ever heard from them again. I forwarded mail during this time to an address she gave me, including bills for their storage unit in Lancaster. When a certified letter came from this place, I called the last number I had for her (both of their cell phones were no longer functioning) and left a message with whoever lived there, but heard nothing. I had to refuse the letter. When we went in to clean the house, my friend Sally and her daughter and I spent five hours—fifteen person-hours—on the kitchen alone, and still hadn't finished. Everywhere was filthy. There were ashes in the mattress, cigarette butts in the heating vents, food ground into the floor. I was disturbed too, but couldn't respond with righteous indignation as could the people who hadn't known them. When we went into the basement we discovered a "grow" room he'd built, to grow marijuana, to warm which he'd diverted a heating vent and the dryer's. As a result the basement tested positive for mold and an "emergency restoration specialist" charged $6500 to clean it. Our dwelling fire insurance policy paid for the bulk of this, but, all in all, we lost thousands of dollars because of this rental. We've always earned just barely enough from the rental to pay the upkeep and taxes[77] and the only reason that my siblings and I weren't left scrounging for money was because the summer before we'd made money from the ash we'd had cut.

People said reassuringly, "If you've rented for twenty years and never had to evict anyone, you've been lucky." "That's just the price of doing business." "Some people have no respect for other people's things." "Face it, some people are just no good." They told me their own horror stories. But in all this, as distressed as I was, as responsible as I felt to my family for the risk I'd taken, as frustrated as I'd been with the tenants, my main reaction was one of uneasiness—an inadequate word for the mix of compassion, self-blame, anxiety for them, and generalized guilt I felt. I was relentlessly aware of all the forces that had come into play to bring about this intractable situation. My advantages versus their lack of them; the increasing unavailability of affordable housing in Vermont; my sympathy pitted against the financial obligations of a property owner,

77 The place now costs yearly more to maintain (taxes, insurance, upkeep) than the 1958 sale price our father worked a second job to scrape up the payments for.

and so on. I'm uncomfortable even writing about my own feelings in the matter—of what relevance are they when thousands of people are homeless? As I've said, there's a discomfort in even writing this book at all, since without having had the luck to be here in the first place I wouldn't have the luxury of worrying about these things. I keep trying to convince myself that the trip from innocence and naivete to a more complex and political awareness allows me still to love the place a little, but I'm not sure if even that isn't specious.

If, in the decades that have intervened between the end of the Republic and now, my awareness of the forces that have shaped life in this village and state has become more acute, it's not least because in the past twenty-plus years I've come to know a group of people who weren't even here until recently, dairy workers from south of the border (the US's as well as ours), who've made their way here because there's no work for them in Mexico (or Guatemala, or Honduras).[78]

These men (mostly men) work twelve- to fifteen-hour days, six days a week, for wages few American workers would accept even if they were willing to do the work—but accepted by people who have in many cases risked their lives to get here and agree to these stringent hours because they can thus send money back to their families and maybe save enough for a business or farm of their own when they return. Though when they do go back, it's often to subsistence work or no work at all. Or to places so ridden by violence that they have to pay someone off to remain safe. If that's even possible.

Most are here without their families and they can't visit their families because they can't get visas, even though the dairy industry in Vermont[79] would collapse without their work. Men who are single have a slim chance of meeting potential partners. Santiago, one of the men I've known the longest, had a daughter he didn't see for twelve years, since she was born after his wife, who came here with him, returned to Mexico. One of the best men I've ever known—one of the most honest, reliable, kind,

---

78 For one, trade agreements with the US forced a privatization of their industries that ended up destroying many of their jobs, and the drug cartels whose violence makes life in many places in Mexico dangerous are largely supported by drug use in the US—thus making freewheeling threats about walls and deportation particularly obscene.

79 As it would in neighboring upstate New York and in other industries throughout the country.

uncomplaining—he was looked up to by everyone, from the farm's owners to his housemates, nearly all of whom were in one way or another related to him. Said the wife of one of the owners, "More men should have more of what Santiago has." She meant his innate gentlemanliness and fortitude, among other things. There's hardly a person of my acquaintance whom I can imagine enduring the kind of privations that Santiago did with so much patience and expressing so little resentment. Maybe it was just with me that he didn't give voice to it, I don't know. But these qualities are not particular to Santiago. All of the workers I know are helping people back home. Another worker, Diego, was on the point of returning to Mexico when his brother crashed the taxi he drove—which belonged to someone else and wasn't insured—and needed thirty thousand dollars. Almost exactly what Diego had saved. So Diego gave it to him, and as a result will remain in the States however many more years it takes to earn the money back. "He's my brother," he said simply, when I deplored his having to do this.[80]

I never drive by the vast cow-packed barns where these men work without thinking of the fact that while I'm on my way to have dinner with friends, to watch a movie, or whatever it is I'm going to do, free to move around at will, they rarely go anywhere, can't feel safe if they do, live under a kind of house arrest—a carceral state in all but name. The fear of deportation is ever present, and with it the risk that children might be separated from their parents and incarcerated separately; immigration lawyers advise anyone to whom they can get a message to establish a US citizen as guardian so this will not happen.

Sometimes, when Santiago was still here, I'd stop and go into the calf barn to see him, and the pregnant cows in the adjacent open-air barn would all turn their heads and watch me go. (Nearly all the cows are in crowded barns; no grazing in green pastures for these milk-producing machines.) I'd speak to the assembled expectant mothers, reminded of Snowy serenading his cows. In the calf barn, the calves are in individual separate pens, or outside in even greater isolation in tiny freestanding huts. They have been taken from their mothers at birth and live in a

80 Knowing them, the claims by former (and now again) president that they are rapists and killers is so entirely ludicrous that I'd like—well, a number of things, most unprintable, but, just for a start, to see him make it through just a single one of their workdays.

carceral state of their own. Sometimes mothers whose calves have been taken from them at birth cry aloud for days. If you hold out a hand to the calves they will attempt to nurse from it. Every time I drive by, I am swamped by pity for them and because I can't do anything to help them; as I turn away from them some quantity is subtracted from my quotient of humanity, just as it is by my inability to do very much for the people who care for them. Whose stoicism, graciousness, and apparent lack of ill will against me for my privilege make me ashamed to give my attention to the things I am generally preoccupied by. It's clear that they do not regard conversations as times of waiting to unload their complaints as it sometimes seems do I and most people I know. Santiago, working his twelve-hour days, six days a week, hearing that my son was working on his cabin said he'd like to help on his day off. It's clear that they do not suffer from the disease of narcissism with which our country in its decadence seems to be terminally infected, from the top on down. I remind myself that I, who have myself always lived paycheck to paycheck, should assign some of the burden of guilt I feel to the corporate capitalists in power who are sailing away in mega-yachts or flying off in private jets to see how construction is coming on their survivalist enclaves, but this maneuver never brings me any closer to exoneration or to knowing what specific action to take to change things.

After fourteen years away from his family, keeping up by telephone and Facebook and WhatsApp (and now there were several grandchildren), Santiago finally went back home. He was there little more than two weeks before his wife, whom he hadn't been able to speak to in person—or look at, or touch—for nearly all that time, was stricken by an infection, and died. The tragic unfairness of this loss (and the likelihood, though I don't know this for a fact, that better medical care might have saved her) can't be adequately described.

Even more recently, and even closer to home, while I was across the ocean working on a manuscript in a café, an email came from a neighbor saying that Stanley Jewell had suddenly died. I had to read the line several times before I could get it to make any sense.

Feeling unwell, Stanley had driven himself to the hospital, where they diagnosed diabetes and heart complications as a result. His condition was so grave that he'd been airlifted first to Concord, then to Boston, by which time he'd lapsed into a coma. After a week, his sister, his closest living relative, gave them permission to take him off life support.

Stanley Jewell died. Even though several years have passed I still can't make sense of those words. I can't conceive of West Delphi without him. We saw each other infrequently, but I drove by his house every time I left and returned to the village, and whenever we did see each other, we talked as readily as we ever had. We disagreed almost entirely about politics—if by that what's meant is how to go about fixing things and who's responsible for them being in the mess they are—but we agreed about what should be done. We could always find common ground in railing against the goddam idiots in Washington and the somewhat lesser idiots in Montpelier, and as I walked along the foreign streets I could think of little else besides Stanley so stalwartly driving *himself* to the hospital, where he died, alone. As he mostly lived, having no significant other except for a brief interval when a woman and her daughters moved in with him; because Stanley kindly drove one of the daughters to school every day so she wouldn't have to take the long ride on the bus, the mother waited until school was out for the year to leave him.

I think of this, and then think back all the decades ago to when I first knew him, when I sat on his father's lap as they hayed, how later on I "helped" with the haying, walking around the field behind the wagon, or went with Stanley to drive the cows in, in the evening, then paced back and forth from barn to milk house as he carried the full milking machines to empty into the gleaming bulk tank—and how he lost all that. The fact that Stanley wasn't alone in losing his family's farm didn't make it any less of a calamity for him.

Afterward he made do with this job and that job, picking up a mail route eventually, raising a couple of beef cows, cutting a few acres around his house with a sit-down mower, as if the habit to be out cutting grass was as hard to eradicate as the wry look at the world that helped him survive. He likely would have qualified for Medicaid, but would have been too proud to use it. If he'd lived through this health crisis, he'd have said something self-deprecating like "the length some people will go to get a ride on a helicopter."

I'd felt sorry for what I thought was his solitary life, but even this, I learned, was a view from a distance. At his memorial service, the town hall was filled beyond capacity, and many people spoke of his kindnesses. The tables were crowded with scores of cards from people on his mail route, for some of whom he'd left gifts or money. His early report cards that were displayed made clear to me only that he'd had inept teaching. Stanley was one of the smartest people I've met. I left that service feeling both happy that he'd had a more companioned life than I'd realized and aware once again how I'd hardly known someone I'd known my whole life. Familiarity is not intimacy, and that is a drawback of living in a tiny place. You think you know all these people, but you actually really don't. As has been said, a building block of intimacy, not to put too fine a point on it, is talking trash about other people; it's necessary and inevitable. If you have a problem with X, and then Y says, Yeah, I know, they do that to me too, you not only feel better about yourself but also feel more generously toward Y. But in a little place, there are so many crisscrossing strands that it can be bewildering. You find yourself calculating hierarchies in a way that you haven't since junior high. Oh, so A invites B to these things but not me even though I introduced them; oh, interesting, C asked me to that thing but not D—self-worth all wretchedly tangled up with other people's half-inadvertent assessments. It's troublingly as if, instead of being friends because we care about the same things, we're friends because we dislike the same people.

Stanley's was a generous and noble nature and against his fate, against the backdrop of unfairness and suffering, the willed obliviousness of some of the fortunate, to revert to thinking of West Delphi in its heyday—this group of inventive and charming but politically unaware and inactive people gathered together in this magical place and making a kingdom of it—is something like recalling the men who donned their topcoats and played waltzes while the *Titanic* went down. Gallantly facing the end but not able to do anything to prevent the ship from sinking. Even if we didn't realize then that our particular ship of state was foundering.

It seems clear that we need to remind ourselves frequently of our fundamental ignorance about other people: we really *don't* know what it feels like to be them, and we shouldn't assume we know why they do what they do.

And just as all of these stories about Vermont are only partial truths, as with the Republic of West Delphi elevating a partial truth to a universal one is the stuff of which republics are made. The founders of the Republic of West Delphi didn't know any of this when we founded ours, of course. We didn't, truth be told, even know we were founding a republic until after it had already happened. The conditions were right and it sprang up like the legendary mushroom about which so much has already been written in these pages. The Republic of West Delphi emerged from an underlying mycelium that circles the globe.

Epilogue

A few summers ago, for the first of what has become an annual occasion, West Delphi held a village potluck. Quite a few new people had moved into the village, but we'd never really had a chance to meet each other. In the field across from the Church, we set up a long table, since what was once the village green is overgrown. I drove around and left invitations in everyone's mailboxes, or knocked on their doors and introduced myself if I didn't know them. But I was afraid people wouldn't come, afraid we'd become a village of people who wanted to keep to themselves and would prefer not to be bothered.

In fact, nearly everyone came. There was so much food that there was hardly room for it on the table. There was a fire to cook meat on. The older kids played football out in the field. The younger ones stayed nearer their parents, keeping tabs. The dogs chased each other in wild circles. The grown-ups introduced themselves and talked. (Note the repetition of the dusk, outside motif.)

It was the most wonderful feeling—to be out in that field with neighbors in the gathering dark. People with a vested interest in the same place—that was what had brought us together. The *place*. We all *lived* there. We could *walk home*.

At one point we were ritually griping about property taxes, gossiping about who (in other parts of the township) had been assessed at what. One of the newcomers from up the hill said, "You know what? I think West Delphi should secede. We'll have our own town meeting. Set our own tax rates!"

I didn't say, That's been tried before. I didn't say anything. I just smiled benevolently and thought, Here we go again.

Appendix

Obituary
West Delphi's Clarence "Corky" Kramer, 1921-2000

by Ben Metcalf

Corky Kramer was the first person I met when I moved to the village of West Corinth in the late spring of 1979. I had turned left out of my driveway, instead of right, and wound up getting lost on the old Birchwood Road. After a half hour of wrong turns, I ended up in his driveway.

Corky came up from his garden and asked if I was lost. We talked for a few minutes and he told me a little about himself.

"Have you met Violet Sleeper?" No, I said.

"Have you met the Jewells?" No, I said.

"Have you met Lois and Rudy Pringle?" No, I said.

He was quiet for just long enough to notice. Then he said, "You're in for a treat." An understatement for sure; these people were such fine people and played a role in all of our lives.

When we met, Corky was in his last years of teaching at Marlboro College. He came up every weekend to get his place ready for the summer. It was a remarkable spot and I wondered if there could be a more perfect summer home anywhere on earth: a rambling yellow building with old plumbing, a noisy freezer, and screen doors that banged when they closed.

It was dusk that first time we met and the sight from his front yard is hard to forget. It was a private view, framed by layers of small hills receding in the variable hazy hues of blue and green, a delicate and magical effect that I've only ever seen in Vermont.

I quickly learned that Corky had a number of unusual interests. He was a philosopher by trade, but was intrigued by politics, the stock market, beekeeping, gardening, and wine-making. I can still see him carefully positioning the antenna on his black and white television so he could get the PBS Wall Street show. I forget what the show was called, but every night at 6 he stopped what he was doing to watch it.

Days later, when I got my first tour of the house, I was surprised by the network of plastic tubing and 5-gallon glass bottles in the living room. "Oh, it's just a hobby." It turned out Corky was an amateur winemaker, frequently inventing recipes using dandelions and other plants from his backyard. Some were quite good. It was a fascinating hobby that with his help I immediately took up. Before long we were making parallel batches of beer and wine, sometimes doing blind tastings to determine who had the best touch.

I remember one of our small triumphs was the creation of the mythical company "Delphi Industries." My little road had no name, so I created the address for Delphi Industries: "1 Mill Street," an address which I believe has since been officially adopted by the town. Our impressive Delphi Industries letterhead permitted us to order supplies for our various activities wholesale: beekeeping supplies, brewing supplies, and a few other things we dabbled in over the years.

I remember when the UPS truck first arrived with a shipment; the driver (a friendly man named Gordon), stopped at my house and asked, "Do you know where I might find 'Delphi Industries'"? with a note of disbelief in his voice.

"You found it," I responded with great seriousness; Gordy looked at me and after a minute we both started laughing. "I've seen everything," he said, and drove away; in subsequent years Gordy delivered lots of packages to Corinth Industries.

But perhaps the strongest memory of Corky is creation of The Threshold Institute, a loosely configured, partially mythological organization, which at various times involved many of the residents of West Corinth. I might be wrong, but I believe that the Threshold Institute was officially conceived by Corky and his daughter Katie and possibly his other daughter Mary. But even as the exact nature of the Institute is ephemeral, so too were its origins.

Katie once explained the philosophical underpinnings of the Institute as pertaining to "that state of consciousness between wakefulness and deep sleep, when you are not sure which state you are in," or words to that effect.

Corky freely delegated Threshold Institute duties to other members of the West Corinth community. For example, I was charged with assisting Violet Sleeper to prepare the "News from the Threshold Institute" which appeared weekly in the local paper, the Lancaster Opinion—to the delight and occasional consternation of other people in the valley. Violet said she would get phone calls all week long from friends asking incredulously, "My goodness, did that really happen?"

Once, over doughnuts and coffee, Violet confided in me, "You know, my life has never been so interesting since I got involved with all of you at the Threshold Institute." It was a compliment that Corky often recited, and I know, cherished.

It is reassuring that I believe the Institute had been passed down to Katie and perhaps Mary and their brother George too, and will find a way to survive. I still have seven or eight precious sheets of Threshold Institute stationery, printed for us by T.R. James and Vanessa Burton on their letter press in Cookeville. At the bottom of the page was a two-color caricature of a wis old man, and under it printed "Dr. Corky Kramer, Our Founder."

He was intellectual in an accessible way that I really loved; he had few airs about his knowledge, which was considerable, or his philosophical views, which were complex. I know little about philosophy, but he was easy to talk to and during the 20 years of our friendship never once did he make me feel uncomfortable because of the disparity in what we knew. I suspect that is why he had been so well liked by his students.

I think Corky may have been most happy in his garden. I'm still amazed at the things he would carry out of that small patch. Hot-house-sized tomatoes; eggplants that were large and beautiful and smooth; plump, sweet watermelons. It seemed so easy for him. I regularly struggled with my own garden, which mainly produced weeds.

The Mexican State Telephone Company also played an interesting role in his life.

One day, I recall it clearly, Corky was wiping garden soil from his hands and said, as though he were quoting a line from The Graduate, "Tom, I have just one word for you."

"What?" I asked.

"Telmex," he said, with great seriousness. "It's only $1.50 a share, and I have a feeling about it."

I remember asking why he thought buying stock in the Mexican telephone company was such a good thing; it sounded nuts to me.

"I've done research.," he said, with an enigmatic tone to his voice, a unique tone that Corky invented and for me was his trademark. "Besides, I have a feeling about it."

Telmex became a regular topic of discussion. All summer it would go up or down a point or two. By the end of that first summer it had settled in at $1.75 and Corky had made a few dollars.

I remember Corky called us "infidels" for not embracing his belief in Telmex. "You just wait," he said.

Two years later Telmex was trading at 33 or 35. And was rising like a thermometer on a hot day. I never knew how much Telmex he bought, but years later, when I asked him about it, I got that Kramer smile—not without a hint of rebuke—and he said, "You see? You didn't believe."

Even after I moved from West Delphi and long periods passed between our visits, I never felt that our connection or our liking for one another diminished.

I saw Corky for the last time about a year and a half ago in Lancaster. We ran into each other at the Village Store. It felt to me that we had just left off from a previous conversation a few minutes earlier. We talked for a while and promised to get together for dinner. We did not, and of course now that leaves me with regret. One more dinner in West Delphi—it would have been fine.

It is not enough to say that I will miss Corky.

It is important to say that much that I know about life I know from him. He had a way of looking quietly at beauty and understanding it. It was a contagious thing, and whenever I see a thing of great beauty today, I think of Corky, beaus he has helped me see it.

And even more. Two of the finest people I know—his daughters Katie and Mary—I met because of Corky Kramer.

It is true; I will miss my friend.

From the Post of…

GENERALISSIMO SNOWFLAKE

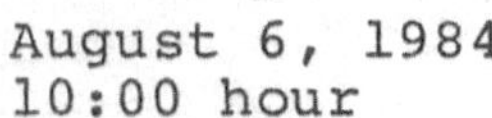

August 6, 1984
10:00 hour

To the Green Army:

This is to announce the promotion of General Kramer to the rank of The GENERAL/ADMIRAL Kramer.

General/Admiral Kramer having demonstrated that the pen is mightier than the sword, is on the verge of moving the world through the principle of Archimedes that, given a long enough lever, the world can be moved.

This promotion is effective immediately. If in a rush, the co-rect abbreviation for General/Admiral Kramer is G/A Kramer.

The General/Admiral Kramer, I salute you.

This promotion is granted pursuant to the powers I have granted unto myself.

At ease, my soldiers:

GENERALISSIMO SNOWFLAKE

APPROVED
DATE
INITIALS
TIME 10:40

THE THRESHOLD INSTITUTE WEST DELPHI, VERMONT

DR. CORKY KRAMER
OUR FOUNDER

Fouth of July Parade

Acknowledgments

Again, my gratitude to the inhabitants of West Delph who were here during the times I write about, and especially to the writers without whose annals published in various journals of the time this book would be sadly paler, particularly "Ben Metcalf," "Violet Sleeper," and the founder of the Threshold Institute. And to Ken Brown, for his illustration of Our Lady of the Large Zucchini. To the many cats and dogs whose companionship has enriched life here over the years. To PTO's garage, where I went over the copyedited manuscript. Next to a certain café in the XIVème arrondissement of Paris, I have found no other place where I can better concentrate. And, last but not least, to the many people whose expertise has enabled me to keep living up here. At night, instead of intoning the Hail Mary, I murmur with gratitude, "I have a plumber, I have an electrician, I have a carpenter; I have someone to plow, to deliver firewood, to cut fallen trees..." Thank you, thank you, everyone!!!

About the Author

Kathryn Kramer has published three novels—*Sweet Water* (Knopf, 1998); *Rattlesnake Farming* (Knopf, 1992); *A Handbook for Visitors from Outer Space* (Knopf, 1984)—and a memoir, *Missing History: The Covert Education of a Child of the Great Books* (Threshold Way, 2015).

Kramer is the recipient of a Guggenheim Fellowship, a Rockefeller Foundation Residency, and a Vermont Arts Council Grant, among others.

She taught writing and literature for many years at the university level, for the last twenty-two years at Middlebury College. She grew up in Maryland and New Mexico and spent many summers in Vermont, where she has lived full-time since 1990.

We Grow Our Books in Montpelier, Vermont

Learn more about our titles in Fiction, Nonfiction, Poetry and Children's Literature at the QR code below or visit www.rootstockpublishing.com.

www.ingramcontent.com/pod-product-compliance
Lightning Source LLC
Chambersburg PA
CBHW030430280726
48872CB00030BA/354
* 9 7 8 1 5 7 8 6 9 3 0 7 8 *